Innovation
IN THE
Community College

Innovation

IN THE

Community
College

TERRY O'BANION

Executive Director
League for Innovation in the Community College

AMERICAN ASSOCIATION OF COMMUNITY
AND JUNIOR COLLEGES

AMERICAN COUNCIL MACMILLAN
ON EDUCATION PUBLISHING COMPANY

NEW YORK

Collier Macmillan Publishers
LONDON

Macmillan Publishing Company
866 Third Avenue, New York, N.Y. 10022

Collier Macmillan Canada, Inc.

Library of Congress Catalog Card Number: 88-8043

Printed in the United States of America

printing number
1 2 3 4 5 6 7 8 9 10

Library of Congress Cataloging-in-Publication Data

Innovation in the community college.

  (American Council on Education/Macmillan series on
higher education)
   Includes index.
   1. Community colleges—United States.   2. Educational
innovations—United States.   I. O'Banion, Terry,
1936–   .   II. Series: American Council on Education/
Macmillan series on higher education.
LB2328.I63   1989   378'.1543   88-8043
ISBN 0-02-897291-0

for Olney and Yolande—
uncommon names, uncommon women

Contents

Preface and Acknowledgments   ix

Contributors   xvii

1. The Renaissance of Innovation   Terry O'Banion   1
2. Curriculum Change in the Community College: Pendulum Swing or Spiral Soar?   Ruth G. Shaw   23
3. Innovations in Teaching: The Past as Prologue   Suanne D. Roueche and John E. Roueche   46
4. The Student Success Systems Model   John Keyser   70
5. Expanding Horizons for Learning and Technology   Kamala Anandam   98
6. Innovative Management through the Use of Communications Technology   Ronald D. Bleed   113
7. Initiatives in International Education   Edmund J. Gleazer, Jr.   136
8. The College/Private Sector Connection: Boom or Bust?   James P. Long   159
9. Innovations in Staff Development   Al Smith   177
10. Entrepreneurial Management: A Fourth Concept of College Management for the Decade Ahead   William L. Deegan   200
11. Governance in the High-Achieving Community College   Thomas W. Fryer, Jr.   215
12. The Costs of Innovation   Peter R. MacDougall and Jack H. Friedlander   244

13. The Future of the Community College:
Premises, Prior Questions,
and Implications for Innovation   Nancy Armes 266

Index   283

Preface and Acknowledgments

Growth and innovation were the hallmarks of community colleges during the 1960s. It was a time of creative ferment in which educators dreamed and risked in ways they had not for decades. The exciting ideas included individualized instruction, management by objectives, the experimental college, encounter groups, humanistic education, programs for new populations, and a host of others. B. Lamar Johnson chronicled the innovative ideas of this decade in his books *Islands of Innovation* and *Islands of Innovation Expanding*.

Sometime during the 1970s and on into the early 1980s, interest in innovation declined. The term "innovation" lost its relevancy and seldom appeared on convention programs or in the literature. The innovative spirit subsided while educators turned their attention to increasing problems of access to higher education, declining resources, changing forms of governance within the institution and at the state level, and the continuing concern for the quality of education.

In the last few years, however, and even more clearly as the late 1980s begin to move toward the 1990s, innovation once again has emerged at center stage in education. At every level of education, in all parts of the country, and for a variety of reasons, there is a renaissance of innovation in the community college.

This book is an attempt to analyze and document the major innovations of the late 1980s that herald what will probably become standard practice for community colleges in the next decade. Definitions of innovation and the processes of innovation, for which there is a considerable literature, are not specifically highlighted, but the careful reader will encounter solid definitions and sound processes in the descriptions of the innovations of the creative educators who prepared these chapters.

This book should prove to be of immense interest to every constituent group working in the community college. Administrators, faculty, board members, and support staff will find here the exciting ideas and programs that make the community college a significant force in American society. Here are to be found tested ideas to serve students more fully, to support faculty more effectively, and to reach the community more extensively. For community colleges planning ahead, here are to be found the programs and practices that will, in great part, define the community college of the 1990s.

The 13 chapters in this book describe and analyze a variety of innovations in a great variety of two-year colleges. The authors followed carefully designed guidelines provided by me to insure this variety. The following is an excerpt from the guidelines:

> This is not a publication by the League for Innovation or about the League for Innovation. It is a publication about innovation in community colleges.
>
> Chapters should be written as useful resources for community college and other higher education practitioners. Therefore, authors are requested to cite examples of innovative practices from at least six community colleges with a broad geographical representation to illustrate points. Attempt to include at least one technical two-year college in the reviewed innovations. No more than three of the examples can be from League for Innovation colleges.
>
> While most authors will tend to cite the well-known colleges in this review of innovations, I hope all authors will ferret out less well known institutions to illustrate points. While several colleges have been cited recently in the national press for their outstanding innovations, I do not want these colleges to be overexposed in this book.

In the first chapter, "The Renaissance of Innovation," I suggest that the community college is an innovative form of higher education that became an innovating institution. In the 1960s, the community college experienced a great surge of the innovative spirit, and the major innovations of this period are summarized. Following this creative period of activity, interest in innovation declined, and the reasons for this decline are cited. In the 1980s, however, the innovative spirit was reawakened in the community college. What I suggest is that this resurgence may even exceed the comparable period of the 1960s. Following an analysis of the reasons for the renaissance of innovation, the chapter concludes with an overview of the major innovations of the 1980s as an introduction to the chapters that follow.

In her chapter "Curriculum Change in the Community College," Ruth Shaw makes the point that change is best viewed as a spiral rather than a swing of the pendulum: "Looking at curricular change as a spiral requires a shifted perspective on the nature of innovation. A spiral, unlike the pendulum, does go somewhere, and it ascends by almost organic power. Curricular innovations, then, are those programs or efforts that are exemplary of the forces propelling the spiral.

They are not radical or dramatic departures that seem by their very uniqueness disconnected from the educational mainstream." Developing this theme, Shaw goes on to note that, during the 1960s, innovation took the shape of curricular diversity while in the 1980s, innovation in curriculum reflects the theme of connectedness and coherence. She describes competency-based curricula, general education, and the new technologies as expressions of curricular coherence. Examples of curriculum connections are critical thinking, writing across the curriculum, and interdisciplinary studies. Shaw then cites developmental studies and honors programs as examples of curriculum continuum and notes that much of the change in the curriculum today is technology-driven. Prior to her selection as the President of Central Piedmont Community College, Ruth Shaw served as a key administrator in the Dallas County Community College District where she co-chaired the Common Learning Committee. In this capacity, she provided leadership for the development of one of the commendable general education programs existing in community colleges today.

Suanne and John Roueche used the rich resources of *Innovation Abstracts** to compile information for their chapter "Innovations in Teaching: The Past as Prologue." Suanne Roueche is Director of the National Institute for Staff and Organizational Development and coordinates an international annual conference on the celebration of teaching. John Roueche has consulted in more than 800 community colleges across North America. Drawing on their extensive experiences in community colleges, they describe "the major teaching innovation of the decade. Simply stated: for their own educational well-being, *students must and should take an active part in their own learning.*" The Roueches describe numerous examples of innovative teaching under the headings of active attendance, active lecture (orchestrate, surprise, keep records, act out, change steps, get feedback, team teach), active testing, active questioning, active teaching and learning strategies, and using practical applications. They conclude their chapter by noting there is much to celebrate in teaching and suggest a number of active roles for the teacher that will insure a kind of teaching worth celebrating.

A former Dean of Students and now President of Clackamas Community College in Oregon, John Keyser is a key national leader in the area of student development. He has played a major role in organizing the Traverse City Conference sponsored by the American Association of Community and Junior Colleges and American College Testing, which have stimulated a great deal of renewed interest in community

---

**A weekly newsletter on teaching tips published by National Institute for Staff and Organizational Development (NISOD), University of Texas at Austin, EDB 348, Austin, TX 78712.*

college student development programs. In this chapter, Keyser places in perspective an emerging new direction for community college student development professionals he calls "The Student Success Systems Model." He cites a number of programs that have implemented various elements of this model and challenges community college leaders to further effort.

Kamala Anandam is the first community college staff member in the nation to serve as an IBM Consulting Scholar. At Miami-Dade Community College where she is Associate Dean for Educational Technologies, she has provided creative leadership for the development of many innovations in instructional computing. She was the moving force behind CAMELOT, one of the first authoring systems to develop instructional technology created by community college staff members. In her chapter "Expanding Horizons for Learning and Technology," Anandam identifies four trends to describe a variety of innovations in instructional computing. She suggests that community colleges are moving from technology-instigated education to education-instigated technology, from uniform information to customized information, from one-way communication to interactive communication, and from a focus on teaching to a focus on learning. She concludes her chapter by noting that an emphasis on faculty development, especially in learning literacy, will be important if community colleges are to bring about the rebirth of innovation that is connected to the use of new technologies.

Ronald Bleed is a frequent speaker at conferences on information technologies. He currently serves as Director of Information Technologies at Maricopa Community Colleges where he helps coordinate a $15 million project developed by the district in association with Digital Equipment Corporation and Information Associates. In his chapter on "Innovative Management through the Use of Communications Technology," he notes that community colleges have been national leaders in higher education in applying the new technology to better manage their institutions. Citing recent data from a special report by the Professional Association for Information Technologies in Higher Education, he illustrates the wide variety of applications community colleges have developed to improve institutional management practices. Selecting from the many programs around the country, Bleed provides more detailed perspectives on systems of library automation, communications, registration, student services, and human resources. He concludes his chapter with a discussion of trends for the future and keys for success for community colleges planning to initiate applications of communications technology.

Edmund Gleazer served as President of the American Association of Community and Junior Colleges (AACJC) for two decades during which time he provided major leadership for a variety of new directions for the community college movement that included an expanding role for community colleges in international education. He has visited dozens of countries as a consultant and has led numerous special excursions to other countries for community college leaders. In 1987, he led a group of adult educators under the sponsorship of the Coalition of Adult Education Organizations and AACJC to the Soviet Union. In his chapter "Initiatives in International Education," Gleazer makes a case for the role of the community college in international education and describes how this development emerged in community colleges. He cites numerous examples of innovative development in international education under the general rubrics of educational partnership, linking international education and business, and internationalizing the curriculum. He concludes his chapter by noting how international education has served to change the community college and how community colleges can participate in helping to change perspectives on the world.

Before he became the Chief Executive Officer of the Community and Technical College of the University of Akron in Ohio, James Long served as the Director of the National Alliance of Community and Technical Colleges. He is also the author of the book *Economic Development in the Community College*. His experiences have provided a unique opportunity for him to know at first hand the major innovations regarding the community college connection with the private sector. In his chapter "The College/Private Sector Connection: Boom or Bust?" Long provides a historical perspective of how community colleges have worked with the private sector and raises important questions regarding this role. He describes a variety of innovative programs including partnerships for human resource development, dual-purpose partnerships, and partnerships for economic development. He concludes by assessing the trends of this new partnership with community colleges and notes that, while there are major benefits to such partnerships, there are cautions that need to be observed.

Al Smith, professor at North Texas State University, has been writing about staff development in the community college for over a decade. In his chapter on "Innovations in Staff Development," he draws heavily on his work as a consultant in staff development to community colleges as well as his experiences as former Director of the National Faculty Evaluation Project for Two-Year Colleges, which was established at the University of Florida in 1980. Smith provides an overview of the early beginnings of staff development in the community college and describes a number of innovative models which have received awards from the National Council for Staff, Program, and Organizational Development. He summarizes the key research on staff development in the community college and concludes his chapter with a discussion of special problems and suggestions for the future.

William Deegan is chairman of the Department of Educational and Psychological Studies at the University of Miami, where he has just completed a major new study on entrepreneurial management in community colleges. He uses the data from this study to describe some management concepts currently in use in community colleges and as a base for discussing a number of issues related to entrepreneurial management. Deegan opens the chapter by noting some of the forces and trends that affect the community college identified in his book with Dale Tillery (Renewing the American Community College: Priorities and Strategies for Effective Leadership). Deegan suggests that these trends encourage new approaches to management and recommends that community colleges examine concepts of entrepreneurial management as important complements to the collegial, political, and bureaucratic concepts that have guided community colleges in the past.

Thomas Fryer, Chancellor of the Foothill-DeAnza Community College District in California, served as the President of the California Chief Executive Officers Association in 1987 and is also a visiting professor at the University of California at Berkeley. He has provided leadership for a recent study of local governance practices in California's 70 community college districts which attempted to identify and describe models of effective governance practice. According to Fryer, "governance is most usefully thought of as those mechanisms and processes for decision making and communication that enable the institution to achieve its mission most effectively. Governance is not an end: it is a means." With this working definition of governance, he notes the factors that complicate an understanding of the term. Following a discussion of the purpose of institutional governance, he suggests a value-driven theory of an ideal governance system. Fryer concludes his chapter by reviewing innovative practices that seem to point in the right direction regarding governance.

Peter MacDougall and Jack Friedlander completed a special study of selected community colleges as a basis for developing the chapter "The Costs of Innovation." They defined cost as "negative consequences that may result when innovations are introduced in community colleges." MacDougall and Friedlander, drawing upon interviews with ten selected institutions and the literature, identified a series of cost categories that will be most helpful to leaders planning new innovations in their institutions. They also call upon their experiences as President and Dean of Academic Affairs, respectively, in which roles they have provided leadership for a variety of innovations at Santa Barbara City College. They conclude their chapter with a helpful checklist for determining potential costs associated with institutional innovations which is likely to become a standard in the field.

During the past two years, Nancy Armes has served as the Executive Director of the Commission on the Future of Community Colleges established by the American Association of Community and Junior Colleges (AACJC). On this Commission, she has reviewed key issues with Ernest Boyer, K. Patricia Cross, Jack Peltason, Frank Newman, and a dozen community college leaders. In addition, she has coordinated testimonies with over 100 selected faculty, presidents, students, and trustees regarding the future of the community college. From these interactions and from her own thinking and writing about the community college, Armes has identified the major premises and prior questions that support and confront the contemporary community college. She draws on this wealth of resources and notes a number of implications regarding the innovative process.

The professionals who wrote these chapters are innovators of the highest caliber. We owe our thanks to them and others like them for the renaissance of innovation in the community college. Through their own vast knowledge, experiences, and accomplishments and that of others they chronicle here, a vision begins to emerge of how the community college will develop and flourish in the 1990s. This book was written in hopes that it will support and encourage others in achieving that vision.

Terry O'Banion
Laguna Hills, California

Contributors

Kamala Anandam—Associate Dean, Educational Technologies, Miami-Dade Community College

Nancy Armes—Executive Director, AACJC Commission on the Future of Community Colleges, Consultant to the Chancellor, Dallas County Community College District

Ronald D. Bleed—Director, Information Technologies, Maricopa Community Colleges (Arizona)

William L. Deegan—Chairman, Department of Educational and Psychological Studies, University of Miami

Jack H. Friedlander—Dean, Academic Affairs, Santa Barbara City College

Thomas W. Fryer, Jr.—Chancellor, Foothill-DeAnza Community College District (California)

Edmund J. Gleazer, Jr.—President Emeritus, American Association of Community and Junior Colleges, Visiting Professor, George Washington University

John Keyser—President, Clackamas Community College (Oregon)

James P. Long—Dean, Community and Technical College, University of Akron

Peter R. MacDougall—Superintendent/President, Santa Barbara City College

Terry O'Banion—Executive Director, League for Innovation in the Community College

John E. Roueche—Director, Community College Leadership Program, University of Texas at Austin; Sid W. Richardson Regents Chair in Community College Leadership, UT-Austin

Suanne D. Roueche—Director, National Institute for Staff and Organizational Development (NISOD); Senior Lecturer in the Department of Educational Administration, University of Texas at Austin

Ruth G. Shaw—President, Central Piedmont Community College (North Carolina)

Al Smith—Professor, Higher and Adult Education, North Texas State University

Innovation
IN THE
Community College

1

The Renaissance

OF

Innovation

Terry O'Banion

AN INSTITUTIONAL INNOVATION

The community college as an institution is one of the most important innovations in the history of higher education. A distinctly American social invention, the public, comprehensive community college is unique in purpose, scope, and design. At no other time, and in no other place, has such a cultural experiment been attempted. The driving premise of the community college—higher education for everyone—is a pivotal educational innovation not just for America, but for the world.

Even the founding fathers of the world's greatest democracy did not envision the community college. Harvard, established as the first institution of higher education on American soil in 1636, was a transplanted form of the English college with all of the accompanying restrictions related to class, sex, and race. Although the land grant college was touted as the "people's college" when the concept became law in 1862, the original land grant colleges did not admit minorities, offered few programs for women, and were inaccessible to many students because of their location. When the German university model, emphasizing research and selective admissions, began to influence the shape of the land grant college, the idea of the "people's college" passed on to the community college.

Not until 1902 was the ancestor of the modern, comprehensive community college established, and that ancestor was very unlike the offspring that came to maturity in the latter half of the 1900s. Joliet

1

Junior College opened in 1902 in Joliet, Illinois, as an institution designed to prepare students for the university (Henderson 1960, 13).
William Rainey Harper, then President of the University of Chicago,
encouraged the superintendent of schools in Joliet to extend Joliet
High School by several grades to establish the "junior college." Harper's faculty at the University of Chicago felt that high school graduates were not prepared for "senior college" and should continue their
preparation by attending the "junior college" for two additional years.
Thus the original two-year college became the handmaiden of the
university, sorting out students who were not qualified to attend the
more rigorous programs of the university (Brubacher and Rudy 1958,
247–51).

In fewer than 50 years, this Joliet experiment had changed completely. Responding to the economic needs of a rapidly expanding
industrial nation and the social demands of a maturing democracy,
the "community college" began to take form. By the late 1950s and
early 1960s, the open-door, comprehensive, community college had
become a major force in American higher education. Firmly established, if not fully accepted, in the 1980s, the community college is
a true innovation—something never tried before—in the history of
human experiments with institutional forms.

AN INNOVATING INSTITUTION

In its 50-year transition from a "junior college" to an institution
offering programs in general education, vocational-technical education, transfer education, developmental education, and community
education, the community college became an entity committed to innovation. This characteristic was a natural development for an institution that was growing rapidly and responding to unmet needs
in a dynamic society. The community college rode the crest of the
wave of expanding opportunity in a society determined to establish
a new order of justice, equality, and economic prosperity. In more
recent years, the community college has become a force that, in part,
pushes the wave of expanded opportunity instead of riding it.

Given this special opportunity to influence and be influenced by
a diverse and dynamic society, the community college had to be innovative. Survival depended on new ideas, but more than that, there
was a rich opportunity for innovation. By experimenting with new
organizational structures, new educational programs, new approaches
to teaching, new ways to serve the community—all new responses to
new students—the community college added "innovator" to its basic
character. An innovating institution throughout its history, the community college reached its innovative zenith in the 1960s.

The decade of the 1960s was a time of ferment as all levels of education changed in response to demands from a changing society. In the "Editor's Preface" to Goodlad's *The Changing American School*, Rickey (1966) observed: "American education is changing so rapidly and on so many fronts that analyses of change from the perspective of today are based on data that will be incomplete next year" (viii).

At the secondary level, the North Central Association of Colleges and Secondary Schools completed a national study of innovative practices in 7,350 accredited high schools and concluded: "High schools have changed their curricula and ways of organizing for learning more in the last decade than in any previous period of time" ("National Innovation Study" 1967, 2).

The same observation held true at the higher education level. Baskin in *Higher Education: Some Newer Developments*, said, "There is good evidence that more significant experimentation is taking place in higher education today than has ever taken place at any other time in our nation's history" (1965, vi).

Foundations in the 1960s gave high priority to innovative developments. The Charles F. Kettering Foundation became actively involved in the school improvement movement and funded a number of programs designed to assist teachers and school administrators to keep abreast of changes in the society. The Ford Foundation supported various plans for making increasingly efficient use of teachers' time and services. In particular, the ESSO Education Foundation supported colleges and universities to help them underwrite innovative experiments, and provided a major grant to establish *Change* magazine at the end of this decade to report on reform and innovation in higher education.

Interest in innovation and experimentation was so common in the 1960s that in 1963 a group of ten colleges organized the Union for Research and Experimentation in Higher Education. The purpose of the Union was to search for new ways and new programs of teaching and learning.

Much of the interest in community college innovation coalesced when the UCLA Junior College Leadership Program and Science Research Associates jointly sponsored the 1967 "Invitational National Seminar on the Experimental Junior College." While the general purpose of the seminar was to advance the development of experimental junior colleges, the selected participants agreed that the word "innovative" was more appropriate for these two-year institutions than the word "experimental." A speaker at the invitational seminar, John Lombardi, said, "Innovation has become as important a concept among educators today as general education was a generation or so ago" (1967, 8). Those attending the invitational seminar represented some of the leading two-year colleges in the United States, and the discussion was rich and exciting as they gathered for the first time in a national forum to discuss their innovative ideas.

Seminar participants established a steering committee to explore plans for continuing and extending their interests in innovation. Stimulated by the opportunities to innovate, and challenged to continue a forum for discussing these innovations, two organizations were created: the League for Innovation in the Community College and Group Ten for the Seventies. Both organizations included 12 to 15 leading two-year colleges selected specifically for their commitment to innovation and experimentation.

B. Lamar Johnson, a distinguished professor of higher education who directed the Community College Leadership Program at the University of California at Los Angeles, has been identified with innovation in the community college more than any other educator. Johnson chronicled the development of innovations in community colleges throughout the 1960s in his books *Islands of Innovation* (1964) and *Islands of Innovation Expanding: Changes in the Community College* (1969).

In *Islands of Innovation,* Johnson described such innovations as teaching aides, the use of television, learning resource centers, programmed learning materials, work-study programs, the use of community facilities, year-round calendars, credit by examination, and cooperative planning with other colleges. Almost all of these concepts have become widely accepted in community colleges today. In his 1969 volume, Johnson elaborated on these innovations and added examples of the systems approach to instruction, games and other simulations, students as teachers, and developmental education as significant areas of innovation.

Johnson's documentation of innovations in the 1960s focused exclusively on the "effective utilization of faculty services" which was and is, after all, the heart of the teaching college. While instructional and curricular development dominated the innovative activity of the 1960s, many other innovations in this decade helped shape the future of the community college.

MAJOR INNOVATIONS OF THE 1960S

Access was the driving force behind the great surge of innovative activities in the 1960s. At the beginning of the decade, the community college was poised to respond to the societal demand for increased participation in higher learning. Throughout this period, improved access for minorities and for other nontraditional students would support experimentation in a variety of areas.

Perhaps the most important innovation of this decade was the expansion of the community college itself as an open access institution destined to become nearly as prevalent and accessible as the American high school. The goal of the community college during the 1960s was to expand so that community colleges would be located within commuting distance of a majority of the citizens in most states. In Florida, for example, community colleges were located so that 99 percent of the populace would be within a 30-mile radius of a community college.

Not satisfied with providing community colleges within commuting distance of the population, many institutions developed outreach centers as another innovative effort to provide services for nontraditional students. Community colleges began to offer programs in rented stores, church basements, and refurbished warehouses throughout the community. In some cases, community colleges purchased and designed mobile vans that could deliver selected services and programs in remote locations of their service areas.

In keeping with the times, community colleges turned their attention to student rights and responsibilities. After Mario Savio's dramatic 1964 speech at the University of California at Berkeley, the students and their rights and responsibilities became a major concern of educators and a ripe arena for innovation. Statements on the subject proliferated, and student codes of conduct were revised to reflect new definitions of student involvement. Most of these activities took place on university campuses, but there were significant developments on a number of community college campuses.

As part of this focus on students, programs in counseling and student development were also major areas of innovation. Counseling was particularly important if the needs of minorities and nontraditional students were to be served, and there were numerous experiments in self- assessment, student tutoring, student leadership, student activities, and what became known generally as human development education.

Programs in human development education burgeoned in response to the students' demand for meaning and relevance in the curriculum. Student development staff offered courses in values clarification, interpersonal relationships, personality development, cultural differences, and assertiveness training. The encounter group process became a major instructional technique used widely in community colleges all across the United States: courses were taught using the encounter group methods, encounter group weekends were provided for selected student leaders, and even faculty and staff participated in retreats led by encounter group specialists.

Because the colleges were expanding so rapidly and providing access for students who had never participated in higher education before, the teachers in community colleges experimented with a variety of new and different systems of instruction. Alternative delivery systems, with a primary focus on individualized instruction, were the major focus for innovation in instruction in the 1960s.

At the University of Chicago, Benjamin Bloom developed concepts of mastery learning which suggested that 95 percent of the students could learn if given time and support. This concept was the ideal complement to the community colleges' commitment to access. Bloom divided the major areas of learning into cognitive skills, psycho-motor skills, and affective skills and encouraged educators to develop behavioral objectives to provide clear directions for student learning in each of these areas.

A number of leaders provided models of application for Bloom's concepts. Samuel Postlethwait at Purdue designed audio-tutorial programs which were applied in hundreds of community colleges, particularly in biology, physics, and business education. Personalized systems of instruction were designed by Keller and other leading educational innovators of the time. Rita and Stuart Johnson traveled across the country teaching community college faculty members to develop their own programmed learning materials.

Many of these concepts supported the development of learning laboratories on community college campuses, particularly in the areas of reading, mathematics, and writing. Basic skills were needed by the nontraditional students if they were to be successful, and community colleges applied with great vigor the new concepts of individualized instruction using alternative delivery systems. One of the major innovations of the 1960s was the experimentation by many colleges with a variety of formats for developmental studies programs.

A number of colleges designed open-entry/open-exit programs which allowed students an opportunity to enter a program when they were ready and to exit when they had completed the requirements. This structure appealed to community colleges because it seemed ideal for many of their new nontraditional students. In practice, only a few of these programs were implemented and usually only in selected areas of technical education.

The use of television—via telecourses—was another major attempt of the decade to provide access to students who found it difficult to attend courses on campus. Several leading community colleges—notably the Dallas County Community College District (Texas), Miami-Dade Community College (Florida), Chicago City College (Illinois), and Coast Community College District (California)—designed and developed some of the major telecourses of the period. They were subsequently used by community colleges and by hundreds of four-year colleges and universities. These colleges were so successful in developing telecourses that they continued into the 1980s as leading proponents of television education.

During the 1960s, colleges also experimented with new management strategies and structures to support the creative learning arrangements designed by faculty and staff. "Management by objectives" was a major attempt at long-range planning and daily management through encouraging staff to prepare objectives for their goals and activities. This approach seemed to provide clarity of direction for complex college operations, but it proved to be a cumbersome process that met with less then enthusiastic response by some participating staff.

Experimental colleges and organizations were also designed in this decade. The College of DuPage (Illinois) was designed as a series of units supporting particular social themes, The Indian Valley Colleges of the Marin Community College District (California) were built as a series of houses expressing major themes. Santa Fe Community College (Florida), instead of using the departments as organizational units, organized faculty into workable units of approximately 15 to 20 staff representing programs in transfer and vocational education. This special structuring of institutions was a bold attempt to encourage faculty and staff to think differently about the purpose and process of education.

Driven by the demand for access, the community colleges of the 1960s grew rapidly and experimented constantly in response to new roles, new needs, and new students. It was a time of intellectual ferment, and many observers today look back on the decade as the finest hour of the community college movement.

THE DECLINE OF INNOVATION

During the middle 1970s and into the early 1980s, interest in innovation declined as complex social and economic forces altered the environment in which innovation had flourished. No single event marked the beginning of this decline. A number of the innovations developed in the 1960s continued to be highly visible during the early 1970s. For example, encounter groups and human development education were popular for a number of years in this decade. Some of the 1960s innovations such as outreach centers and the use of television found widespread acceptance in community colleges and continue today as accepted activities.

But "innovation" gradually lost its relevancy and seldom appeared on convention programs or in the literature during the 1970s. Foundations no longer supported innovative and experimental programs as they had in the previous decade, and centers of innovation established as special units in universities and community colleges were quietly absorbed into the structures of their institutions.

Group Ten for the Seventies struggled to survive and finally disbanded. In 1977, the Board of Directors of the League for Innovation in the Community College entertained a recommendation from a charter board member to delete the word "innovation" from its name. The Board recognized that innovation was not currently highly visible and perhaps not even a respected idea in education. Board members stood by their name, however, noting that in such seemingly unimaginative times it became more important than ever to support and encourage innovation.

Analyzing this period in an article "Community Colleges on the Plateau," K. Patricia Cross put forth the thesis

> that the late 1970's and early 1980's represent a plateau between two periods of high energy and a sense of mission in the community colleges. The old ideals that sparked enthusiasm and the sense of common purpose in community colleges have receded, and new ideals have not yet emerged to take their place. Meanwhile, community colleges sit, not altogether comfortably, on a plateau assimilating and consolidating the social changes of the 1950's and 1960's, concerned about what the future holds. (1981, 113)

There are many reasons for the decline in innovation in community colleges. One of the more obvious is the scarcity of funds for new programs and new ideas. There was no lack of funds to build the hundreds of community colleges and to establish the thousands of new programs needed in the 1960s, but in the mid-1970s plentiful funding began to disappear. There was little start-up money for new programs or "seed" money to support faculty in their creative ideas.

In the 1960s, some community colleges captured national headlines because the size of their student enrollment doubled each year. In the 1970s, student enrollment stablized and in some cases declined. It is difficult to initiate new programs when there are not increasing numbers of new students who need them. Colleges were also frantically—and sometimes unsuccessfully—trying to manage the new programs that had been initiated in the previous decade. There was less time and less inclination to initiate new programs in the 1970s. Germinating the ideas was creative and stimulating; implementing an innovation was grueling work.

Other factors related to the decline in innovation include the changing faculty perspective and the rise of faculty unions. Faculty members in the 1960s were hired, often fresh out of college, as part of a bold new adventure. Their energies and sense of mission complemented well the social energy and mission of the community college. Unfortunately, few of these faculty were well trained to design innovations that were sound, much less manage them well and evaluate them carefully. In the 1970s, faculty members began to abandon innovations that did not seem to work or that required more energy and responsibility than had been imagined when first initiated.

With fewer funds, stabilized enrollments, and dwindling energy, faculty members began to seek security in unions. Unions were also a response to the inattention and neglect from administrators regarding the needs and concerns of faculty members. In the resource-rich growth era of the 1960s, administrators did not have time or did not take the time to pay attention to institutional climate and faculty issues. In the accountability-driven constrictions of the 1970s, faculty wanted some protection regarding decisions that affected their welfare. Little creativity occurs when faculty members are preoccupied with issues of personal security and institutional fairness.

Innovation also waned because of a growing national apathy and cynicism described by Cross as a "plateau" for the community college movement. A national conservative swing to the right, an increasing public critical attitude toward education, and a tightening of taxpayer purse strings led to diminished community college programs, services, and staff. It was not a time in which innovation prospered.

The touted innovations of the 1960s had created a certain cynicism, too. A number of them failed to deliver promised results and were viewed as fads. Part of their failure can be ascribed to the top-down nature of their implementation. The great community college builder-presidents of that decade were generally visionary authoritarians who provided primary leadership for the changes of that decade. Eventually, faculty members who were not involved in the innovative ideas at the grass-roots level became disenchanted. Without faculty support, innovations do not long survive.

Students of the innovative process have come to understand that it is much easier to launch an innovation than to implement and evaluate one. Many innovations begun in the 1960s were pet projects of individuals and had little effect on the total function of the institution. Seldom were any of these activities evaluated to provide data for correcting their directions and strategies. Many were left to die a lingering death, consuming resources and becoming institutional white elephants.

Finally, the innovative spirit seemed to falter in the leaders of the time. The building pioneers of the 1960s had become tired. There were no new colleges to build, and managing the existing colleges became routine and boring. Sometimes the tasks of the following decade were simply ill-suited to the skills of the 1960s leaders.

Risk taking, a necessary part of the innovative spirit, was more dangerous in the late 1970s than it had been in the late 1960s. Boards of trustees had become more active, citizens had become more watchful, and faculty members had become more organized. With stable enrollments, a suspicious and disheartened faculty, and fewer resources, boards of trustees looked for managers rather than leaders to run the institutions. In this climate, the innovative spirit could not thrive.

THE RENAISSANCE OF INNOVATION

As the 1980s pass into the 1990s, innovation is returning to center stage. At every level of education, in all parts of the country, and for a variety of reasons, there is a renaissance of innovation. One of the most visible and powerful changes is occurring in the application of the computer to improving learning, teaching, and institutional management. Providing sophisticated services for sophisticated businesses and industries is an arena for innovation seldom imagined 20 years ago. The expansion of international education, the attention to staff development, the changing nature of governance and management, the need to recruit and retain students—these are areas in which creative and committed college staff are experimenting in new and exciting ways. And some of the old ideas are being recycled and refurbished: honors programs, general education programs, and developmental studies, to name a few. The resurrection and redesign of student assessment, advising, placement, and progress monitoring are case studies in the resurgence of innovation.

The innovative spirit, reflected in a deeply held conviction that there is a better way and a strongly held commitment to find that way, has once again brought a sense of mission and renewed energy to the community college movement. This spirit is alive and well in community colleges and promises to make the coming decade as exciting and challenging as the 1960s.

While innovation of the 1960s was driven by access, current innovation is motivated by the complementary concept of "access with quality." Today's community college is an institution committed to access and insistent on quality educational experiences.

The quality reformation that permeates all of higher education, coupled with the societal requirements of an information age, provide a framework for the new interest in innovation. Shocked out of the doldrums of the 1970s by dozens of national reports on the decline in the quality of education, community colleges, along with other institutions of higher education, are committed to overcoming the problems of a past decade. College leaders and faculty are beginning to recognize, on the one hand, the lack of quality in their programs and, on the other hand, the need for increased quality if the very nation is to flourish These factors are driving forces for innovation.

In addition, the changing demographics of American society, with a resurgence of new clienteles to serve, are forces that shape the renaissance of innovation. Just as new groups of students in the 1960s stimulated faculty to design new programs, so do new groups of students in the late 1980s stimulate such design. The new immigrant populations have encouraged the establishment of an array of new programs in community colleges. The number and variety of immigrants coming to Miami-Dade Community College served there as a major force for institutional reform and renewal.

Underprepared students have always flocked to community colleges, but their increasing numbers and their increasing visibility have focused attention on their needs. Community colleges are responding with innovative programs, particularly to the challenges of providing successful opportunities for large numbers of students who are illiterate.

Changing demographics have also resulted in increasing numbers of older adults, displaced homemakers, single parents, and other special groups that are receiving increasing attention from community colleges. The needs and visibility of these new groups have challenged the innovative spirit of community college faculty who are beginning to respond with renewed interest.

In the last decade and a half, community colleges have learned to build alliances with other segments of education and with other agencies in the community and nation. In the 1960s the community college was still struggling for its own identity and throughout much of that decade acted in isolation.

Now community colleges are building strong alliances with high schools in two-plus-two curricula, in joint efforts to serve minorities, and in joint efforts to serve gifted students. With four-year colleges and universities, community colleges have developed sophisticated transfer agreements and joint service compacts. A number of innovative institutions sponsor joint degree programs and special exchange opportunities for their faculty.

New alliances with business and industry have provided community colleges with one of their most successful innovations in the late 1980s. In the early part of this decade, community colleges began to be seen as a major partner with business and industry in the training and retraining of American workers. With leadership from the American Association of Community and Junior Colleges (AACJC), the project "Putting America Back to Work," which later became "Keep America Working," signaled the growing maturity of the community college as a major job training agency for American society.

Community colleges are now being viewed by state governments and other agencies as major players in the economic development of regions, states, and the nation. These new alliances with business and industry would be sufficient to make a case for the renaissance of innovation in this decade.

In some cases, the renaissance has been fueled by new resources that have been made available to community colleges. Some states have provided additional funds, particularly for special programs such as economic development. In many cases, community colleges have become more entrepreneurial, developing their own foundations and providing services for profit. Community colleges have learned to reach out to business and industry for equipment and start-up funds as a basis for innovative developments.

A new sense of efficiency and productivity in the community college movement also fuels innovation. Perhaps spoiled by society's largesse in the 1960s, community college leaders felt rebuffed and spurned by the withdrawal of support in the 1970s. The leaders of the 1980s, determined to become more productive and efficient, began to explore more effective ways to utilize staff and facilities, and to reduce energy consumption. Necessity guided community colleges to new methods and strategies, many of which were innovative in character.

The new technology designed to improve learning, teaching, and institutional management has also been a driving force in the renaissance of innovation. The communications technology available to community colleges today is infinitely more sophisticated than the technology of the 1960s. Computers, interactive videos, compact disks, telephone technology, and dozens of other applications have encouraged and stimulated a tremendous variety of innovative programs. Technological innovations are highly visible, can be applied in almost every educational area, and have great appeal in an increasingly technological society. For these reasons, technology is a major force for innovative development in the community college in the 1980s.

Through technology and through new alliances, community colleges have learned to participate in networks with other groups. In some states, all community colleges are linked through technology. Project ACCESS, of the AACJC, now makes it possible for all community colleges in the nation to be linked through a computer. Some community colleges have developed specialized consortia to support international education, minority projects, and even innovation. As colleges learn from each other and from a variety of new partners, innovation is often one of the outcomes.

The renaissance of innovation is also stimulated by increased competition from four-year colleges and universities for community college clientele. In the 1960s, community colleges did not need to "market" their institutions; today there is hardly a community college in the country that does not have a committee on marketing. Proprietary institutions and specialized educational programs designed by business and industry also compete for the same students who might attend community colleges. This sense of competition encourages innovation.

In the last several decades, educational researchers have added to the knowledge base on the assessment of learning problems and prescriptive programs to address those problems. New knowledge of human behavior, coupled with increased use of technology, have helped educators to experiment with new programs and practices to better serve students.

Finally, the faculty members hired in great numbers in the 1960s, who led the innovations of that decade, and who suffered the growing pains of the community college, are being replaced by a new generation of fresh innovators. It has been estimated that approximately one-third of all community college faculty members will retire in the next five years. As new faculty are employed by new administrators, the results are likely to be energetic faculty members with great interest in innovative programs designed to increase access and quality for students in the community colleges.

THE INNOVATIONS OF THE 1980S

Any overview of the innovations of the 1980s must be incomplete because of the sheer number of changes, and somewhat inaccurate because of the many ways to organize the innovations under a variety of rubrics. The chapters that follow provide considerable detail regarding the major innovations of community colleges in the 1980s. This section is intended as a template for understanding the kinds of innovations that have developed in this decade and to support the thesis that a renaissance has occurred in the community college.

Innovations reviewed here are described under two categories. *Refurbished innovations* are those that were popular in previous times, particularly in the 1960s, for which there is renewed interest today. Reburbished means "to polish up again," "to brighten," and "to renovate"—apt descriptions for what community college staff members have done to these earlier innovations.

The second category is that of *new innovations*, and those discussed here are exactly that, *new*. Although their roots can be traced to the 1960s, they have emerged in the 1980s with such different characteristics and style and so much more fully developed that they deserve the designation "new."

REFURBISHED INNOVATIONS

Three major areas of refurbished innovations are evident in the 1980s: curricular innovations, systems of student induction and monitoring, and staff development programs. Most of the refurbishing has occurred in curricular innovations, with renovated programs in general education, honors programs, collaborative learning, writing across the curriculum, and critical thinking.

In the 1950s and early 1960s, almost every community college in the country had a general education program. General education had its finest hour in the 1950s with almost all institutions of higher education designing a selected core of "common learning for the common person." In the 1960s, required curricula, including the required general education core, gave way to elective curricula as colleges responded to student demands for free choice regarding their education. Many community colleges continued to list general education requirements in their catalogs, but these were no more than distribution requirements in which students were required to select one or two courses from 15 or 20 in several designated areas. Many community colleges today continue this format under the mistaken impression that they are offering general education.

General education is an ideal concept for the diversity of students and programs that comprise the community college. In the report of the Commission on the Future of the Community College, established by the AACJC in 1987, there are strong recommendations that general education be reinstituted as a major feature of the comprehensive community college.

Unfortunately, only a handful of community colleges in the 1980s have recommitted to the concept of general education. The Dallas County Community College District (Texas), Los Medanos Community College (California), and Miami-Dade Community College (Florida) are examples of colleges that have developed authentic programs of general education based on the historical concepts of this important idea.

Four-year colleges and universities, on the other hand, have been most active in redefining general education. Since general education is such an appropriate concept for the community college, and since it is being strongly recommended by the AACJC Futures Commission, it is included here as a refurbished innovation of the 1980s even though only a few colleges have developed major programs. Given the obstacles to general education (O'Banion and Shaw 1982), it is not likely that a great number of community colleges will redesign general education programs for the coming decade.

Honors programs in community colleges share a similar pattern to general education programs. Honors programs existed in almost all community colleges in the late 1950s and early 1960s, gave way to the spirit of democratizing higher education in the 1960s, but unlike general education are experiencing a major comeback today.

In 1983 there were only two honors programs in California community colleges, but in the fall of 1987 there were approximately 60 such programs. Foothill College (California) has designed a freshman core colloquium, a freshman arts language core, and a sophomore core colloquium for honor students. Frederick Community College (Maryland) offers honors programs in general and by department. The Maricopa County Community College District (Arizona) has allocated $3 million to recruit able students for honors scholarships; 40 percent of the top 15 percent of Maricopa County high school graduates attend the district as a result.

Collaborative learning is another curricular innovation that has been refurbished for the 1980s. In the 1960s, a number of community colleges attempted collaborative models by having the same instructor teach two different classes comprised of the same group of students. In other models, students took two or three classes together, and the instructors of those classes collaborated on common teaching strategies and interdisciplinary content. Still other colleges organized programs around basic themes and worked together to help students understand larger concepts that cut across courses.

An outstanding example of collaborative learning in the 1980s has been designed by the Washington Center. Housed at Evergreen State College, the program is a joint effort of community colleges and selected four-year colleges and universities in the state of Washington to improve undergraduate education.

Valerie Bystrom, an English instructor at Seattle Central Community College (Washington), described collaborative learning or coordinated studies in a recent issue of *The Washington Center News*:

> When you talk about coordinated studies, you immediately begin to talk about active and interactive learning. The atmosphere of both workshops and lectures is radically different because of so much power being transferred to the students. In coordinated studies there are so many power shifts: no longer is the teacher the one, the lone authority in the room. The teacher is a colleague, with other teachers! And the students are being asked what they think! The students are being asked to develop meaning with the teachers and with one another. Because of these changed roles, we begin to see one another as different people. (1986, 7)

In the Washington experiment, community colleges and universities work together and exchange faculty to team teach a variety of formats. For example, at Seattle Central College the coordinated studies program maintains a 16-credit thematic curricular structure, a team of three or four faculty who are jointly responsible for 60 to 80 students, a multimethod teaching format with a heavy emphasis on seminars and communication skills, high expectations of students and faculty, and the use of challenging primary texts.

There were attempts in the 1960s to encourage faculty to assist students with writing skills, regardless of the discipline. Writing across the curriculum, however, was an innovation that was not nearly as developed as general education and honors programs during that period. In more recent years, writing across the curriculum has received a great deal of attention, and many community colleges have college-wide committees attempting to implement this innovation.

Critical thinking has always been a key interest of educators, and considerable attention was given to basic concepts during the 1950s and 1960s. In this decade, new attention has been paid to critical thinking. A small movement is emerging in higher education with leading spokespersons, national conferences, and a developing new literature. There are also attempts to develop the concept of critical thinking across the curriculum.

A second major area of refurbished innovations is that of processes related to student induction and monitoring. All colleges must design processes to admit, assess, advise, place, orient, and register students. The technology available to colleges in the 1960s for these processes now seems primitive. Rolling tub files, McBee sort systems, color-coded paper, and eventually IBM punch cards comprised the technology to enroll millions of students every term in colleges across the country.

In the 1980s many are beginning to design completely computerized student processing systems in which students can explore their values and vocational interests through such computerized programs as SIGI and Discover, become oriented to the institution through an interactive video they review in the library, be assessed with a new College Board adaptive testing program that individualizes the test for the student's level of ability, have programs suggested by the computer based upon assessment scores, and register by a voice-synthesized, touch-tone telephone system. The goal is to provide these various services to an individual student at one location in one brief time period rather than over a period of time and days at a variety of locations with information supplied by a variety of staff members. The one-stop student processing system is currently being field-tested at several institutions around the country.

Staff development is a third refurbished innovation. Community colleges have provided "in-service training" for many decades, particularly for new staff, as a way of introducing them to the college and acquainting them with the particular culture and programs of the college. In the 1960s, all colleges provided an in-service day at the beginning of the year for this induction process. In the early 1970s, staff development became a high priority of community colleges with support from foundations and national leadership from the AACJC. A major study of the time, *Teachers for Tommorow: Staff Development in the Community-Junior College* (O'Banion 1972), commissioned by the President's National Advisory Council on Education Professions Development, helped place staff development as one of the key concerns and issues of the 1970s. There was a flurry of staff development activity for several years during the late 1960s and early 1970s, but the state of Florida was the only state that institutionalized staff development by providing a special fund in each of its community colleges.

The declining resources of community colleges in the late 1970s was the primary cause of the lack of support for staff development. In the early 1980s, staff development reemerged as a refurbished innovation and will continue to grow and develop in the coming years. Faculty members need assistance in using the new technology effectively and in teaching new immigrants and the large number of underprepared students more effectively. There are further opportunities for development in the new alliances with business and industry and countries abroad. Staff development will also provide the means for selecting and orienting the new faculty who will be needed to staff community colleges of the future.

As outlined above, some of the refurbished innovations of the 1980s are: curricular programs of general education, honors, collaborative learning, writing across the curriculum, and critical thinking; processes for student induction and monitoring; and staff development. These innovations have been around for decades, but, as will be seen in subsequent chapters of this book, they have been "polished up" for the 1980s.

NEW INNOVATIONS

Some new innovations have roots in the 1960s, but their new characteristics, purposes, and structures and fuller development in the 1980s mark them as "new." The new innovations include alliances and partnerships with business and industry, high schools and colleges, and government agencies; applications of computing and communications technology; and programs of international education.

Although community colleges offered programs for business and industry in the 1960s, these programs were primarily the traditional, on-campus programs leading to a two-year degree in the applied sciences. In the 1960s few colleges ventured beyond their campuses to provide contract training and other forms of service that today are commonplace.

One of the most creative and exciting forms of innovation in today's alliance between community colleges and business and industry is the specialized technology centers built on community college campuses. Moraine Valley Community College (Illinois) has constructed a multi-million-dollar Contemporary Technology Center in which various business and industry agencies will occupy "pods" to teach high technology programs jointly with college staff. In many cases, the business and industry agencies provide sophisticated equipment and specialized training for college staff. The new Unified Technologies Center at Cuyahoga Community College (Ohio) is part of a major partnership with the Cleveland Advanced Manufacturing Program which links resources of the state of Ohio with Cleveland State University, Case Western Reserve University, and many private businesses. The new $15 million center is a central component to the manufacturing revitalization efforts underway in Ohio.

A Michelin Tire Center offering high-tech programs has been built on the campus of Greenville Technical Community College (South Carolina). Similarily, Johnson County Community College (Kansas) is building an Industrial Technical Center to be completed in 1988. The center is designed specifically to serve the technical training needs of the nation's largest railroad, Burlington Northern. The college will pay one-third of the cost of the facility, and Burlington Northern will pay two-thirds. Under an unusual agreement with the City of Overland Park, Kansas, which issued industrial revenue bonds to finance construction, the building will belong solely to the college in ten years. Burlington Northern and the college each will control a third of the facility and will share the remaining third. This is an unusual partnership involving a community college, a national corporation, and local government.

These centers reflect the community colleges' commitment to assisting in the economic development of this country. In some states, community colleges are recognized by their state governments as major partners in economic development. South Carolina is a model state in which regional centers have been designed by community colleges and the state government to serve new high-tech industries.

Danville Area Community College (Illinois) initiated the Industrial Survival Project to ensure Danville's future success in a declining manufacturing environment. Danville is a small community, where the college, under the direction of its visionary leader, is committed to assisting the community in its redevelopment with a perspective that relates the local community to national and international issues.

Danville President Ronald Lingle described the challenge to community colleges, communities, and to business and industry representatives:

> The Industry Survival Program is based on several very simple premises. First, and foremost, is the fact that this community's economy and the way of life it supports are dependent upon our doing everything humanly possible to keep our core industries healthy, productive, and profitable. Second, virtually all of those industries not only have domestic competitors but international competitors as well. To survive in today's global markets, they must not only turn out a superior quality product, they must do it in the most efficient and cost-effective manner possible. Third, many of the companies we are competing with have tremendous advantages in terms of cheaper national resources, lower labor costs, and, in the case of those in Western Europe and Japan, more modern and up-to-date manufacturing technology. And, fourth, to overcome those advantages, we must rely once again on the most basic and invaluable resources we have—the ability of our workforce to find better and more efficient ways to produce a quality product. (1987, 1–2)

In these alliances with business and industry, the community college is forging a number of highly innovative new programs and practices. The community college has added a major new mission and is capitalizing on this opportunity to serve its communities in productive and creative ways.

New alliances with high schools and colleges are another major area of innovation for community colleges. In the 1960s community colleges certainly communicated with high schools in their service areas and with colleges to which their students transferred, but few real partnerships were developed. In the 1980s, community colleges have become full and respected partners and have been the leaders in building alliances with other levels of education.

A few community colleges have developed two-plus-two programs with area high schools which allow students to complete a four-year integrated program consisting of the last two years of high school and the first two years of community college. An example is the two-plus-two agricultural program developed by Bakersfield College (California) and area high schools served by the college.

Many community colleges have developed joint programs of enrichment for gifted students who are currently enrolled in high schools. Richland College (Texas) provides special summer workshops for gifted students in the arts, computers, and the sciences. Some community colleges have developed model joint efforts to recruit minority students to engineering and science programs by identifying them at the 9th and 10th grade levels and providing special opportunities for them to participate in selected activities at the community college.

Similar programs have been designed between community colleges and four-year colleges and universities. Monroe Community College (New York) has developed a cooperative program with a number of area four-year colleges and universities that guarantees a student's transfer and enrollment in the four-year college or university at the time of entrance to the community college. The Maricopa County Community College District (Arizona) has worked for a number of years to design an outstanding program to facilitate the transfer of students between the community college and Arizona State University; the electronic transfer of student transcripts is one feature of the cooperative program.

Computing and communications technology is a second major new area of innovation in the community college. The application of communications technology is, of course, affecting all levels of education, but the community college, with its zeal for innovation, has embraced the new technology in some exciting and creative ways.

In addition to the use of technology to improve student processing systems described earlier in this chapter, the new technology provides for networks and access to information that will change the way educators think and function in the institution. For example, in several leading community colleges, students and faculty are able to exchange electronic mail messages; call up bulletin board notices; receive and complete course assignments; write research papers; retrieve database information from files, libraries, and campus directories; and receive course instruction. Because of the national databases available, community colleges and their students now have access to major libraries and other resources far beyond what innovators could imagine in the 1960s.

Computer-assisted instruction and computer-managed instruction are important new developments in many community colleges. Some courses in community colleges are offered totally through computers with special support provided by faculty monitors and tutors. Most of the learning labs of the 1960s are now equipped with computers for drill and practice. Interactive video has been used successfully in business and industry and is beginning to be used for selected vocational and technical courses in community colleges. Programs are now being designed in a variety of disciplines, and community colleges will use this new technology to serve their students better.

Programs in international education deserve their distinction as a third area of "new" innovations in community colleges. In the 1960s a few colleges managed to send a few students on summer-abroad programs, a few faculty visited other countries under special college programs, and a few colleges opened their doors to international students on an exchange basis. These programs are commonplace in community colleges today, with many of the programs supported and coordinated by three or four major consortia on international education designed by community college leaders. Community colleges have gone far beyond these "traditional" international education activities. A number of colleges have been involved in major efforts to serve international students. In the early 1980s, for example, the League for Innovation signed a contract with the Republic of Mexico to train approximately 250 students over a period of several years in high-tech fields in the League colleges. Several colleges have participated in programs to prepare large numbers of students from Nigeria and Central America. Many colleges are currently designing language institutes through which many international students would become oriented to American culture and learn English basic skills.

Community colleges have also learned to take advantage of international opportunities to expand their staff development programs. It is not uncommon today for groups of faculty members from a single college or a collection of colleges to spend the summer abroad studying various cultures and designing instructional materials for use back home. Through these means and others, community colleges are beginning to internationalize their curricula.

A few community colleges are beginning to explore roles of educational service and economic development with foreign countries. Recent visits by leaders to such countries as Russia, China, and countries in Southeast Asia and South America have helped stimulate programs designed to provide expertise to assist these countries in achieving their goals. There is beginning to be a transfer of technology and instructional techniques between countries. Humber College (Canada) has faculty members working in over 35 foreign countries to provide technological expertise, to assess program needs, and to train faculty. Through these innovations, the "community" of the community college has expanded considerably beyond the geographic service area to which community colleges were confined in the 1960s.

These, then, are the practices, refurbished and new, that herald the renaissance of innovation in the 1980s in the community college. In one sense it is *déja vu* for the community colleges as they rekindle the innovative spirit so prevalent in the 1960s. This time around, it is hoped that community colleges will study the innovations more analytically, implement them more carefully, and evaluate them more thoroughly. If not, in the year 2000 community colleges will be refurbishing, once again, programs of the past and implementing new programs with great gusto and without much forethought. Such innovative times can be highly stimulating for faculty and administrators in the institution; without thoughtful leadership, however, the impact on students will be slight.

REFERENCES

BASKIN, SAMUEL. 1965. "Preface." In *Higher Education: Some Newer Developments*, edited by Samuel Baskin. New York: McGraw-Hill.

BRUBACHER, JOHN S., and WILLIS RUDY. 1958. *Higher Education in Transition: An American History: 1636–1956*. New York: Haper and Row.

BYSTROM, VALERIE. 1986. "Model Program in Depth: Coordinated Studies at Seattle Central." In *Washington Center News* (Evergreen State College) 1, no. 2 (Fall).

CROSS, K. PATRICIA. 1981. "Community Colleges on the Plateau." *Journal of Higher Education* 52, no. 2, (March/April).

HENDERSON, ALGO D. 1960. *Policies and Practices in Higher Education*. New York: Harper and Row.

JOHNSON, B. LAMAR. 1964. *Islands of Innovation*. Occasional Report no. 6. Junior College Leadership Program. Los Angeles: University of California-Los Angeles.

———. 1969. *Islands of Innovation Expanding: Changes in the Community College*. Beverly Hills: Glencoe Press.

LINGLE, RONALD. 1987. "Parade of Winners Series: Nummi." Opening Remarks. Danville Area Community College, Wednesday, September 16.

LOMBARDI, JOHN. 1967. "The Experimental Junior College. In *Innovation: The American Junior College*. Palo Alto, Ca.: Science Research Associates, Inc.

"National Innovation Study Indicates Broad Attack on School Weaknesses." 1967. *North Central Association Today*, Special Issue XI (May).

O'BANION, TERRY. 1972. *Teachers for Tommorrow: Staff Development in the Community-Junior College*. Tucson: The University of Arizona Press.

———, and RUTH SHAW. 1982. "Obstacles to General Education." In *General Education in Two-Year Colleges: New Directions for Community Colleges*, edited by B. Lamar Johnson, no. 40. San Francisco: Jossey-Bass, (December).

RICKEY, HERMAN G. 1966. "Editor's Preface" In *The Changing American School*, Sixty-fifth Year-book of the National Society for the Study of Education, edited by John I. Goodlad, part II. Chicago: University of Chicago Press.

2

Curriculum Change
IN THE
Community College

PENDULUM SWING OR SPIRAL SOAR?

Ruth G. Shaw

Curriculum innovation. Many would label this phrase an oxymoron, a combination of terms such as "military intelligence" which are obviously contradictory. "Innovation" suggests freshness, change, movement, creativity. "Curriculum" is the solid educational backbone, rigid and little given to change. Woodrow Wilson, during his years as president of Princeton University, described changing the curriculum as more difficult than moving a graveyard. Instructional approaches are tried and discarded almost as freely as sample soaps that arrive in the mail. Their individual nature makes it easy to experiment and take risks. To revise a curriculum, however, requires institutional movement and a judgment that the change has the prospect of enduring.

Given the difficulty of innovation in the curriculum, community colleges have experimented boldly in the last two decades. During the 1960s and 1970s, innovations took the shape of curricular diversity (or, critics would observe, incoherent variety). The 1980s have seen a renaissance of curricular connection.

Understanding the impact of major curricular innovations spanning the last two decades depends upon a recognition of this gradual shift from fragmentation to coherence. The American Council on Education (ACE) has reported that about half of American colleges have completed a review of their curriculum within the last five years, and most of the rest are currently doing so. Emerging from this widespread curricular activity is a strengthening of general education and a new emphasis on writing, math and computer-related skills, and other competencies ("ACE Releases . . ." 1987, 1). However, without an awareness of the gradual shift in curricular focus, issues and innovations produced by all this activity would be viewed by the "staying and graying" faculties of community colleges, who have been around for more than a generation now, as old issues that have simply come around again.

Undoubtedly, some of the curricular "innovations" of recent years have reflected the sort of repetitive pendulum swing that has come to mark cycles of curriculum reform. But while some changes may reflect a mere return to yesterday's practices, much of the curriculum change underway in the community college is better compared to an ascending spiral. The movement of a spiral is circular and in that respect is similar to a pendulum since it passes over the same territory, again and again. But a spiral covers the same territory in a new context, on a new and different plane, with each pass, and thus affords abundant possibilities for new combinations.

Looking at curricular change as a spiral requires a shifted perspective on the nature of innovation. A spiral, unlike the pendulum, does go somewhere, and it ascends by almost organic power. Curricular innovations, then, are those programs or efforts that are exemplary of the forces propelling the spiral. They are not radical or dramatic departures that seem by their very uniqueness disconnected from the educational mainstream. Some curricular experiments do, in fact, stand alone, but they seldom survive. Innovations that endure, seem, in retrospect, so natural that it is difficult to envision them as innovative.

The curriculum is a complex, interconnected organism that moves with direction. To understand what is truly innovative today, one must know that direction and be able to see individual efforts, not in terms of their oddity, but in terms of their symbiotic connection to the spiral. The curriculum is a complex system composed of interactive components. Only from this perspective is it clear why, for example, a competency-based curriculum today is not only different from, but better than, an objective-based curriculum of the past; why computer-based education is, in fact, a generation ahead of computer-assisted; and why such phenomena as general education, interdisciplinary studies, and writing across the curriculum are re-emerging, after a virtually dormant generation, with their greatest likelihood of success ever.

The pendulum/reform concept of curriculum change implies that old solutions are brushed off and trotted out to address new problems, returning the curriculum to precisely where it was before. The spiral/ renaissance view holds that revisiting today's curricular problems with solutions a generation old could not work because various components of the curriculum system and the context within which it operates have irreversibly changed. Indeed, if the application of an old tool to a truly new task is judged successful, it is largely a matter of having used the tool in a new and different way. Innovations in curriculum thus may appear to be one more iteration of an old idea, when closer scrutiny reveals that the innovation has built on the best of the past, but has moved far beyond it.

As Axelrod (1968) pointed out, the curricular-instructional system is made up of the interrelated components of content, scheduling, certification, interaction, experience, and freedom. Therefore some of the curriculum innovations described in this chapter appear as changes in curriculum content, instructional delivery schedules, or degree requirements. Others appear as attempts to connect student learning experiences both across the breadth of the college experience and with the complex world within which the college exists. The use of computer technology, for example, may profoundly affect content, scheduling, and other aspects of curriculum even though the use of computer technology per se may be viewed as just another instructional medium.

The whole point of curriculum change is, of course, to improve student learning. In the early 1970s, this goal was pursued by segmenting learning and describing it in terms of what could be observed and measured. The innovations in curriculum of the 1980s clearly follow a different path, though they share the emphasis on evaluation. The new path is most decidedly toward coherence. Innovations of the last 20 years can be understood in terms of how they fit in a spiraling continuum from fragmentation to integration, from a narrow focus on parts to a broad focus on the whole, from a curriculum segmented for clarity to a curriculum interconnected for college-wide meaning, from measurement based on achievement of specific objectives to assessment based on educational effectiveness.

There are a variety of organizing principles through which to analyze the innovations of the last 20 years. However, given that the direction of curricular change is toward coherence, one logical group of innovations is that which has provided the impetus for this direction; that is, those innovations which, by their very nature, require greater integration of learning. General education, competency-based curricula, and the new technology are in this group. Although these will be seen as individual approaches, they must be understood in terms of the principles behind them, for these principles are the same ones that undergird the new search for coherence. A second group of innovations are those that should be seen more as products of the changes in curriculum focus than as causes of those changes. These efforts (e.g., critical thinking courses, writing across the curriculum, and interdisciplinary studies) have shifted in viability as the educational focus has shifted. And finally, there is a third group of innovations within enduring tools or programs that have enjoyed new or different emphasis through the focus on curriculum coherence. Honors programs, for instance, are nothing new in the community college, although they receive greater or lesser attention from time to time based upon how well they align with the catchwords of the day. It is difficult for an honors program to get a slot in a forum about access, but much easier to be included in one devoted to the topic of excellence.

The following sections examine curricular reform of the last two decades in the context of the spiral's soar to coherence.

CURRICULAR COHERENCE

The 1960s marked the heyday of community college growth and innovation, and the hundreds of colleges born into that rich, turbulent era reflected both their heredity and their environment in the curricula they offered. Their very existence was an innovative departure from traditional colleges and universities with their monopoly on higher education. Building their missions upon access rather than selectivity, the community colleges would satisfy the demands for an educated democracy in ways that would never be achieved by traditional curricula and traditional colleges.

The new purpose and mission were not, however, entirely altruistic. Business and industry were clamoring for a new wave of technically trained workers with the new skills required for a rapidly expanding technological society. To meet these demands, colleges needed to be responsive, unbelievably adaptable, and willing to pursue new ways to teach a new population of students who never acted like, nor considered themselves, students. Traditional students in traditional colleges and universities in the 1960s were taking to the streets and demanding relevance in the curriculum with only a vague notion of what they were demanding. Many new students in the community colleges, on the other hand, knew exactly what it meant: "Will what you are teaching me help me get or keep a job?" For back-up, these students had the full support of the business/industrial community, demanding of the colleges, "Are you teaching the skills we need?" As more and more necessary skills were identified, time-tested core curricula and general education requirements were abandoned, to be replaced by an array of options that honored the student's right to choose—and sometimes abandoned the institution's responsibility to decide.

Access and vocationalism became twin masters that demanded more and more curricular choice. If underprepared students who entered through the open door could not complete one set of requirements, then the college would create another option to enable them to succeed. If the standard English composition course was not "relevant" for management students, perhaps "Communications Skills for Business" would be more to the point.

The 1960s and early 1970s seethed with curricular activity, much of it indeed innovative. But however worthy the motives of those responding to the demands of access and vocationalism, however necessary the transition from rigidity to relevance, the result was an inevitable fragmentation that led Arthur Cohen to comment that "community colleges have long been in the forefront of instructional innovation, but some of them have confounded individualized instruction with a curriculum for each individual" (1979, 107). Renewed emphasis on competency-based curricula, general education, and the integrating power of the new technology are reviving a coherent curriculum.

Individualized curriculum was epitomized by the "educational supermarket" at Portland Community College (Oregon) in the early 1970s. Numerous community colleges adopted this cafeteria approach, which allowed students to sample small curricular modules and arrange these snippets to meet their individual needs. Harold Hodgkinson noted early that no one ever chose to eat in a cafeteria for its quality, but access, convenience, and individual appetite were the market demands that drove the cafeteria approach (1974, 192).

COMPETENCY-BASED VERSUS OBJECTIVE-BASED CURRICULA

Simultaneous with this development, systematic, individualized, objective-based instruction moved into ascendancy in the community college. This movement increased the fragmentation of the curriculum by casting teachers as selectors of objectives in the service of the curriculum, rather than as vital connecting links between student and curriculum. The system's movement also fostered the development of specific objectives which attempted to break the curriculum into its most discrete units, generally translated into demonstrable skills.

Competency-based instruction and objective-based instruction are alike in that they are both techniques or principles for specifying exactly what a student is expected to learn at a given point in his or her instruction. But they are as different as the two ends of a telescope.

Specific objectives focused narrowly on the most discrete units of learning. An objective-based curriculum, then, was literally a string of specific skills performed by a student in isolation. If these skills are the basis for assessment of student learning, there is little impetus for synthesis even within a course, much less across course lines. A specific objective may be as simple as "the student will be able to spell 50 vocabulary words with 80 percent accuracy"; or, "the student will be able to arrange facts supplied by the instructor into a five-paragraph theme with an introduction, a conclusion, and three support paragraphs, each with a minimum of five sentences, with no more than seven mechanical errors." Both of these examples place emphasis on the form rather than the substance of the student's learning. The 20 percent allowable spelling errors may, in fact, be the most important words in the student's occupation, and the student may be able to write an acceptable five-paragraph theme without actually learning the cognitive skill of classification of the objective intended.

Competencies, in contrast to objectives, attempt to describe what a curriculum actually requires of a student and to that extent must be focused broadly enough to incorporate many varied learning tasks. A competency may be that "the student will demonstrate an ability to use the vocabulary of the occupation appropriately." Although the vocabulary may be taught in the communications skills course, the competency is certainly required in virtually all the curriculum courses. Consequently, the student's performance on this competency is continually assessed as the student moves through the program.

Instead of requiring a student to write a five-paragraph theme, a competency may state that a student will be able to synthesize and organize information and communicate it clearly. Again, a single course may "own" this competency, but it is cross-disciplinary and could be assessed throughout the curriculum.

With an objective-based curriculum, the student rarely is encouraged to see the connection between the skill and the total educational experience. (And this approach was promoted on the heels of the 1960's cry for relevance in the curriculum!) With competency-based curricula, the student knows that the knowledge and abilities he or she must acquire and exhibit in one course are also what is needed to become college-educated.

GENERAL EDUCATION

The renewed emphasis on general education in the community college is related to the integrating power of a competency-based curriculum. The best-known general education reforms, including those of Miami-Dade Community College (Florida) and Dallas County Community College District (Texas), have been built upon models that define essential competencies for associate degree recipients. Where general education has been genuinely revisioned, it has begun with the fundamental question: "What ought every graduate of this community college to know?" which echoes Ralph Tyler's first fundamental question, "What educational purposes should this school seek to attain?" The answer to that question has taken many forms, from common core curricula to sets of clearly defined competencies that may be acquired in a variety of courses.

Certainly no question has been asked more frequently in recent years, as commission after commission decried the loss of curricular coherence and called for a core of common learning for all students. When Senator Nancy Kassebaum admonished the new Commission on the Future of Community Colleges to avoid overspecialization of education and to move instead toward a more general approach, she cited the 1947 President's Commission on Higher Education (1987, 31). This call, however, requires nothing less than a redefinition of what it means to be an educated person in contemporary society and a specific delineation of the role a college should play in contributing toward that essential knowledge.

In their 1987 report "Core Curriculum: Emerging Challenge for the California Community Colleges," the Task Group for the Commission on Instruction sets forth a proposal for the California community colleges to adopt a core curriculum for all degree students. Their report clearly distinguishes a core curriculum from distribution requirements, and further notes that many models for a core curriculum are acceptable.

Elements and Principles of Core Curriculum

The core curriculum will be based on a different set of principles from those underlying breadth requirements. Breadth is a pattern for a distribution of courses selected from traditional fields of knowledge; on the other hand, core curriculum is a group of courses that will provide an integrated educational experience with common elements.

Elements of Core Curriculum:
1. Core curriculum is unified by a set of principles.
2. Core may satisfy breadth but breadth does not necessarily satisfy core.
3. Core is more specific than breadth and more detailed.
4. Core is internally cohesive based on a common set of experiences. The courses within core should reinforce and echo one another.

5. Core is crafted internally, while breadth generally satisfies external requirements.
6. Core models will reflect the characteristics and needs of individual colleges but express the core principles delineated above.
7a. Core courses will satisfy common criteria such as the following:
   1. Communication skills
   2. Problem solving
   3. Critical thinking
   4. Appreciation of the arts
   5. Ethical implications
   6. Cultural pluralism and awareness of diversity
   7. Modes of inquiry (scientific methods)
   8. Interdisciplinary methods
   9. Creativity
7b. Core courses will be taken by all students seeking degree and general education certification.
7c. Core should not be preemptive or have negative effects on vocational programs. Colleges need a way to encourage vocational students who get a certificate to complete a degree. The key factors impacting on this will be their willingness to take core courses and the capability within vocational programs to elect core courses. (Task Group 1987, 4–5)

These elements represent an innovative beginning in their differentiation from the distribution requirements which were long confused with a general education core. The recognition that many curriculum models may address the general education core is also distinctive. The report mentions a nine-unit core, an interdisciplinary core, a survey course model, and a model combining core and breadth. Surely it is more renaissance than reformation when creative leaders accept that more than "one right way" exists to address the core of learning.

It is interesting to note that one curriculum model overlooked in the California report is a curriculum-spanning general education competency approach. Though it presents special difficulties in implementation, this innovative model is being used successfully in a Georgia college.

Clayton Junior College (now Clayton State College, a four-year institution) defined its new general education curriculum as outcome-based, identifying two skills and eight perspectives for students to acquire, apply, and integrate. The innovative aspect of the Clayton program is not the skills or perspectives identified (a task each institution must perform for itself), but the fact that the general education outcomes are not associated solely with particular disciplines or courses. They are developed across the college curriculum, "emphasizing the coherence of the general education program as it is taught and as students experience it" (Doig, Corse, and Horne 1986, 2).

The curriculum innovators at Clayton recognize the complex assessment challenge presented by this approach. Each outcome or competency is repeatedly assessed in different disciplines and courses throughout the curriculum. This process reinforces student learning and validates assessment information, though it is complex to manage. The common criteria and standards applied to the outcomes assessment increase student understanding of the outcome, as well as build a strong "sense of the coherence of the general education experience" (1986, 3).

The "new" general education found in the 1980s community college curricula shares a common tradition with the time-honored liberal arts curriculum which 1960s leaders so pointedly attacked as irrelevant. But the innovative programs are not reactionary returns to the past. Any individual liberal arts course could be viewed as irrelevant if the only criterion is whether it specifically prepares one for the immediate demands of life. Likewise, a liberal arts curriculum, when viewed as a series of disconnected, purposeless choices, could be viewed as irrelevant, and worse, as a sentimental attachment to values no longer meaningful in the contemporary world. The emphasis of the California proposal and of Clayton State's general education curriculum is coherence achieved through interrelated courses within a curriculum. Learning that is interrelated across course lines is inherently relevant.

Truly meaningful education, of course, must be relevant to life outside the educational environment. Recent curricular innovations in general education requirements and core curricula are studies in relevance to life. Most educators and educational critics agree that knowledge and skills taught today will be outdated soon. An integrated, coherent general education curriculum prepares a student to be a learner, and that will enable the kind of adaptability life today demands. An integrated curriculum not only gives a student a more solid foundation on which to build than does a fragmented one, it teaches the student that learning is something more than what is measured by a single test, and that learning transcends the experiences occurring within a single course. It is this "knowledge" that enables a student to become a lifelong learner.

Far from being a return to the past, these innovations answer enduring, fundamental questions in new ways within a new context to prepare students for a complex future. The best answers provide a sense of connection to the past, integration of learning, and the invaluable capacity for lifelong learning.

Curricular efforts at this integration are not new. PROJECT CHANCE operated from 1976–80 at Brooklyn College (New York) and was described as a reentry curriculum for ethnically diverse low- and middle-income women in the Brooklyn community. This innovation serves as a good example of the emerging attempt at integration in curriculum at the halfway point in the 20-year cycle. The students who entered PROJECT CHANCE found themselves developing their learning materials through autobiographies, art, poetry, tapes, and newsletters. They found a new educational philosophy in which students and teachers saw themselves as "co-investigators" of their experience.

Although much more limited in scope than general education requirements or a core curriculum, this experimental project was similar in that it attempted to prescribe a common experience for an identified group of students, and to make that experience totally integrated. With community colleges firmly committed to accessibility, especially for "nontraditional" students, it is understandable why PROJECT CHANCE had a narrow target population. But already its leaders saw that students needed to feel a personally relevant connection not only to what they were learning, but even to those from whom they were learning. Unfortunately, the students were operating from an earlier mindset about learning and expected the teacher to be the authority; they would be the passive participants. Although this experiment did not continue past the duration of its grant from the Fund for the Improvement of Postsecondary Education, projects like this one a decade ago enabled the integrated curricula emerging today.

While PROJECT CHANCE was still basically a response to the heterogeneity resulting from increased access, its leaders had recognized what academics in the 1980s accept: the educational mission of acculturation is best served by shared goals, by curricular connection, by connection of individuals to each other and their shared experience. The role of the community college in the acculturation process is likewise changing.

Judith Eaton observes that community colleges are less willing to be unstructured, undirected "course colleges" and are striving to create a "purposeful, powerful learning climate that provides clear signals about educational values" (1985, 9). While the community college continues to offer a cafeteria-style range of courses for the student wishing to sample its wares, those institutions in the forefront of innovation make unequivocal statements about educational values through their approaches to general education. They bring every resource of assessment, advisement, and instruction to bear as they support this central core of learning in ways that help assure student success. They acknowledge that curriculum is a complex system integrally related to instruction and student support. This comprehensive approach spirals upward; it does not signify a pendulum swing to the curriculum of yesteryear.

THE NEW TECHNOLOGY

The impact of technology on curriculum over the last 20 years is so great that it will be discussed in a separate section later in this chapter. It is presented briefly here, however, to establish how the change in the use of technology in business and industry has necessitated a similar change in education. Innovations in general education and competency-based curricula have brought a new definition of what it means to be educated, and this has fueled the upward spiral of curricular change. But nothing has contributed more to the pace and direction of this change than the explosion in technology, and especially the growth of the microchip.

A great fear of the 1950s and 1960s was that technology was in the hands of narrow specialists who understood only small, discrete parts of the whole. Consequently, according to the myth, technology was out of control. It is obvious today that narrow specialists cannot exist in the new technology, which is why technical curricula increasingly share courses and why lifelong learning is essential.

It is also a false notion that students today have to know more, be smarter, or start higher than students of the past. Students have always had to know theory and know skills. So the content may be different, but it is not necessarily harder or more abstract. That can be demonstrated by tracing the trend from vacuum tubes to microchips in electronics technology. To be knowledgeable about vacuum tubes, which may seem primitive today, students had to learn the specifications of literally hundreds of kinds, and be able to accommodate the fact that two of the same type could have slightly different characteristics. A microchip, on the other hand, is exact. With microtechnology, more than two dozen laser tracks can be set in a space the width of the edge of a piece of notebook paper. Throughout this rapid change, colleges had to design the curriculum to prepare students for technical jobs, and to do so within degree programs of reasonable demands and duration.

The learning is different, however, in that students learned *about* vacuum tubes, *about* transistors, but they learned to *make* ICs (integrated circuits). Now, with EPROMS (erasable, programmable, read-only-memory), they are able to use software to create hardware (a chip—which is called firmware); essentially they create as well as design electronic components. Consequently, what a student learns is no longer separate from how he or she learns.

Technology now demands integration of method and content. A student who learns how to machine an aluminum candlestick using a Bridgeport numerical control machine or who learns accounting using Lotus 1-2-3 learns more than just machining or accounting; he or she learns a new technology. In the early 1970s computer-assisted instruction (CAI) was based on the belief that computers offered better ways to teach content. The students did not use the computers; they merely responded to them. In the new marketplace of the 1980s, however, microprocessors are so much a part of life that innovative colleges now enable students to learn to use them as they learn content.

Cuyahoga Community College's Metropolitan Campus (Ohio) loans laptop computers to students for an academic quarter, so they can do word processing anywhere, even on the bus. The results show that students are writing more and have a greater understanding of the mechanics of writing, from basic sentence structure to the composing process. The only difference between now and before is the change from paper and pen to computer. Just as electronic numerical control cannot be separated from machine tool processes, and information processing in electronic spreadsheets cannot be separated from accounting, electronic word processing is becoming an integral part of written communication.

The integration of learning as a result of the new technology is not limited only to the integration of method and content. Technological curricula of the 1980s are more interdisciplinary, by necessity, than are the general education curricula. The shift from specialized curricula to those that cross departmental lines can be seen by looking at the development of technical curricula at a single college.

At Central Piedmont Community College (North Carolina), the Architectural Technology program came about because of the need of architect firms for technicians with more drawing skills. This program drew heavily from the Civil Engineering program. Likewise, the Electrical program gave rise to the Electronics program, and they both contributed to the Computer Technology program. The Mechanical program led to the Manufacturing program, and, now, there are so many shared courses that the dividing lines between programs are arbitrary at best.

This approach reflects industry practice. When Eastman Kodak recently contacted Central Piedmont to provide training for the optic-recording technicians in its subsidiary company Verbatim, the college responded, not with a new curriculum, but by adding only five new courses to the existing ones. A technician at Verbatim who is in charge of a block of production must have some knowledge of robotics, computers, hydraulics, pneumatics, electronics, as well as electrical systems, to name a few. In other words, what Verbatim needed, and the college could accommodate, was actually less technical specialization even though electro-optic technology is one of the most recent specialties.

In the 1960s and 1970s, a technician who took electronics engineering learned to work on TVs using electronic analog or digital readout devices. A computer seems, in several ways, to be similar to a TV. However, the difference is that computers are always connected to something else: a keyboard, software in a diskdrive or hard disk, a robotic welder, or an optical scanner. The technician who works on the computer has to have some practical familiarity with the technology of these other processes and instruments as well. Likewise, in manufacturing, a manufacturing engineer will design a system for drilling holes for a cam shaft. A computer engineer will have to develop the software to run the system, and an electronics engineer will have to maintain the system. But each individual will have to have some understanding of the whole process, and the curricula that trained them will have to accommodate this need.

The fear of the early 1960s that technology was in the hands of narrow specialists who understood only a small part of the technological whole has proven unfounded. The nature of technology itself, at least as it has developed into the 1980s and seems to be headed into the future, requires a greater integration of knowledge across specialty lines than could have been imagined two decades ago. No one then could have foreseen that this chapter would, 20 years later, be developed in a microchip, projected on a CRT, stored on a floppy disk, printed on a laser printer, and enhanced with a snack heated by microwaves. The curriculum today reflects this same integration of technology and learning.

Other, more traditional curricular connections are playing a key role in the resurgence of curricular coherence.

CURRICULAR CONNECTIONS

The fragmentation of the 1960s and 1970s curriculum was not without its casualties. The focus on discrete objectives and the attention on specific skills, usually one skill at a time, did not foster synthesis, so critical thinking, always a concern of educators, became less and less a working value in the curriculum. Likewise, the early entrenchment of departmental boundaries worked against the integrated learning fostered by interdisciplinary studies. With courses and departments increasingly accountable for specific content and skills, curriculum-spanning efforts such as writing across the curriculum also were pushed further into obscurity.

Gradually, however, the voids became unacceptable and colleges recognized that their graduates, having received narrow educations, were not satisfying the more generalized needs of business and industry. The pressure from the marketplace shifted from technical training only to technical training with the ability to think and to communicate. Midway in the last 20 years of curricular change, individual programs aimed specifically at improving thinking and communication skills began to reappear, often with notable success. These are now giving way to the more integrated approaches fostered by competency-based education.

CRITICAL THINKING

Faced with students often lacking basic skills and frequently lacking cognitive skills, several community colleges emphasized critical thinking in the late 1960s and 1970s. One well-publicized effort was designed by Ellen Korn at Jefferson Community College (Kentucky) in the mid-1970s. Her cognitive model program attracted widespread attention because it was designed for students who lacked basic skills as well as critical thinking skills. The program emphasized audiotutorials, games, and computer tests designed to improve students' thinking skills—and it used them in a remedial learning laboratory setting.

This approach and other similar designs were aimed at responding to the familiar lament: "It's not just that they can't read. They can't *think*!" But the reviews on critical thinking programs were mixed. While students were able to master the particular course assignments, they frequently were unable to transfer the critical thinking skills they had supposedly mastered to other areas of endeavor. When taught as a separate skill, critical thinking became an exercise without intellectual connections outside the context of its own discrete learning unit.

Mortimer Adler (1987), that intrepid proponent of integrated learning, sums up the case of many critics in an article entitled "Why 'Critical Thinking' Programs Won't Work." He argues forcefully against courses with texts and teachers that develop decision rules and pseudosystems for critical thinking and offer it up as yet another skill to be "mastered" for course completion and forgotten. Adler prefers a coaching approach that reinforces critical thinking in every course. Some of the more exciting work in community colleges follows this advice.

The Learning Strategies Program at Johnson County Community College (Kansas) is a recent development designed to help students use "cognitive and meta-cognitive" skills to become more effective learners. Adler would undoubtedly see this as a critical thinking program, but he might have some hope that it would work because it develops cognitive skills along with content, rather than attempting to teach critical thinking in abstract isolation. The program has three phases. The Strategic Learning System, Phase 1, coaches students in eight task-specific strategies applied to a content course in which the student is currently enrolled. Phase 2, Generalization, concentrates on the transfer of the strategies to other content courses. The final phase, Executive Strategy, encourages students in the development of their personal strategies for critical thinking.

Even more acceptable to Adler would be the Clayton State approach, in which critical thinking is one of two skills identified as part of the outcomes approach to general education. The Clayton curricular strategy holds out the promise for critical thinking as a cohesive agent for the curriculum.

WRITING ACROSS THE CURRICULUM

It is no accident that the second skill in the Clayton State College program is communication. Communication skills, and particularly writing skills, are currently popular integrating devices in a curriculum overloaded with multiple-choice tests and depleted of regular writing experiences. National furor over declining reading and writing skills precipitated this emphasis. Teachers of composition, properly incensed that all deficiencies in student writing were laid at their door, protested that writing skills should be reinforced across the curriculum, and thus began a national movement. More accurately, thus began a national movement again.

Since World War II, writing-across-the- curriculum (WAC) programs have surfaced from time to time, burning brightly with the fire of inspired leadership before fading with the departure of the leader. The most recent wave of WAC programs has been somewhat unique in that certain states, such as Florida, have issued legislative fiats requiring certain quantities of writing. While it is too early to make judgments on the effectiveness of such "innovations," it is predictable that WAC programs will continue to encounter the obstacles of specialization and departmentalism that have plagued them in the past.

As with most cross-disciplinary or interdisciplinary efforts, insular department structures and specialized curricula present formidable obstacles. Community college programs face special barriers with many faculty members in occupational or vocational areas who do not see writing as a way to learning and who are unable to develop meaningful writing assignments that help students learn.

In fact, one WAC director observes that the most important element when beginning a writing-across-the-curriculum effort is identifying an "apostle" in each department. Others agree that this accurately reflects the nature of the conversion it takes to institute writing across the curriculum.

Southeastern Community College (North Carolina) is one example of such a conversion. This WAC effort depends highly upon a single committed and resourceful leader, but at present the entire college seems to agree that the attitude toward using more writing in all classes has changed completely. Part of the effectiveness of this effort can be traced to three workshops offered to the faculty. The first helped faculty to understand what is meant by "good" writing, without relying on English-teacher terminology. The second helped faculty understand how to use writing as a mode of learning, and the third attempted to get faculty who do not teach English to approach student writing from an assessment point of view rather than one of strict grading. Writing at Southeastern is now a part of most courses.

Another successful model is found at Bakersfield College (California). Their WAC manual states that writing across the curriculum is "an attempt to return writing—wherever possible—to its former, more significant, place in the pedagogical process" (Stansbury and Palitz 1985, 2). Writing is integrated into the learning process at Bakersfield. Their success is demonstrated at the end of the manual with sample assignments, each one requiring the student to synthesize the content through writing from courses as diverse as career counseling, nursing, geology, math, and chemistry.

The success of WAC programs of the past did center, unfortunately, on a dynamic leader. But the reason they were less than successful was not only that the leader, or the dynamism, faded; it was that the writing was never fully integrated into the student's learning. Many programs simply asked faculty to require more writing, such as essay tests or research papers. (At least one was even set up so that the English faculty would grade for mechanics, the course faculty for content.) Others, some that survive today, put writing-intensive courses in the curriculum. And some approached writing across the curriculum by instituting minimum numbers of words the students would write.

These attempts to remedy the writing wasteland developed as a result of the fragmentation of curriculum and resulting focus on objective-based learning. There simply was little place for writing in those days except in the isolated communications courses. The newer approaches, however, seem much less personality-dependent because they attempt to make writing an integral part of day-to-day learning. When this type of integration occurs at a college, it is very likely that writing will remain fully entrenched as a learning tool, at least through the next spin of the curriculum spiral.

INTERDISCIPLINARY STUDIES

The emphasis upon integration and coherence in the community college curriculum has created a renewed emphasis upon interdisciplinary studies as well. Several of the major general education revisions have included some dimension of interdisciplinary effort, Miami-Dade notable among them. Most institutions have been too unwilling, too unwise, or quite simply unable to provide the time, resources, and environment required for the success of interdisciplinary efforts. Where these have been provided, as at Miami-Dade, the success is remarkable.

The Dallas County Community College District included one interdisciplinary course in its general education core revision. Based in part upon a survey of employers which emphasized outcomes related to human relations and oral communications, the Dallas District designated a speech communications course that combined aspects of the traditional speech curriculum and the traditional human development curriculum. Instructors from both disciplines collaborated in the design of the course, and it is frequently taught by a team. Heavy enrollments and high levels of student satisfaction indicate the positive effects of such collaboration.

Colby Community College (Kansas) has adapted science courses to emphasize the visual arts. Science content is maintained, but students' assignments build upon an artistic perspective. For example, drawing from live models is the basis for learning human anatomy. Lab time is used for drawing as well as experimenting, and faculty from both science and art fields are available to discuss student approaches to the assignment.

Some of the interdisciplinary approaches go so far as to redefine the roles of teacher and learner. Tacoma Community College (Washington) has a "Bridge Program" with Evergreen to prepare students for upper division work at Evergreen's downtown Tacoma campus. The program takes a thematic approach (in this case, the theme of "The City as Cultural Mirror") and brings together the faculty of both colleges. Evergreen, however, has begun an experiment of its own using the "federated learning community model" in which three courses are linked by a theme, and the faculty member becomes, instead of a teacher, a "master learner." The role of the master learner is to take all the courses along with the students and to lead weekly integrating seminars.

Despite the difficulties of these cross-disciplinary or interdisciplinary approaches, when well-done, they kindle an enthusiasm unmatched by more linear, traditional curricula. North Seattle Community College (Washington) found its interdisciplinary "American Values" program so stimulating that students were arranging study parties to pursue the new, complex ideas they were exploring. Study parties? A curriculum approach with this much ability to excite the modern community college student is an innovation worth perpetuating!

CURRICULAR CONTINUUM

Neither developmental studies programs nor honors programs are new to the community college. But they have often been seen as outside the regular curriculum, sometimes with little connection to it. Developmental studies programs of the 1960s and 1970s, for example, sometimes awarded grades based on attendance; the goal of building self-esteem overrode any academic goal. Most of the previously described innovations provide integration across subjects or curriculum areas; they provide ways to connect history to English or to integrate computer applications across the horizontal curriculum continuum.

Developmental studies and honors programs may be described as points on a vertical curriculum continuum, moving, for example, from basic studies in writing, to regular composition courses, to honors courses. No longer is separation of the developmental or honors curricula acceptable; means to span the boundary to the regular curriculum are fundamental to today's innovations.

DEVELOPMENTAL STUDIES

Developmental studies have been a special curriculum purview of the community college, and the past two decades have been marked by dramatic developments in how adults learn basic skills and how developmental curricula can be designed for greater effectiveness. Increasingly, developmental studies curricula are becoming part of a network of programs designed to help assure success for underprepared students. These studies are rarely viewed in today's community colleges as single-shot courses designed simply to improve a skill. Instead, developmental studies programs are curriculum boundary spanners, helping move students up the vertical curriculum axis. Two examples illustrate this emphasis upon connection to the regular curriculum.

Midlands Technical College (South Carolina) created a Developmental Science Program designed to enable nontraditional students to move into mainstream curriculum science courses and be successful. The Developmental Science Program is divided into three phases called Developmental, Transition, and Spanning for Success. In the Developmental Phase, the student assists in generating a prescription that includes a working schedule and planned dates for completion. During the Transition Phase, the developmental instructor meets with the mainstream instructor and works out a schedule for the student to begin auditing part of the mainstream science course. During the Spanning for Success Phase, the student enters the mainstream course but retains the developmental instructor as tutor (National Institute for Staff and Organizational Development 1985).

Laney College (California) created Project Bridge to allow students the "opportunity to 'bridge' into academic or vocational programs." Bridge I offers classes in reading, writing, math, and two content courses developed for 4–7 grade reading level. Bridge II offers the same classes at a higher level. Bridge III is a study skills class with small-group tutorials and counseling support for students who are simultaneously enrolled in regular classes. The most important features are content classes, primacy of natural (spoken) language, a student-centered classroom, and a learning community. The program is built on the premise that, "if teacher information is to become student understanding, the students must filter it through their own experience and express it in their own words."

HONORS PROGRAMS

Honors programs lie at the other end of the vertical continuum. Once hotly debated as elitist or worse, honors programs have been experiencing a resurgence in popularity on the crest of the quality wave. Such programs have been touted as a means to encourage student achievement and foster academic excellence, and they have taken many forms. Some have merely been special "stretch" assignments made as part of regular courses. Others have been developed as fully coordinated curricula. Ironically, just as earlier developmental studies programs tended to isolate students from the curricular mainstream, some honors programs may have precisely the same effect. Well-developed programs, however, may benefit not only the honors students, but the overall curriculum and thus all students.

The program at Frederick Community College (Maryland) certainly has this potential. The culminating course in their departmental honors program is an independent study and forum. The student proposes an independent study project that is approved by a committee. Working closely with a faculty mentor, the student prepares the project and periodically meets with other honors students and presents his or her work. The final project is reviewed by the committee and then presented orally to the college and the community. Copies of the project are bound and become part of the learning resource center collection.

About their general honors component, Frederick staff say, "We believe that learning takes place in a social context . . ." (Lindblad 1987, 31). The foundation of the program is a series of team-taught interdisciplinary seminars. After one of these courses has been taught three times, it is modified for one instructor and becomes part of the general college curriculum.

Rather than seeing honors programs as narrow, Frederick Community College sees theirs as providing "greater opportunities to experiment with subject matter, and increased latitude to improve teaching techniques." Their students affirm the importance of the social dimension of learning when they say the honors program provides them "opportunities to study with others who are intellectually inclined, to be exposed to instructors who demonstrate a high level of interest in their progress, and to be academically challenged" (1987, 31).

CURRICULAR CHANGE: TECHNOLOGY-DRIVEN

Earlier in this chapter, the ways in which technology has contributed to the integration of curricula were discussed. Unquestionably, more curriculum change has occurred in technical/occupational curricula as a consequence of changing technology than in all the general education, interdisciplinary, and honors areas combined. And it is on this type of change that the following section will focus. These changes are so commonplace in community colleges that they are rarely regarded as innovative, but they embed many of the most significant innovations of the last two decades.

Rapid changes have generated new courses or new course content that have made the curricula of the past obsolete, or the changes have resulted in totally new curricula. A student who dropped out of a secretarial science program in the early 1970s lacking only, for example, an accounting course, could not complete the program in 1988 without taking perhaps 20 additional hours that simply did not exist before. These include training in not only the obvious, such as word processing, but also on office machines, which existed then as a course, but with entirely different content than today's course.

Probably as much as 20 percent of today's automotive technology program did not exist in the early 1970s. As automobiles became more and more electronic, service depended more and more upon technical training. The industry set up ways to provide training to automotive technology instructors who, in turn, revised existing courses and added new ones to make the curriculum reflect the state of the technology. Donald Petersen, CEO of Ford motor company, points out that 1987 Fords have 58 engine configurations, 43 transmission combinations in 10 transmission families, 33 axle assemblies, and 56 unique powertrain calibrations. Recognizing that "the ability to learn and adapt and keep our knowledge current will be crucial," Petersen says that Ford has established ASSET (Automotive Student Service Educational Training) as a two-year cooperative education program between Ford and ten colleges. By the end of 1988, he expects one in each of Ford's 29 districts throughout the country ("Ford, Change" 1987, 25).

Community colleges have historically developed new curricula to meet the demands of new technology. Programs developed across the country in robotics, laser optics technology, automated manufacturing, and more, reflect this continuing trend. Community colleges must be adaptable. Future demands may warrant an entirely new curriculum, such as the Optical Engineering Technology program implemented at Monroe Community College (New York) to train technicians to manufacture disks produced by Kodak. Or the demands may warrant only the addition of a handful of new courses added to an existing curriculum, as was the case with Central Piedmont Community College (North Carolina) and its arrangement with Kodak discussed earlier.

Another interesting impact of technology is the inverse of the technological breadth required of students. It is the dramatic increase of specialized courses, typically in the extension or noncredit areas developed to meet immediate and specific needs, which often arise from the rapid advance of technology. Shifting courses that could be credit to the noncredit area is the community college's entrepreneurial response to rapidly changing market demands. And community colleges across the country are witnessing the burgeoning growth of their extension operations—sometimes at the expense of their credit offerings.

In diverse ways, technology is changing the technical curricula of the community college.

CONCLUSIONS

If the fundamental trend in community college curricula over the past two decades has been toward greater integration and coherence, then surely the next significant emphasis will be upon evaluating curricular outcomes and modifying curricula based on these assessments. The Southern Association of Colleges and Schools has taken the national lead in the institutional effectiveness movement. This approach may call for more fine-tuning of curriculum, based on continuing assessments.

This next step is an important one if community colleges are to have confidence that the curricular changes of recent decades represent real improvement over what went before. Already, some critics see the emphasis on general education and honors programs as reactionary returns to a university model rather than bellwethers of continuing progress in the community college curriculum. The response to such critics should come in the form of a report on results achieved, not another hollow philosophical debate.

Some changes presented by their champions as curriculum innovations are pendulum swings toward a tired, exclusionary past and some may appear that way because of the observers' myopia. But many of the new general education programs, the interdisciplinary studies, and the integrating technologies represent that spiral moving ever upward over the same familiar—and fundamental—ground of community college mission. The best of these innovations is helping the curriculum bring meaning to the excellence that gives access its value.

REFERENCES

"ACE Releases 'Campus Trends, 1987.' " 1987. *Higher Education & National Affairs* 36, no. 16 (Aug. 10).

ADLER, MORTIMER J. 1987. "Why 'Critical Thinking' Programs Won't Work." *Education Digest* (March):9–12.

AXELROD, JOSEPH. 1968. "Curricular Change: A Model for Analysis." *The Research Reporter* 3 (University of California-Berkeley, Center for Research and Development in Higher Education).

COHEN, ARTHUR M. 1979. "Issues in Curriculum Formation." *New Directions for Community Colleges* VII (Spring):101–13.

DOIG, JAMES; LARRY CORSE; and CHRISTINA HORNE. 1986. "Teaching and Assessing General Education Outcomes across the Curriculum." Paper presented to the 1986 AACJC Convention, Orlando, Florida, April 13.

EATON, JUDITH. 1985. "The Challenge for Change at the Community College." *Educational Record* (Fall):5–11.

"Ford, Change and Community Colleges." 1987. *Community, Technical and Junior College Journal* (Aug./Sep.):25–27.

HODGKINSON, HAROLD. 1974. "Commentary: Educational Supermarkets, Flathead and Portland Community Colleges." In *New Colleges for New Students*, edited by Harold Hodgkinson. San Francisco: Jossey-Bass.

KASSEBAUM, NANCY. 1987. "Renewed Focus on Community Colleges." *Community, Technical and Junior College Journal* (April/May):30–32.

LINDBLAD, JERRI. 1987. "Having It Both Ways at Frederick Community College: Departments and General Honors in the Context of a Two- Year Program." In *A Ren-*

aissance of Innovation, edited by Terry O'Banion. Irvine, Calif.:Association of California Community College Administrators.

National Institute for Staff and Organizational Development. 1985. *Innovation Abstracts* 7, no. 29 (Nov. 15).

STANSBURY, DON, and MERRIEM PALITZ. 1985. "Writing Across the Curriculum: A Manual for Teachers." Bakersfield College, Kern Community College District, 2.

Task Group for Commission on Instruction. 1987. "Core Curriculum: Emerging Challenge for the California Community Colleges." Report, March 31.

3

Innovations

IN

Teaching

THE PAST AS PROLOGUE

Suanne D. Roueche and John E. Roueche

IDENTIFYING THE REALITY

Hindsight is such a curious phenomenon: insightful, thoughtful, bright individuals are regularly humbled by its ability to make clear in retrospect those events so elusive in progress. A review of the last two decades is such a humbling experience. One can now identify, with 20/20 vision, the events that were gathering strength and developing into a more familiar educational predicament. The predicament is simply: higher education must address the needs of the majority of entering students who are unable to perform at the so-called "traditional" skill level and must creatively respond to the vast majority of those students presently enrolled who cannot negotiate regular college work. Simultaneously, it must address the needs of the more "traditional" student and the honor student, providing them with the high level of instruction that they need and deserve.

Using hindsight as a guide, it is clear that the road to this predicament was more clearly marked for those involved in researching or teaching developmental/remedial courses for 20-plus years than for those teaching/researching traditional students and classes. It is then from such a perspective that this discussion begins.

In the early 1960s, a problem—seemingly unique to community colleges—was receiving widespread attention. "New students" who had never before considered going to college were arriving to enroll, and their skill levels were clearly inadequate for successful college work. Many colleges were testing these students in the areas of reading, writing, and math to determine whether they should enter regular courses or remedial/development classes that had been organized to receive this new clientele. Faculty were being recruited and/or commandeered to "develop" these students and courses.

Early on, those who taught remedial/developmental courses could only wonder how it was that when skills tests indicated a need for remediation or development in basic skills, only a small percentage of those students so identified enrolled. On registration days, students—who were unable to find space in the developmental courses or who were ignoring a counselor's suggestions to take basic skills courses—enrolled in regular academic and vocational classes. It was suspected that these students would be leaving college very soon; but there was no tracking system for verifying their academic progress, and at best there was only speculation about their fate.

But the fact that instructors of remedial/developmental courses could sit and watch this unfolding with little more than mild amazement—and only some annoyance—suggests that no one had begun to comprehend the severity and the magnitude of the possible disasters that this early indifference and commitment to the problem of student unpreparedness would create. The general feeling in those days was that remedial/developmental faculty and courses were just strange and unexplainable phenomena that would likely go away, just "flash-in-the-pan" efforts to attack a temporary problem that had no clear form or significance.

However, not too many years had passed before this curious brand of instruction was developing some popularity. Many of those students whose registration decisions were puzzling and annoying were alive, but not so well, at the college. Instructors from other disciplines were requesting help with their (most likely these) students, for example, in teaching the rudiments of math, tutoring in the writing of complete sentences and useful paragraphs, teaching mnemonics for spelling and defining technological terms, providing tips for using the dictionary, and so forth. As help for individual students expanded to include instruction for larger groups of students, it was clear that the academic transfer and technical/vocational instructors were having to teach more and more students who appeared to be much like developmental students.

Moreover, those who taught both academic and remedial/developmental courses could not ignore the mirror-images effect; developmental students were becoming peculiarly similar to those enrolled in so-called "regular" courses. It was becoming increasingly difficult to identify the "developmental" students. Greater numbers of high school graduates were appearing in remedial/developmental courses, where but a few years before there had been a majority of GED recipients and high school drop-outs. The newest enrollees, these high school graduates, were rather deficient in basic skills to have earned diplomas. An unbelievable and unfortunate scenario was unfolding— slow motion in those days, but rapid-fire in retrospect.

During this decade, those teaching remedial/developmental courses were experimenting with a multitude of instructional strategies. Faculty experimented with self-pacing, only to find that it worked best with highly motivated and self-directed students, of which there were few. Others developed instruction using peer counselors and tutors, paraprofessionals, media, tape recorders, and so on. In a flurry of activity, less and less attention was paid to what others in the academic and transfer areas were doing and more attention paid to the problems and to the literature currently describing the "new" phenomenon of developmental education.

Tunnel vision was the result, and most educators were in fact missing the early rumblings of the ground swell: the talk about poor skill development was no longer limited to discussions about the "new" student. Descriptions of these underprepared students and responses to them had broadened considerably. Furthermore, community colleges were no longer the only scenes of the controversy. Four-year colleges and universities, and even high schools, were struggling with what they described as a "new" student. Developmental educators were shocked, but a mental review of the last decade left them unsurprised and very unsettled.

Parallel in time, the research, literature, and teaching experience documented that three distinct situations had a frightening momentum: "new" students were continuing to arrive at community college doors, bringing with them disturbingly poor skill levels, the likes of which terrified the average teacher and led to the creation of remedial/ developmental courses; more and more "traditional" students were arriving with high school degrees that had not prepared them for college work (and/or for the world of work); and scores of students were already sitting in college courses for which they were academically unprepared, and the faculty were overwhelmed with the new instructional responsibilities created by their presence.

Admitting the severity of the problem has not been easy or come quickly, but colleges and universities are slowly coming to grips with the fact that they have a peculiar bed to lie in. Whether or not they have contributed significantly to the making of this bed, they nevertheless have to go about rearranging it. In fact, they are beginning to think differently about *all* students who arrive at their doors and about some common charge to drive their instructional efforts.

The findings of *College Responses to Low-Achieving Students: A National Study* (Roueche, Baker, and Roueche 1984) identified a massive problem and a varied assortment of instructional and programmatic strategies for dealing with underprepared students. Most colleges and universities could describe efforts to identify and attack the problem, but generally their approaches were fragmented and not yet well defined and/or proven.

More recent research, specifically *Profiling Excellence in America's Schools* (1986) and *Access and Excellence: The Open-Door College* (1987), investigated the successful, excellent behaviors of institutions and individuals who were making significant contributions to education. The findings of these investigations documented strategies for educational success.

Research and experience with successfully innovative practitioners have created a tapestry of the very best in the educational enterprise. There is a common thread in the fabric of these practitioners' successes. This common thread has been so obvious as to be overlooked, so simple as to be ignored by assumption. This strategic thread can now be identified as the "what's new in teaching" or "the innovation of the decade."

MEETING THE CHALLENGE

If they have accurately assessed current trends, educators are looking square in the face of the major teaching innovation of the decade. Simply stated: for their own educational well-being, *students must and should take an active part in their own learning.*

From a cursory review of teaching strategies, it is obvious that Socrates had the quintessential teaching strategy: to teach is to ask. Activity, by design, was the outcome of this strategy. Somehow over the years, that idea has become misinterpreted, as teachers have done more and more of the talking and less and less of the asking and listening. Socrates' notion has been diluted to the point that, in many classrooms, students could have lockjaw, be in immovable body casts, and/or be brain dead, and these physical conditions would make literally no difference in their activity level in the classroom.

This is a rude, tongue-in-cheek way of reflecting on the state of teacher expectations/demands and of student performances over the last decade or so, but it is one version of the truth as told through research and experiences. Now face to face with the documentable reality that the activities required of students in the classroom have *everything* to do with how well they will perform there, the next step for educators is to meet the challenge that this innovation creates.

There is a renewed interest in staff and organizational development, driven by concerns that faculty must be prepared to deal with the student wave of the future. The National Institute for Staff and Organizational Development (NISOD), at the University of Texas at Austin, is an international consortium of colleges and universities committed to pursuing their own styles of excellence. It is founded on the principle that faculty want to improve their own and their students' performance. To that end, *Innovation Abstracts*, a weekly teaching tips newsletter published by NISOD, provides practical and successful ideas that are being implemented in community colleges, four-year colleges, and universities across the United States and Canada. The following examples of successful classroom strategies are taken from a review of *Innovation Abstracts*, written by college practitioners implementing their best designs for student involvement in active learning.

ACTIVE ATTENDANCE

The active component in learning begins at Bloom's lowest cognitive level, the act of attending, or just *being there*. The age-old student question "I can't be in class today; will I miss anything?" is the frequent reminder of a "learned" attitude about the classroom experience. If by not being there, the student misses nothing, teacher and student are both in trouble. Attendance is the lowest—and the most basic—cognitive level, but it is crucial to the learning process *if* instructional activities that require the presence of students' minds and bodies are planned and carried out. Engagement in classroom activities can only occur if the student is present!

John Weber, former Dean at Central Oregon Community College, described a telephoning procedure intended to improve student retention rates. FUD—or the Follow-up Desk—is staffed by faculty members whose tasks are to call students who have missed a class or two (from lists prepared by all faculty), arrange for their return to class, and make appointments for them with their instructors and/ or counselors. This college effort has contributed to significant increases in returning students.

John Easton wrote that City Colleges of Chicago, determined to improve student retention, studied the relationships between attendance and achievement. They prepared histograms from a study of these patterns and determined (1) that those students who attended class frequently at the beginning of the semester received higher final grades than did those who missed classes, and (2) that the attendance and final grades continued to be related to each other over the entire semester—with A and B students attending between 90 and 95 percent of their classes, B and C students attending between 80 and 90 percent, and D or F students attending only 70 to 75 percent. Faculty share these data with students in an effort to strengthen the students' sense of control over course outcomes.

ACTIVE LECTURE

Disrupting a class in the midst of active discussion is antagonistic to learning. It is even more harmful to terminate these conversations when the intent is to initiate one-way communication. Consider these data: a review of findings from learning and memory retention studies indicates that people retain 10 percent of what they read, 20 percent of what they hear, 30 percent of what they see, 50 percent of what they see and hear, 70 percent of what they say, and 90 percent of what they do and say. One conclusion is: teaching methods that include the widest variety of the senses will keep students most stimulated and involved.

Still perhaps the most common method of teaching in colleges and universities, the lecture is designed to bring large groups of students together and give them contact with an instructor. It has, however, taken several new directions that make this teaching technique more useful, and palatable, to students; these directions reflect some responses to the foregoing data.

ORCHESTRATE. "The less the teacher talks, the more the students learn." Joan Zumwalt, at Yavapai College (Arizona), found this comment in an old notebook, and she wrote that it led her to consider her own teaching strategies in a new light. She knew that students who were good listeners, effective note takers, and conscientious reviewers *did learn* from lectures that are lively, well organized, and liberally sprinkled with relevant and interesting examples. But because most of her students did not have these characteristics, she decided to make her lectures more useful for the kinds of students she did have. She:

1. prepared mini-lectures or broke long lectures into 5- to 15-minute presentations;
2. gave the mini-lectures only on student demand; and
3. created that demand.

She suggested the following procedures for creating the demand for lecture:

1. before each learning unit, give students hand-outs with questions covering important content;
2. after the learning unit, ask students to identify questions they were not sure they could answer on a test and would like to discuss;
3. write the requests or the numbers of the questions on the blackboard until there is a starting place for a possible lecture;
4. ask the students if they can answer the questions;
5. never give the answer to the students but rather guide them toward the right response; and
6. when the sufficient answer or set of responses is given, begin the mini-lecture.

She discovered that answering one study question at a time and resisting the temptation to go through a more standard lecture encouraged more questions from students and improved their retention of the material.

SURPRISE. Sandra Allaire and Nancy Wilhelmson, at the University of Minnesota Technical College, suggested a strategy for keeping students involved in the progress of the lecture. The strategy is called "microwave problem solving." The instructor breaks the lecture from time to time by pausing and then throwing out a problem that may be related to the specific lecture or to the course in general. The students have five minutes to respond in writing with some solution to the problem that she has proposed. She finds that students remain more alert and attentive during the lecture (she may throw out one or two problems during the lecture time) and that the strategy leads students toward a sharper sense of the procedure for solving problems and gives them significant amounts of practice in thinking through the problem and proposing/explaining solutions in a compressed period of time.

KEEP RECORDS. Edna Boris, at LaGuardia Community College (New York), described classroom minutes as a valuable teaching device. Each class period a different student is assigned the task of taking notes; overnight the notes are prepared by the student and then read at the beginning of the next class meeting. Minutes become a formal, systematic way of recording the class sessions. They remind students of the materials that were covered and provide an opportunity for the instructor to review material missed by the note taker. The minutes also provide an opportunity to monitor how well the notetaker understood what happened in class and how well the class assimilated the information by observing their reactions to the reading of the minutes. Boris further discovered that the minutes became a springboard for discussion of learned material and of material that had been omitted from the previous class session. In addition, the minutes signaled the beginning of class for the students, and they could focus their attention on some common points of recollection from the previous instruction.

The students, knowing that they each would be required to keep and recite the minutes for at least one or two class periods during the semester, began to attend to the skills of listening, note taking, organizing, and selecting important information. They were consciously aware of the importance of developing good notes. (The format of the minutes was laid out early and clearly by the instructor, and the individual student's minutes were graded.) Side benefits to keeping good minutes were the identified qualities of doing neat work, checking over work before presenting it to the instructor, and consulting models of good note taking for further direction. The instructor could easily assess the writing and listening skills of the entire class at the beginning of the course when everyone submitted trial minutes. Students quickly identified careless and sloppy work as a convenient and speedy way to receive poor marks, and neat and polished papers were sure indications that the student was making great effort and working hard to sharpen these skills.

ACT OUT. Vicki Mitchell, an art history instructor at Colby Community College (Kansas), combined her acting skills and her interest in providing a realistic view of history into a teaching strategy that made lectures come alive. She acts out the roles of women in art history; her ability to engage students in real-life situations makes the experiences, the events, and the concepts more memorable. Mitchell's role essentially is that of lecturer; but the fact that the lecture is presented in the first person dramatically changes the traditional format, tone, and the impact. Wearing the clothes and portraying the emotions of those personalities, she follows an outline, provided earlier to the class, that serves as a summary of the most significant material. The content in the lecture is included in other instructional activities and later serves as a review for exams, but it is provided for the students initially in the first person.

CHANGE STEPS. Dwight Oberholtzer at Pacific Lutheran University (Washington), described students as "silent partners" in a teacher's lecturing career. Lecturers want to believe that students are engaged in the process, when in fact most are merely sitting quietly glassy-eyed in their seats. While their silence may be a compliment to a dazzling lecture, it can conceal a multitude of processing schemes that may not be identified until the first test or the first assignment. From Oberholtzer's review of findings from studies of short-term memory (students use short-term memory when listening to lectures), he found that students can hold a total of only seven units of information at any one time. He designed a new lecture strategy by arranging lecture material into "chunks" or combinations of units to expand the total amount of information that students could absorb during the lecture session. He then sought:

1. to change the pitch of his voice;
2. to shift the intensity or the pace of the presentation; and
3. to change facial expressions or movement frequently to bring the student's attention back to the lecture and the lecturer.

He further suggested that:

1. supplying students with the instructional objectives and/or outline for the lecture enables them to glean more information than those who are simply listening willy-nilly;
2. confronting students with some absolute gaps in their own picture of the world in the lecture's first ten minutes or so will stimulate their curiosity about what the lecture will contain;
3. highlighting these connections, asking questions to stimulate new syntheses, and encouraging personal applications will create helpful relationships for improved retention; and
4. collecting student lecture notes and assessing the degree to which students are translating or summarizing, reporting or spotting new connections will get at the heart of what is really happening while students listen to a lecture.

GET FEEDBACK. Jefferson Community College (Kentucky) circulates an in-house publication, *Full Classrooms: 95 Practical Suggestions to Guarantee Student and Teacher Success*, to all faculty. Some of the suggestions pertain specifically to using the lecture method. Two suggestions not yet mentioned here are: when a student asks a question, the instructor should verify that the answer is understood by having the student *repeat* the answer in his or her own words; and the instructor should place his or her own lecture notes in a file in the library or the study skills center for student use.

TEAM TEACH. Sandra Quinn and Sanford Kanter, at San Jacinto College (Texas), reported that they found team teaching to be an effective alternative to lecture fatigue. Students get involved as they watch a dynamic interplay of two minds and two personalities weaving through a subject. In team teaching, two instructors draw from each other, and from themselves, factual and conceptual knowledge that might otherwise never surface when a lecturer is speaking in isolation. These authors stated:

1. team teaching is best accomplished when friendship and/or confidence, which comes from respect and the understanding that two people have for each other's capabilities and knowledge, are the bases for creating the team;

2. a friendly compatibility does not require that individual teaching reputations or styles be equal;

3. team teaching may require that one individual is the lead teacher for the day and the other is on the sidelines as a responder, a moderater, a commentator, or simply as an observer who from time to time will interject his or her own opinions or supporting information;

4. the team approach is usually least workable when the instructors are at opposite sides at different lecterns on the same stage (and the class appears to be watching a tennis match); and

5. it should be a well-orchestrated team effort.

ACTIVE TESTING

Standard features in most college classrooms include some testing procedures whereby students can demonstrate their grasp of course content. Test makers are developing tests with new characteristics, particularly in light of research disparaging the use of short-answer, true/false, and "multiple guess" tests. There is increasing emphasis on student demonstration of basic skill development and content acquisition, more demands for analysis, synthesis, and evaluation.

Carolyn Roth, at Northern Virginia Community College, described a new testing procedure she termed "tandem testing." She found that providing opportunities for cooperation in the classroom, and more specifically at testing time, spurs students to do more thinking, collaborating, and communicating about important issues and information than is possible when students are tackling questions alone. She discovered that when she gives two students one copy of a test, requires them to collaborate on the answers and turn in one answer with both their names on it (both receive the earned grade), students are encouraged and directed (1) to improve their communication skills (as they express their ideas to each other), (2) to improve their skills of persuasion (persuading others to accept their own answers), and (3) to improve their ability to provide detailed explanations and examples that support their own statements. Students commented that they felt less anxious about tests when they knew they were sharing the testing with another student, *unless* their partner had not prepared for the test. In this event, they would be understandably miffed; to the contrary, if they had not prepared well themselves, they would feel that they had let their partner down.

Barbara Lester, at Ashland Community College (Kentucky), termed her version of this testing strategy "partnership exam." She allowed her students to select their partners and then change partners throughout the semester, if they wished, to find the right mix-and-match. She discovered that many of the advantages of partnership testing were as obvious in a general psychology course as in a math course; students had to develop collaborative skills and had to be prepared to the point they would be assets, not liabilities, to their partners. Beyond the testing situation, however, she discovered two other important outcomes of student collaboration: many of the pairs designed study strategies together, and they accommodated each other's learning and problem-solving styles—the partner who was significantly better at one or another stage of problem solution would take over at that point and be the teacher for the other.

ACTIVE QUESTIONING

Most educators acknowledge that the Socratic method of teaching—that is, the teacher asking questions and the students responding—is an old and well-respected teaching activity. Tessa Tagle, at San Antonio College (Texas), wrote that using the method successfully depends upon asking the *right* questions. She distinguished between the acts of *questioning* and *inquiring*. On the one hand, questioning suggests the Socratic method of teaching: students are asked direct questions, and there is a generally assumed correct spoken or written response. Inquiry, on the other hand, is a systematic form of questioning that gets at another level of knowledge. If the questioning sequence is always directed at the right answer, and there is no inquiry sequence directed at getting the students to higher level thinking, then the students do not have to think for themselves and process information for new ideas. Research findings indicate that teachers who are trained in questioning techniques ask higher order questions themselves, and their students achieve and retain knowledge at a significantly higher level than those taught by teachers untrained in questioning techniques.

Joe Anthony, at Lexington Community College (Kentucky), wrote that, while asking the right question is important, the *process* of asking is also. The response or wait time between the question/inquiry and the response drives more and improved student responses. Anthony noted that most of his colleagues are good question answerers, particularly of their own questions in their own fields; and they are always eager to share their knowledge with their students. Unfortunately, their impatience with student delay and the excitement and confidence they themselves bring to answering questions often overshadow the purpose of asking. Students should be allowed appropriate time to prepare their responses to questions—a pause of at least three to five seconds is a baseline delay. At that point, the instructor may begin his or her own response or comment.

ACTIVE TEACHING AND LEARNING STRATEGIES

Claire Weinstein, a Professor at the University of Texas at Austin, has written and researched learning strategies—behaviors in which a learner engages during learning and that are intended to influence the learner's knowledge acquisition processes. She lists eight major categories of learning strategies for students:

1. rehearsal strategies for basic learning tasks, such as repeating names of items in an ordered list;
2. rehearsal strategies for complex learning tasks, such as copying, underlining, or shadowing the material presented in class;
3. elaboration strategies for basic learning tasks, such as forming a mental image or sentence relating the items in each pair for a paired-associate list of words;
4. elaboration strategies for complex tasks such as paraphrasing, summarizing, or describing how new information relates to existing knowledge;
5. organizational strategies for basic learning tasks, such as grouping or ordering to-be-learned items from a list or a section of prose;
6. organizational strategies for complex tasks, such as outlining a passage or creating a hierarchy;
7. comprehension monitoring strategies such as checking for comprehension failures; and
8. affective strategies such as being alert and relaxed, to help overcome test anxiety.

Weinstein suggested that instructors who use instructional methodologies that demonstrate, cue, and reinforce the use of these learning strategies can implement what might be called a learning strategies "metacurriculum." Instructors implement a "metacurriculum" by analyzing the regular course curriculum and the learning demands it places on students and translating the findings of that analysis into the instructional methods for the course. For example:

- pausing to review and answer student questions within a lecture is an excellent time to talk about self-review and the role self-testing can play in bringing about new learning and identifying areas of misunderstanding and confusion;
- announcing a class test is an excellent time for presenting strategies for test preparation as well as for coping with test anxiety;
- discussing negative self-talk and how to turn it into a positive experience can introduce students to a very powerful self-management skill; and
- using analogies to make a concept more meaningful will create the opportunity to pause and discuss the rationale for using this technique as a teaching strategy.

In addition, humorous and/or entertaining recollections and sharing of experiences serve to provide important and excellent asides to teaching. They make points that students do not forget, and they lead them toward fashioning some useful learning strategies for themselves.

Walter Pauk, at Cornell University (New York), told the story of his own student days in an Egyptian History class. Unable to grasp the content that the rapid-fire lecturer delivered and realizing that his frantic scribbling and note taking were going nowhere, he decided to experiment with a new idea: write on every other line of his paper in class and fill in those blank lines after class with additional information he might recall. He noted that at first it was difficult to remember most of the lecture; but as the days passed, he became more successful at filling in his notes. He also remembered when he began reciting the day's lecture to himself; he discovered that in trying to make the presentation as smooth as possible, he was grouping his ideas into topics and subtopics. Then he began creating test questions for himself. He humorously concluded this story: the history instructor abruptly changed a lifelong habit (of which Pauk was unaware) of giving short-answer examinations, and he gave an essay test requiring students to analyze and synthesize. Pauk passed with flying colors, and he credited his "peculiar" study strategies, fashioned out of survival hysteria, for his success.

Linc. Fisch, formerly at Lexington Community College (Kentucky), teaches mathematics. He wrote that during a college football game one afternoon he began to compare his strategies for teaching mathematics to the coach's strategies for coaching football. A follow-up conversation with the coach identified the following: (1) the coach worked primarily with individual students, but often with students in groups; (2) he asked the athletes to perform every day, under observation, and gave them immediate feedback to correct their performance; and (3) he required athletes to practice the corrected performance repeatedly until it was correct and then move on to another. By contrast, Fisch noted that in his own classroom he typically showed students how to work problems, laying out the steps in carefully ordered and logical sequence. He would watch the students nod, assume that they understood, and then he would move on. He compared his strategy to that of a football coach who would throw passes and run plays *himself* while the players watched and who then would expect his players to do as well on the day of the game as *he* had done "in practice." Fisch could not provide individual students the amount of individual time that he wished, but he did invite them to come for one-on-one coaching sessions in his office. Moreover, he found himself making positive written comments on students' exams before returning them, keeping morale high and giving them confidence and support. He encouraged students to work together on homework problems and allowed them more time in class to work together on individual problems.

He began to think of himself as a coach; he was far less willing to allow students to fail, providing practice exams just as the coaches conducted final scrimmages. Above all, Fisch noted that students became more interested in successful performances—on the football field it was winning the game, and in the classroom it was passing the examination.

USING PRACTICAL APPLICATIONS

In order to get students more actively involved in their classes, instructors are turning to classroom activities directly related to what students will find in the "real world." Richard Crowe, at Hazard Community College (Kentucky), remembered his own experience with the Commerce Clearinghouse and the employee manual that highlighted these words, "We pay for results, not effort." He assigned his educational philosophy to those few words and his instructional strategies to the design that they suggested. In effect, he attempted to teach practical theory in the classroom, combining his perception of the world of work, psychological learning principles, and effective methods in teaching.

Crowe begins a typical business law class with a fictitious scenario, involving students in the roles of local business managers/owners in the middle of a contract, bailment, or agency dilemma. The class then discusses the problem and makes recommendations for action; the homework is around cases reinforcing the principles involved in the classwork. He developed a "dollar grading system" for his tests, assigning a worth of $40 to each of the four tests that he gave during the term and $100 to the comprehensive final exam. In addition, each student completes assigned legal research and participates in classroom activities for another $40. In total, students must have earned $270 to be awarded an A, $240 to earn a B, $210 to earn a C, and $180 to earn a D. Also, they are provided opportunities to work overtime, by presenting an oral book review, thereby earning as much as $15 extra. The same monetary system applies as Crowe docks each student $15 for each class absence beyond the three allowed by the college. A side effect of this monetary system: students no longer plead for more points; they appear to find it more difficult to ask for gifts of dollars than for gifts of points.

Phillip Venditti and Robert Bahruth, at Austin Community College (Texas), sought to improve the competence of their ESL students. They described a unique instructional strategy, "interactive errands." ESL students are sent into the community on these errands to build up linguistic, sociolinguistic, and informational capabilities which were designed to help smooth their adaption to life in the United States. The interactive errands were labeled "idiom searches," "human bingo," site visits, and "team quests." In "idiom searches" students take a list of English expressions, have two or three native speakers explain these expressions, and give examples to provide a context for their meanings. The site visits and "team quests" send students in groups to gather facts about historical locations and community organizations. The "human bingo" is used to involve students in meeting others; they obtain the signatures of several individuals who fit a number of descriptions revolving around a common topic, gathering enough signatures to fill up a row or a column on their bingo cards. Students share and describe their encounters in class after they have completed an interactive errand. Venditti and Bahruth believed that the out-of-class interactive language errands made major contributions to this comprehensive pedagogical program.

IMPLEMENTING INTERDISCIPLINARY PROGRAMS

Elizabeth Hodes, at Santa Barbara City College (California), wrote of her interdisciplinary course for honor students, "Ethical Dilemmas and the Scientist." The course was designed to include students in the sciences, social sciences, and health professions. It was intended to acquaint students with currently debated moral and ethical issues pertaining to the scientific community as well as provide more experience with research, writing, and analytical reading. A different category of problems was examined each week. The class met for one two-and-one-half hour session and one one-and-one-half hour session each week; the longest session introduced the topic and the shorter session rounded off the discussion and drew some conclusions. The students read background materials on the subject of the particular category, and the class period included guest lecturers and video presentations.

The unplanned reward was the sense of camaraderie developed by the students. They began to be actively involved in their work as though they were a small community, often sharing copies of readings when there were not enough for everyone and creating discussions in which they learned more about each other's beliefs and experiences. Because each student had to lead the discussion once in the semester, all students were actively involved in trying to make it easier for the leader to do a good job. They actively assisted others in locating materials for classwork and for their individual research papers. At midsemester, they met to share difficulties, get reactions to written work, and provide moral support for continuing the semester. Hodes' students enhanced their general education about humanities and the sciences, strengthened their skills in writing and logical analysis of issues, and fostered independent and critical attitudes by examining issues for which rote answers and memorization simply would not serve.

Vernon Wranosky and Kenneth Mitchell, biology and art instructors, respectively, at Colby Community College (Kansas), described their unique courses in anatomy, botany, and microbiology that instructed art students in the "hard" sciences. While scientific jargon was used for all assignments and students were required to understand terms and concepts presented in the lectures, the art students translated this jargon into drawings and paintings; in fact, science became art!

In anatomy, each assignment included factual information related to how the bones affect body shape and muscle contours. An assignment example: Use the human head as a measuring device, and draw to scale the outline of a human from right side, coronal plane view, lateral from midline. In botany, emphasis was placed on the internal anatomy and cellular detail of plants. An assignment example: Generate a botany textbook cover; the theme can involve artistic license along botanical lines or actual botanical material. The microbiology course was the most difficult subject to teach, given that students often could not visualize an abstract concept. An assignment example:

Draw a microbiology scene depicting each of the following: (a) infection, (b) sudden death, (c) abortion, and (d) diarrhea.

They found that students attended class more regularly, were more interested in homework, and learned more new techniques than did those in traditional biology courses. Moreover, the art students approached difficult subject matter with a desire to learn and gained an appreciation for a discipline most of them disliked or at best found only casually interesting. Art students found themselves doodling botanical thoughts, microbes crept into their designs, and conversations about art assignments became studded with scientific terms. Art students and science students became friends; and one student considered training to teach art and science in high school.

REQUIRING WRITING ASSIGNMENTS

The majority of the strategies included thus far have involved the writing process, but developing writing skills is of such importance that it should be more than obliquely addressed. Therefore, two distinctly different strategies are included here to emphasize the critical role that writing plays in active learning.

Gary Budd, of Modesto Junior College (California), explained the writing assignments he used to deal with the problem of absence and give his students additional occasions to write. He required students to write out their excuses for class absences. However, just any trite excuses, no matter how truthful, would not be accepted. The excuse had to be outrageous and was to be read to the class upon the student's return. Even when students missed class, they were involved with it—composing.

John Greening, at College of the Sequoias (California), wrote that the biologists at his college decided to change instruction in the beginning biology classes. Students were to write a number of short essays, verifying that they understood the material in the reading assignment and responding to a question in which they had to analyze some part of that assignment. Different testing procedures were prepared for the biology majors and the general education students, but both procedures included traditional quizzes and one-to-two-page essays which were to be completed during the testing time or prior to the date of the more traditional quiz. Students were provided with a format for answering the essay questions and directed to write their answers as though they were explaining to a fellow student who had not understood the assigned reading. Questions were designed to lead students to consider how different parts of a reading assignment are connected, how material can be applied to a new situation, and how they might seek other sources of information to support their answers. Several acceptable answers for each essay were posted to demonstrate to students that there is not just one way of answering each question and to allow them to compare their work with others'.

Greening found that, with these strategies in place, student performance on essay exam questions improved considerably. It was first apparent that the number of questions left blank, or answers consisting of a few disconnected sentence fragments, were reduced and that answers became more organized and easier to read. In addition, performance on questions requiring more elaborate answers distinctly improved.

Greening's efforts to align appropriate learning and students are clear in the following sample exercises. A general education biology student would be asked to respond to the following: "During the breeding season, male antelope exhibit a very stereotyped fighting behavior. Through this fighting, they establish dominance among themselves and breeding rites. Use the activities of the nervous system and the current model of instinctive behavior to explain how such fighting begins." A biology major would be expected to respond to the following: "There are rumors that the U.S. Navy has contracted with Zooeapon (Zoological Weapons) Inc., to breed giant attack planaria for use against enemy ships. This camouflaged flatworm would sink these ships either by wrapping itself around the ship or by sucking a hole in its hull. Evaluate the feasibility of such a weapon based on size, waste removal, and so on." Greening agreed that the success rate of his students in responding to these exercises, both in content and format, has improved and that writing does actively engage students with the subject.

RESPONDING TO STUDENTS' WORK

As students are expected to be more active in their own learning, instructors must be more active in responding to that learning. David Jenrette, editor of *Lifelines*, from Miami-Dade Community College North (Florida), wrote that there are tremendous differences between "feedback" (as educators have come to term their responses to students' work) and "calibration." He makes these distinctions: "feedback" is an instant, just-as-it's-happening response to an error condition; "calibration," on the other hand, is an after-the-fact adjustment. Feedback is a term educators borrowed from sound systems. For example, if the volume of a loudspeaker is too high and the microphone begins to screech, there is an immediate rush to correct the problem. Feedback is instant! Calibration, however, might be best described using an example from ballistics. A rifle is fired through a series of rounds, and a study is made of the resultant pattern of holes; the pattern is studied to determine if the shots are too high or too much to the left or to the right, the rifle sights are adjusted, and more rounds are fired until the sights are calibrated properly. Once there is continual feedback from the target that the rifle is firing properly, it is assumed that the weapon has been calibrated and that with proper aim the rifle will fire perfectly at the target.

Jenrette suggested introducing elements of feedback and calibration into classes. Feedback strategies could include:

- in all disciplines, making more use of open-book quizzes in which students can get their answers from hand-outs, class notes, or textbooks;
- in math or in other problem-solving disciplines, giving the students the answers, or making partial answers available.

Calibration strategies might include:

- as each student completes a task, an immediate copy of the correct answers should be provided and reviewed immediately;
- prior to an essay exam, students should be provided with a large number of essay questions that they might answer and check out ahead of time, and the actual test questions can even come from these;
- after students have taken a test, they should be required to correct every item with an explanation of why the right answer is right and the wrong one is wrong.

He concluded and emphasized that feedback is instant; if it is not instant, perhaps it is not feedback, but rather calibration. Both are crucial to keeping students active and on- target.

IN SUMMARY

No earth-shattering strategies have been described here. In fact, they are merely rational, common-sense responses to otherwise ho-hum, primarily inactive teaching situations. They bring thoughtful responses to the questions of how students might be most active in their own learning. But the future of these strategies—and the innovation that drives them—is dependent upon the imagination of those individuals who have been identified as the *keys* to successful active teaching and learning.

CELEBRATING THE FUTURE

There is much to celebrate in teaching! The instructional strategies described, if they are truly the emergence of a major teaching trend, have a celebrative feature in common: they tease out of instructional activities those sparks of enthusiasm and interest that get

students active in, and excited about, their own learning and simultaneously get *instructors* active in, and excited about, their roles as
performers and creators in the classroom. Teachers have always been,
and will continue to be, the *keys* to the success of this innovation.
This awesome responsibility deserves some special attention.

Several years ago, Roland S. Barth, at Harvard University, wrote
that the lack of collegiality between teachers and teachers, teachers
and administrators, and all school people and parents is a major threat
to excellence in education. He contrasted the absence of collegiality
he witnessed in schools to the highly organized cooperation he witnessed in his bee colony. How remarkable it was that these little creatures, with their astonishing acts of communication, sharing, and interdependence, created enough honey during the spring and summer
to feed themselves, the entire family, and many friends through the
winter!

Barth identified a good working definition of collegiality in
schools—a definition he attributed to Judith Warren Little, a researcher at the Far West Regional Laboratory in San Francisco. Little
described educational collegiality as the presence of four specific behaviors: talking about the practice of teaching and learning; observing
each other teaching and administering; working on the curriculum
together; and teaching each other what each knows about teaching,
learning, and leading. With Little's definition and Barth's concerns
as a springboard, the following offers some documentation (all described in *Innovation Abstracts*) that *collegiality* is working its way
into college classrooms and dramatically affecting instruction.

TALKING AND OBSERVING

Bill Shawl, at Golden West College (California), devised many
strategies for getting faculty involved in their own growth and development. He offered the following inexpensive and convenient sug-
gestion. All interested faculty are invited to gather weekly for a regularly scheduled brown bag lunch; this is an informal meeting during
which the week's *Innovation Abstracts* and/or any institutional/in-
structional issue of particular value to the group may be discussed.
Shawl found that the sessions were well attended, that faculty felt
free to exchange ideas, and that a significant number of college innovations came from discussions at that roundtable exchange.

Earl G. Bloor, at Alberta Career Development and Employment
(Canada), described the format and objectives of the Instructional
Skills Workshop, an intensive four-day workshop conducted *by* community college instructors *for* community college instructors. Participants each conduct a 10-minute mini-lesson, and each acts as a
learner while other participants give their mini-lessons. The lessons

are videotaped, and the instructor receives feedback following his or her mini-lesson: 7 minutes via guided feedback forms; 13 minutes for an unstructured sharing of experiences. The feedback session focuses on three questions: what did the instructor do to help you learn; what did the instructor do, if anything, to hinder your learning; and what suggestions do you have for more effective instruction? Bloor noted that a tremendous sense of teamwork develops among participants during the workshop, and it continues throughout the teaching year as workshop participants visit each other's classes and meet afterward for debriefing. Through this collegial interaction, valuable interdepartmental rapport within the college is established, and the changing needs of teachers and students are successfully addressed.

Cynthia A. Barnes, at the Community College of Aurora (Colorado), explained the mentoring system developed at her college to support the sizable number of new part-time instructors. The Faculty Mentor Program is staffed by full-time instructors/coordinators and part-time lead teachers who have been chosen to act as mentors. Each mentor is assigned to a new part-time instructor in his or her own discipline. With classroom observations (each visits the other) and discussions on the new instructor's strengths and weaknesses, an action plan is developed and specific objectives for enhancing classroom performance are outlined and discussed. The Faculty Mentor Program has fostered a constructive, creative alliance between new and more experienced faculty members and has helped to maintain an enviable level of instructional quality at the college.

WORKING TOGETHER AND TEACHING

Julie Bertch, at Maricopa County Community College District (Arizona), described the Maricopa Writing Project, a summer faculty development program that draws faculty from a variety of content areas to improve student writing performance across the entire curriculum. Faculty share successful classroom practices and techniques and devise new ones. Engaging in these activities, they become a working community of writers who discover that not only are they planning for improving their own students' performance but that they are improving their own thinking and writing skills as well. Furthermore, they have found that:

- most faculty know very little about what their colleagues do in the classroom;
- writing is more demanding and threatening than they had remembered; and
- writing is a satisfying, useful experience for building both their own and the students' confidence.

At the end of the project, these faculty

- are available as resources for writing- across-the-curriculum programs in their own colleges;
- serve as witnesses to the value of writing both for students and teachers;
- bring a renewed enthusiasm to programs already in existence; and
- lend an important impetus for a competent beginning at those colleges with no writing programs.

Bertch placed the spinoff from this program in perspective: when 25 faculty participate in a summer writing program, well over 3,000 students will be affected in just the following semester; over a five-year period, as many as 30,000 students could learn how to use writing to improve their learning.

Joseph F. McCadden, at Burlington County College (New Jersey), wrote of the team-teaching approach to instruction in the College Skills Program. Each team includes a social science, reading, and English teacher, and a counselor, all working to reinforce what is being taught in the others' classes, to apply what is being learned in other classes to their own, and to deal collaboratively with instructional problems. The reading teachers, for instance, help students comprehend reading material assigned in social science classes, and the reading and social science professors coordinate their writing assignments with the English teacher. Faculty members unanimously felt that the team membership made them better teachers, they appreciated the feeling of cooperation that they got from the shared venture, and they relished the supportive attitude of their peers. They also believed that the teamwork helped broaden their perspective on students and the instructional process. Finally, they felt that frequently involving students, those doing well and not so well, in the team meetings was a sound way of helping students confront their own problems and work out potential solutions with the team. The result: the Program's students have higher grade point averages in their regular college courses than do those entering the college with no diagnosed skill deficiencies.

Donald Jung, at Castleton State College (Vermont), described a faculty development program based upon mentoring relationships between teachers of basic skills and faculty from traditional liberal arts disciplines—theatre arts, philosophy, Spanish, music, geography, and French. Upon completion of the instructional phase of the program, newly instructed faculty teach in the basic skills program as part of their normal teaching load and serve as catalysts for curricular change. In their own departments, they use the expertise gleaned from this relationship to revise required general education courses. The result is that fundamental linguistics and computational concepts that have been introduced in the basic skills classes are systematically reinforced across the general education curriculum.

Instructors learned how to assist students in discovering and recording topics for development, and they learned strategies for editing students' work. The faculty who had been instructed in basic skills teaching and had taught a developmental section or two found a marked improvement in the quality of their students' writing and a comparable improvement in the content of their essays. Jung wrote that, having viewed the inside of college writing through his own exposure to basic skills teaching, he is convinced, as are his peers, that the entire curriculum should be demanding competent writing and the demonstration of basic skill development.

And, finally, Bob Miller, at Eastern Kentucky University, provided background and rationale for an unusual team-teaching event that occurs each semester in his department—in the interest of following Socrates' admonition that *passion* must be intimately involved with a search for truth and knowledge. Convinced that passion is often the missing ingredient in students' learning and that instructors have an obligation to provide some sense of this passion for their students, Miller and his colleagues asked themselves: "How can we turn our students to philosophical ideas?" and agreed to "do something that combines philosophical thinking with drama, or if not drama at a high level at least raucous atmosphere."

They decided to choose three positions on a topic (e.g., "Is there life after death?"). They then put on their academic robes and march into the debate room. Using a structured debate format (stating initial positions from prepared manuscripts, followed by rebuttals), they proceed to yell at and insult each other, and get the crowd to laugh at opponents, boo and hiss them, and cheer when a debater makes a good point. Miller wrote: "They (students) have too long associated cleverness with quietness, deep-thinking with dull tones. I should like them to experience those exciting moments when a flesh and bone human being 'slam dunks' an idea right over the outstretched objections of an opponent—and, if necessary, rakes him across the face going down. I want the heart to race and a yell to go up for that." Miller and his colleagues believed that students ought to see excitement in learning and that instructors, by getting excited themselves, having a good time, and sharing that good time with their students, can create an atmosphere for learning that gets their students and themselves intimately involved as partners in a most passionate experience!

IN SUMMARY

Necessity may indeed have been the mother of invention. Perhaps it is too simplistic to draw this strong link between the problems that underprepared students introduced into higher education and the renewed interest in teaching strategies that focus on active learning. But the perspectives created by 20/20 hindsight would strongly suggest some dramatic relationships.

However, it is not nearly so important to draw out and analyze all of the possible cause-and-effect relationships as it is to capitalize on the outcomes. And in this regard, what might the future hold? From all accounts, it appears that it holds an awesome variety of strategies for active teaching and learning. The strategies included here have been designed by teachers whose most creative thinking has gone into improving their instruction, hence inspiring (demanding) more learning from their students. Such thinking has not yet created a great ground swell of change, but it has caused exciting, documentable rumblings.

REFERENCES

ROUECHE, JOHN E., and GEORGE A. BAKER. 1986. *Profiling Excellence in America's Schools.* Arlington, Va.: American Association of School Administrators.

———. 1987. *Access and Excellence: The Open Door College.* Washington, D.C.: Community College Press.

———; and SUANNE D. ROUECHE. 1984. *College Responses to Low-Achieving Students: A National Study.* Orlando, Fla.: HBJ-Media Systems Corp.

Further information about cited issues of *Innovation Abstracts* may be obtained by writing to Suanne D. Roueche, Director, The National Institute for Staff and Organizational Development (NISOD), The University of Texas at Austin, EDB 348, Austin, Tex. 78712.

4

The Student Success Systems Model

John Keyser

> No genuine consensus exists about the nature of, need for or direction of community college student service programs. A model for change seems to elude most leaders . . . leaders of community colleges and student services staffs agree on one point: the student service function needs an infusion of new ideas, new approaches, and a new reason for being. (Elsner 1983, 139)

It is time to put this oft-quoted statement to rest.

In recent years, a number of innovators have changed the tradition-bound student services function and have developed new and better ways of thinking and doing. These innovators have worked with common assumptions, significantly different from the assumptions made by their counterparts of the past decade. They operate under a new paradigm, described as the Student Success Systems Model. Student success is defined as the discovery of, and commitment to, the pursuit of career and educational goals. "Systems" defines the primary concept or approach used to achieve this purpose. The challenge of creating environments where students have the maximum opportunity to succeed is just as difficult as before, but the methods and techniques for achieving this goal are much more sophisticated. The paradigm shift which has occurred is in an embryonic stage of understanding and acceptance. This chapter is written with the hope of elucidating the emerging model and accelerating its acceptance.

A BRIEF HISTORY

Between 1900 and 1950, most present-day community colleges did not exist. Those that did were extensions of high schools or junior

70

colleges attempting to establish their own identity. It wasn't until the 1950s that the community college movement began to expand nationally, and for much of the 1960s, one community college a week opened its doors. The professionalization of student services and counseling paralleled this extraordinary growth. The faculties of higher education graduate schools developed specializations in student personnel services. At the core of these programs were two loosely defined models which have remained fundamental frames of reference for community college practitioners.

The Student Services Model did not have strong philosophical underpinnings. It was based on the assumption that experts needed to be trained to assist students with admission, registration, financial aid, health services, counseling, advising, out-of-class activities, and job placement. Student services personnel were trained to provide maintenance functions, leaving to students the initiative of seeking out those services for which they had an interest or need. Student services was commonly defined as a series of services. Even today, the states of Washington, Maryland, and California have published student services manuals which list and describe a taxonomy of student services recommended for community colleges.

The Student Development Model used the Student Services Model as a foundation. These services were to be provided, but within a holistic perspective for the total development of students. Holistic was understood to mean the reintegration of personal, social, moral, and intellectual development activities. Student personnel workers or "student development professionals," which some prefer to be called, were viewed as facilitators who could assist students in bringing about this integration.

The theories of developmental psychology, on which this model was built, suggested a proactive role of intervention in students' lives to ensure that they progressed toward educational and personal development goals. However, during the 1960s and early 1970s, most community colleges were pressed to cope with rapid growth. It was not practical to do more than accommodate the self-declared intentions of students who waited in long registration lines. It was accepted that students had the right to fail. Access, the great cornerstone of the community college, meant keeping the doors open to provide classes for all who desired them.

Leach summarizes the difficulties with both of these models:

> Many of these new student development approaches, influenced by the human potential movement and its focus on affective learning, were not well understood by faculty or decision makers within the institution. Practitioners were often perceived by their faculty colleagues as "mystical do-gooders" who, at best, were on the periphery

of the educational enterprise and, at worst, were perceived as coun-terproductive to the educational process.

On reflection, one might observe that while the *In Loco Parentis Model* was too narrowly institution-oriented, both the Student Ser-vices Model and the Student Development Model were too narrowly student oriented. Moreover, many instructional colleagues were in-censed by the idea that a small group of counselors or student de-velopment specialists would attempt to take credit for student de-velopment, whereas they perceived the primary role of instruction to be student development. (1985, 14)

Both the Student Services Model and the Student Development Model *were* too narrowly student-oriented. The Student Development Model was a step forward, giving new practitioners a more sophis-ticated understanding of the complexities of student behavior than was characteristic of those subscribing to the student services phi-losophy. It also gave the first generation of student development professionals a sense that they should be proactive in the design of strategies that would facilitate and promote student survival.

SYSTEMS THINKING

Sometime in the late 1970s and early 1980s, the Student Success Systems Model began to emerge. This model had its roots in the sys-tems thinking which was taking place in many disciplines. Environ-mentalists pointed to the interdependency of all living things. Inter-nationalists expounded on the thesis of interconnection among all nations of the world. The word "system" as a group of "interacting, interrelated, and independent elements forming a complex whole, with all elements being functionally related" became a fundamental part of society's vocabulary. It has become one of the best descriptions for a complex reality.

"Systems" was also used to describe a method for purposeful ac-complishment in a complex environment. The "systems method" was based on a cycle of planning, implementing, reviewing, and correcting for error. It depended on the sequential steps of setting general goals, defining specific objectives, designing activities necessary to achieve these objectives, evaluating the degree to which objectives and goals were met, making adjustments suggested by the evaluation, and re-peating the process. The Student Success Systems Model is broadly integrative of systems theory and the systems method. As applied to the desired outcome of student success, it is based on these assump-tions:

- There needs to be a comprehensive design for how human and fiscal resources are used systematically and deliberately to support students as they work to achieve their goals. A basic rendition of this is a student flow diagram which tracks a prospective student from the point of contact through the point of transition to a job or another college.

- Enrollments can be increased, student retention can be improved, more learning can occur, and community support can be secured if the interrelationships of student support programs are commonly understood by college staff, and if they are continually refined toward the common purpose of maximizing the potential for student success.

- Students will have more potential to succeed if they have clarified their goals, if they are directed into courses for which they are adequately prepared, if their progress is carefully monitored, and if intervention strategies are implemented when students deviate from desired performance.

- All staff (faculty, management, classified) have the common mission of creating an educational environment in which students have the maximum opportunity to succeed. Further, all staff should see themselves as agents who help link the array of community organizations (schools, churches, business, and government) with this mission of student success.

- Since any college is a system whose various subsystems are interdependent, changing one subsystem will change all other subsystems. This reality demands that all who work with the system define their role in relationship to all others.

A major implication of these assumptions is that there is more role similarity than role difference among student development staff, teaching faculty, and instructional administrators. All are educators who work together to provide the best opportunities for students to realize their potential. All have importance in the formula for student success.

Student development professionals have defined their role around the theme of student advocacy. The notion has existed among some of these professionals that they must be watchdogs for the protection and defense of students, acting to prevent them from being victimized by a heartless bureaucracy.

The Student Success Systems Model assumes that all college employees are actively engaged in a process of meeting the many special needs of community college students. This vision means that all community college staff are student advocates, sensitive to the unique characteristics and needs of students and disposed to respond in a helping and caring manner.

The Student Success Systems (sss) Model assumes student centeredness, but clearly states standards and expectations for student performance. It represents a balance between extending opportunity and insisting that students meet certain responsibilities as a contingency for success. The SSS Model is firmly linked with the quality movement in contemporary education. In the broadest sense, it is a way of thinking, planning, and problem solving which aims to respond systematically to the needs of students and the community.

Paralleling the development of systems thinking was the increasing sophistication of computer technology. Computers are now the tools that enable educators to be holistic generalists rather than specialized experts. They become adjuncts to human thought, with the potential of multiplying exponentially the capacity to conceptualize, design, implement, and improve student success systems.

The computer has probably changed the environment outside the classroom more than it has inside the classroom. Great masses of data have been translated by hardware and software into useful information. As a result, decision makers have a new-found capacity to be much more knowledgeable and to make better judgments in monitoring and supporting the goal achievements of students.

Three developments have dramatically increased the usefulness of the computer to managers of student success systems. First, the size and cost of hardware have decreased. Second, machines have become "user-friendly," making it possible for all staff, regardless of training or expertise, to use them. Third, networking technologies have facilitated data and information management. These developments have made it possible to translate systems thinking into a tremendous variety of sophisticated practices. The result has been improved quality of service and increased productivity of personnel. The placement of responsibility at the user level for generation and maintenance of information files has created a new sense of responsibility for timeliness and accuracy of data. The increased access to common information has also minimized the potential of suspicion between offices, and fostered an atmosphere of trust and mutual respect among staff members. Thus, the computer has become a potent catalyst for the development of effective human information networks.

The League for Innovation in the Community Colleges (Armes, Griffith, and Trout 1984) has published a handbook which sets guidelines for applications in student admissions; assessment, advising, and counseling; student registration; academic alert monitoring; degree audit; transfer program requirements; and student follow-up. This handbook is largely based on the systems perspective. It also points to the importance of maintaining the balance between using new technologies and staying sensitive to individual differences.

FROM VISION TO REALITY

Each community college has at least the semblance of a student success system. What differs from campus to campus is the degree to which these systems are defined, understood, monitored and, over time, improved. Central Oregon Community College has implemented a version of an sss Model. The results have been impressive. Enrollment has increased, student retention rates have improved, and there is a strong sense of purpose among staff.

William Lindemann, Dean of Students at Central Oregon Community College, is one of the prime architects of this system. His conceptual model is presented in a handbook entitled *Student Success: The Common Goal* (Lindemann, DeCabooter, and Cordova 1987). He recently collaborated with the American College Testing Program to conduct national workshops which describe in some detail how this model can be implemented. A key component of his thinking is the integration of student service functions within the college's total educational process. This handbook is an excellent resource, providing a framework for each community college to develop and refine a student success system in its own context.

Lindemann's model, as shown in Figure 4.1, includes six integrated systems, all with the common mission of supporting student success:

- Potential students are initially contacted through the *institutional access system* (the student outreach and contact plan).
- The *inquiry/admit system* provides personalized attention to prospective students as soon as they respond to college outreach and contact activity. The system monitors the students as they receive information about financial aid, career selection, assessment, orientation, and advisement.
- A potential student becomes a student through the *registration system*.
- The *educational programming system* delivers courses, labs, seminars, and other learning experiences, such as student activities, so that students acquire knowledge and skills that enable them to achieve their educational and career goals.
- The *feedback system* asks students to evaluate their experience before and after leaving the college. It also seeks evaluative input from a variety of sources throughout the campus.
- The *institutional information system* supports the entire educational process by providing data upon which institutional leaders and planners can make decisions about elements of the other five systems.

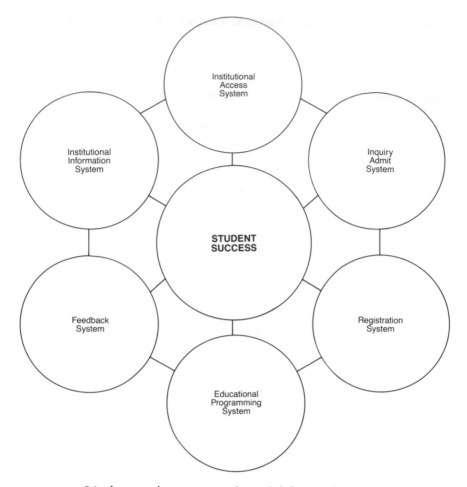

FIGURE 4.1. Lindemann's conceptual model for student success.

Lindemann's handbook presents guidelines for defining these six systems and discusses the elements and issues important to each.

Miami-Dade Community College (Florida) was one of the first community colleges to implement a comprehensive student success system. Their pioneering effort stimulated many other colleges to begin developing their own version of this system. Because of its size and the magnitude of change that was made in a short period of time, Miami-Dade's effort has been cited as a prototype. Generally, students are thoroughly assessed for appropriate course placement, carefully monitored for progress toward program completion, and given the benefit of special intervention programs. A highly computerized sys-tcm is used to accomplish this purpose. After students are tested, they attend an orientation session which describes the services and academic programs of the college. A document that indicates the results of the basic skills assessment and courses students should take is produced "on-line" for each student. The Academic Planning Manual is used by students to plan a course of studies consistent with their career goals. Students leave this initial orientation session with a program advisement sheet, specifying the courses to be taken.

Both faculty and counselors have a well-defined role in advising students in program and course selection. New students and continuing students who have a declared major and no basic skills deficiencies are referred to teaching faculty for advisement. Undecided students, transfer students, and students with basic skills deficiencies are directed to counselors.

In the Miami-Dade system, counselors monitor a series of computer warning signals to manage the advisement process. The computer is programmed to insure that students correct basic skill deficiencies and complete general education core courses early in their program of studies. Students are not allowed to enroll in mathematics courses if they have computational difficulties; nor can they take social science or humanities courses without completing the core course sequences in these areas. About one-third of the way into the semester, counselors activate the Academic Alert System. This system uses progress and attendance reports supplied by each teacher to generate a letter to each student. The letters, written by the computer, advise students to seek help at different campus offices to overcome deficiencies. This same system is used to identify outstanding students and give them messages of encouragement.

At the end of each term, the Standards of Academic Progress Support System is used to flag students who have weak academic records. If GPA requirements are not being met, a conference with a counselor is required before the students are allowed to register for the next term. Students with less than a 1.5 GPA are suspended and those with between a 1.5 and 2.0 are placed on a warning or probationary status.

The Advisement Graduation Information System electronically realigns students' transcripts by degree requirements rather than by semesters, and, taking into account current and future term enrollments, checks graduation status. A counselor can see at a glance how close students are to meeting graduation requirements without manually checking transcripts against program outlines. This system also produces information regarding transfer requirements for 72 different programs to 13 Florida universities and colleges. Students receive mailers which inform them what courses are needed for their intended degree and for transfer in a particular major. If they are not on track to graduate, they are so informed and asked to visit the counseling center.

A subsystem called Course Sequencing Pathways is a sophisticated computer advising system which aids students and advisors in selecting appropriate courses based upon test scores, graduation requirements, intended major, and university-specific transfer requirements. The report that is generated lists suggested and required courses, course prerequisites and corequisites, all registration holds that the student will encounter when attempting to register, and career information which relates to the listed major.

Beaufort Technical College (South Carolina) is an example of a much smaller community college in a much different setting which developed its own student success system. The Miami-Dade prototype served as a benchmark that helped inspire Beaufort's efforts. Ultimately, however, Beaufort staff had to design their own system within parameters unique to their situation.

In 1981 the staff of Beaufort began to design and implement a comprehensive assessment and course placement strategy to enhance student success and retention. They selected the ASSET system which is marketed by the American College Testing Program. Staff believed that the ASSET assessment instrument would be consistent with their philosophy of maintaining open admission while promoting quality instruction, high academic expectations, and strong interactive support systems. The instrument would stimulate and guide the improvement of instruction and the personal and career development of students.

Prior to Fall 1984, the college had in place various components of the present model, but the system was not integrated with instruction. Problems were numerous: lack of immediate feedback to applicants resulting in feelings of academic inadequacy and low enrollment rates; no compulsory orientation; no identification of student needs to evoke proactive support strategies; no follow-up on statistical data; and minimal feedback of assessment information to academic advisors.

To address these concerns, the college adopted a personalized, career-based admissions model. The ACT/ASSET program served to integrate the primary components of the entry process with assessment, academic advisement, and educational planning information. Follow-up was conducted by the student development staff on student needs identified in the entry component. Student development and instructional programming were modified based on testing information, other identified needs, and research provided by the ASSET service.

The main goal of the personalized admission/advisement model has been to provide students a systematic, positive, humanistic approach as they begin their college decision-making process. Additional objectives have been:

- to assess academic skills in reading, writing, and mathematics for proper course placement;
- to support a comprehensive, compulsory student advising program;
- to generate information on student plans, educational goals, and perceived needs for follow-up and evaluation of outcomes;
- to provide a database for programming planning;
- to orient the student to college activities, program resources, and procedures; and
- to serve as a retention tool, since proper advisement, appropriate course placement, and adequate support services enhance the student's chances for success.

Gail Quick, Beaufort's Dean of Student Development, reports a much closer integration of student development and instructional efforts in promoting student success throughout the student flow process. She also reports impressive results which are statistically corroborated (Rowray 1986):

- Before ASSET was implemented in 1984, only about 75 percent of those who applied for admission actually enrolled for classes. After 1984, the enrollment jumped to between 85 percent and nearly 92 percent, depending on the term.
- Before 1984, about 45 percent of applicants who took the college's self-designed placement test enrolled for classes. In dramatic contrast, 88 percent of those who took ASSET enrolled for classes.
- Before ASSET, there was a 70 to 75 percent term completion rate for entering freshmen. With ASSET, the term completion rate jumped to 88 percent.
- Before ASSET, only about 16 percent of entering freshmen returned for the second term. With ASSET, this return rate jumped to 67 percent!

At Beaufort, the ASSET assessment appears to be satisfying the purposes for which it was administered. Placement of students is reasonably accurate. Students are better prepared for courses they are entering and more knowledgeable of appropriate support services. Counselors and advisors have more accurate information on students' backgrounds, needs, and academic abilities and, as a result, can provide better academic advisement. College administrators are provided with a comprehensive student data profile for analyzing the impact of various student retention components.

STAYING STUDENT CENTERED

The Student Success Systems Model could be misunderstood as a computer-based, social engineering program which sacrifices sensitivity to the uniqueness of each individual for the sake of controlling and directing students. The key feature that most implemented models attempt to employ, however, is a balance between technology and student-centeredness. All computer-based systems should be measured against this "high tech–high touch" criterion. Ultimately, the desired goal is to individualize student delivery systems more than ever. In theory, this should be possible as the technology releases professionals from the mundane role of data processing and routine information exchange to perform the higher order tasks of developing and maintaining human support systems for students.

Assessment programs are particularly vulnerable to charges of dehumanization. Certainly, any assessment strategy must be implemented with the understanding that there is a certain amount of imperfection involved. How should assessment programs be structured so they do not deny access to students, but facilitate their proper placement in courses where they will have the maximum opportunity to attain their goals? How can they be individualized so that they enable students to succeed rather than restrict and confine them?

One encouraging answer can be found at Central Piedmont Community College (North Carolina). In 1984, Central Piedmont was selected to pilot-test Computer Placement Testing (CPT), developed by the Educational Testing Service and marketed by the College Board. CPT is used to place students in communications, reading, and mathematics courses. Like ASSET and other course placement systems, it gives educators the opportunity to design more easily an integrated student flow model.

The CPT is unique because assessment is administered on the computer, and the questions are individualized for each student. The software is intended to be very user-friendly.

- The computer chooses at random one of the middle-difficulty-level questions.
- Depending on whether the student answers correctly or not, the computer selects an item from either the least difficult questions or the most difficult questions.

- The computer continues to monitor responses and chooses from questions of appropriate difficulty until it finds questions that focus on the student's skill level.
- Adaptive choice of questions at each difficulty level ensures that no two students see the same set of items.

At Central Piedmont Community College, students and faculty have expressed their liking for the convenience and adaptability of the test. On a questionnaire, 74 percent of the students preferred CPT; 16 percent found no difference compared to pencil-and-paper tests, and 10 percent preferred pencil-and-paper tests.

The CPT runs on IBM computers, 256K, with color monitors. Individualized reports may be printed, or the Educational Testing Service has programmed standard reports which may be printed after testing is complete. Students may take any section of the test without the other sections. Testing time may be a few minutes or a few hours depending on a student's speed and the number of tests taken.

Some advantages of computer testing include:

- Each student may work at his or her own pace.
- Immediate scoring and printout are available at completion of the test.
- Appropriate questions are selected for individual students.
- Test security is provided by individual selection of questions.
- Text anxiety may be reduced because tests are not timed.
- Retesting is easily accomplished.

Perhaps the most outstanding benefit of CPT is the flexibility of scheduling. CPT is available on a drop-in basis. The student who applies for admission is directed to the Testing Center where CPT is administered, results are printed upon completion, and the admissions process may continue through counseling and registration. The entire process may be completed on the student's first visit to the campus. With more working students or those with family responsibilities, the completion of admission in a single campus visit saves time and energy. The convenience of CPT may be the key factor when a student decides to proceed with enrollment.

Another example of how SST thinkers are staying student-centered can be found at Mt. Hood Community College (Oregon) (Keyser 1980–81). Here, a different type of assessment is employed to empower students to assume responsibility for their own learning. A Cognitive Style Mapping (CSM) questionnaire is administered to the majority of full-time students to assess nine dimensions of learning style. The computer printouts are used in group and individualized interpretive sessions to answer questions for each student. Some of these questions are:

- How do I use my senses in teaching-learning situations?
- How do I communicate with others?
- How sensitive am I to people and things?
- Do I perform motor skills according to recommended form?
- How sensitive am I to time expectations?
- To what degree am I influenced by associates, family, or authority figures in making decisions?
- To what degree do I use classifications or rules as the basis for accepting or rejecting a hypothesis?
- Do I reason by making comparisons and seeing differences or by discerning relationships and similarities?

The four-week orientation program, which incorporates CSM as part of a goal-setting process, received high marks from program completers.

- Ninety- four percent of the students responded that they could describe how they preferred to learn (a 91% improvement from the pretest); and 84 percent could identify who had the greatest influence on their learning (an 89% improvement from pretest findings).
- Eighty-five percent of the respondents could describe the process they used in making decisions (a 67% improvement from pretest findings).
- Eighty-four percent of the respondents "strongly agreed" or "agreed" that the "map" gave them useful information about how they get and use information.
- Eighty-five percent of the respondents indicated they could describe their "map" to another student with the help of the student guide.
- Eighty-one percent of the respondents would recommend being mapped to other students.

The orientation course in which the Cognitive Style Mapping questionnaire is used places responsibility on students to develop an awareness of their learning style and employ this awareness as a survival skill. Well over half of the full-time faculty of 150 at Mt. Hood Community College have participated actively in teaching orientation classes, interpreting learning style "maps" to advisees, and discussing their own learning style preferences in classroom settings. A number of faculty have found CSM a useful approach to individualizing and personalizing instruction. For some, it has been a mechanism for translating learning style information into instructional improvement. At the very least, CSM has stimulated interest, discussion, and focus on the important variables of teaching and learning styles.

Orientation programs have become common elements of student success systems. They are examples of efforts to devote more resources and energy to the task of getting students started in a way that maximizes their chances for success.

An example of a student-centered orientation program is found at Northwestern Michigan Community College. Lornie Kerr, Vice President of Student and Administrative Services, and his staff developed a computerized orientation program. Similar to a number of innovations in other student success systems, the development of this program was funded by federal dollars under Title III. The program is required of all first-time students who are taking six credits or more. The class is taken for credit and students must receive a passing grade or repeat the course. The course is designed to complement Northwestern's regular academic advising program. This computerized success program is designed to ensure that students are aware of the facilities and resources in the college that will help make them successful. The program introduces students to a topic, informs students why knowledge of the topic is important, identifies sources of information, and quizzes students to ensure that knowledge of the topic has occurred. Computerized modules include topics on career planning, study skills, time management, values clarification, college facilities, student activities, academic advising, and philosophy of education. Interaction with the instructor occurs in one class meeting, but all other interactions occur between the student and a computer. This approach is designed to make better use of professionals by ensuring that all first-time students are knowledgeable about how, when, and where to find the professionals they need. The computerized orientation program was combined with other elements in the Title III project at Northwestern. The use of ASSET testing and a much more integrated approach to advising were other key subsystems. After one school year, over 700 students had participated in the program. Preliminary studies showed that the target group of students enjoyed more than a 15 percent increase in retention.

A SYSTEMS APPROACH TO THE ACCESS PROBLEM

The systems approach has been applied at Prince George's Community College (Maryland) to improve its marketing-retention effort (Lewis, Leach, and Lutz 1985). Figure 4.2 diagrams the college-wide

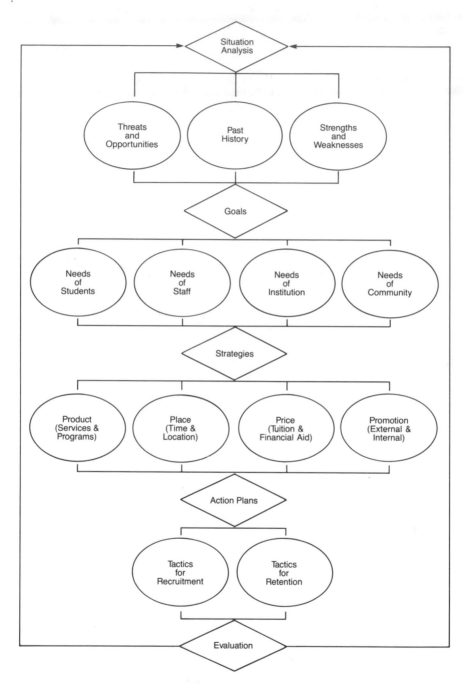

FIGURE 4.2. Marketing-retention system.

plan for being systematically aggressive and systematically supportive in reaching a number of target groups.

- The *situation analysis* is the result of a continuing process of evaluation. Strategic questions such as, "How fast should we grow?" and "How fast can we grow?" are addressed. The college's history, its internal strengths and weaknesses, and threats and opportunities in the "external" environment are profiled. The market, the student consumers, and the competition are described in detail. An institutional research report summarizes student pass rates by course, discipline, and division.

- In response to needs of specific market segments, 96 marketing and retention *goals* were approved. Goals were written to address the needs of the institution, the community, students, and staff. For each marketing goal, success indicators were developed in advance. These indicators were designed to serve as criteria for evaluating goal implementation and results. Completion rates, and term-to-term retention rates, provided general indices of the success of retention strategies. At Prince George's Community College, these indices continue to be published each semester and are distributed to administrators, faculty, and staff. This needs-based approach depends on the concept of improving the fit between the consumer and the product or service. It is assumed that there must be a mutually beneficial relationship between the consumers and the college as a provider of programs and services. The student-consumer must be sufficiently benefited to continue, and the college must be sufficiently compensated to stay in operation.

- *Strategies* are developed in the four equally important areas of marketing—product, place, price, and promotion. Product strategies for student retention included the modification of existing programs and services and the development of new programs or services to respond to identified needs of the student-consumer. Distribution or place strategies were developed to assure that programs and services were available at convenient times, in accessible locations, and in formats that responded to student preferences. Although tuition and fees are fixed at public institutions, price strategies promoting financial aid were used to discount the real cost to students. Promotion strategies, while usually directed toward recruitment, also were used effectively to respond to student retention needs.

- *Action plans* include both tactics for recruitment and tactics for retention. Action plans are continually modified based on the evaluation process.

The success of an early 1980s marketing program at Prince George's was demonstrated by the continuation of 1,000 more students from Spring to Fall than for any similar period in the previous five years.

Prince George's system goes well beyond selling and promotion. Its comprehensive marketing plan accounts for the complex needs and motivations of diverse consumers through a sophisticated approach of market segmentation. The plan balances the needs of the consumers against the needs and realities of the college. This same concept extends through all entry services, support services, and transition or "exit" services at Prince George's. It is a broad, system-wide view of marketing which encompasses all instructional and noninstructional functions. It is also a practical planning process which results in improved student retention. This approach assumes that student attrition is a dynamic phenomenon and that, without a systematic process for the collection and use of information, institutional retention rates cannot improve significantly. It also assumes that simple, tactical approaches for improving enrollments or retention cannot be easily borrowed. There is too much diversity found within, and among, institutions and student populations. What works well in one organization for political, financial, and logistical reasons may not work well at another.

What is adaptable, however, is the system that Prince George's has so successfully employed. This system holds significant potential for addressing the access problems faced by disadvantaged populations.

Although special support programs for disadvantaged populations have been successful for many community colleges, they also present a considerable challenge. In a recent letter to college presidents and other leaders of the largest educational associations, Dale Parnell (1988) said:

> We have reason to be concerned about declining enrollments of disadvantaged and minority students in higher education. Yet we know that educational opportunity programs work. U. S. Department of Education studies show that students enrolled in pre-college programs like Upward Bound are four times as likely to receive a baccalaureate degree as comparable students. They also indicate that poor and minority students who receive appropriate counseling, tutoring, and remedial instruction in a Student Support Services Program are twice as likely to remain in college.

To avoid the continuing trend of greater division between the educated majority and uneducated minorities, there must be a concerted effort to build partnerships to improve the access, opportunity, and success of high school students as they move to community colleges and on to four-year colleges and universities. Several innovations, representing systems thinking, are important reference points for developing these partnerships.

As reported by Ellison and Smith (1987), the Ford Foundation's *Urban Community College Transfer Opportunity Program* (UCCTOP) is an important work from which to build. UCCTOP is designed to assist urban two-year colleges in the development of models and programs that facilitate the successful transfer of minority students from two-year to four-year colleges. One of its goals is to engage high schools and senior colleges in strengthening the transfer process. Among the projects undertaken by the five urban community colleges that received three-year grants in 1984 are: curriculum revision to provide credits required for senior college acceptance; consultation with graduates now studying at four-year institutions to determine the best preparation for advanced study; skill improvement in reading, writing, and mathematics; orientation programs and tutoring for 11th and 12th graders planning to go to college; and faculty mentorship programs to provide potential transfer students with academic and personal support.

The Community College Transition Program (CCTP) is a partnership between the Office of Minority Affairs at the University of Washington and ten community colleges, mostly in the Seattle area. When applicants to the Educational Opportunity Program do not meet university admission requirements, they are given a prescription for meeting deficiencies through the community college. Depending on the nature of their deficiency, they are asked to attend a community college for two quarters and achieve a 2.0 minimum grade point average in transfer courses, or attend a community college and take one or several English composition courses.

Upon completion of these alternatives, students are assured of admission to the University of Washington. The community college option is presented in a supportive manner by university staff. Community college staff guarantee that special attention will be given to the students in satisfying their needs for admission, course placement, and financial aid. Students are told that their progress will be tracked by the community college and the university, thus reassuring the student of the continuing interest of the university.

Students are informed of the potential advantages of participating in the CCTP. The community college is aggressively marketed for its cost advantage and for its supportive academic environment. Community college students who have been successful in making the transition to the university are used as role models.

NATIONAL, REGIONAL, AND STATE NETWORKS

A number of national, regional and state networks reflect the concepts of the sss Model and the enthusiasm for implementing improved strategies for student success. The growth of these networks is, at least in part, attributable to the recognition that student development in the community college is distinctly different from student development at the four-year college or university. The national organizations that serve primarily four-year universities, such as the National Association of Student Personnel Administrators and the American College Personnel Association, have been criticized for not meeting the needs of the community college professional.

One of the networks that has attempted to fill this gap is the National Council on Student Development, one of the affiliate councils of the American Association of Community and Junior Colleges (AACJC).

In 1986 the National Council on Student Development, under the sponsorship of the American College Testing Program, joined forces with the National Council of Instructional Administrators, the American Association of Women in Community and Junior Colleges, the National Council on Black American Affairs, the National Community College Hispanic Council, and the National Association for Developmental Education to produce *Toward Mastery Leadership in Access, Assessment, and Developmental Education* (Keyser and Floyd 1987). The breadth of this partnership is, in itself, a good example of the systems approach. The recommendations were built upon, and added to, the framework for student success systems. This partnership developed new concepts of access, assessment, and developmental education. In 1987 this approach became nationally accepted when the AACJC Board approved position papers developed by these councils.

According to the new concepts, access is a process to ensure student success. It is assumed that the "open door" is really a "revolving door" unless programs are in place to direct and support students toward successful goal attainment. The "freedom to fail" notion so prevalent with the student services/student development thinking of the 1960s and 1970s is rejected as irresponsible. It is also understood that community colleges will aggressively seek out disadvantaged and unserved populations, developing support programs to facilitate their entry into the institution.

Reflecting this broader definition of access, assessment is defined comprehensively to include constructive measurement of motivational levels, study skills preparation, educational readiness, self-concept, and past performance. It is a combination of systematic efforts and educational tools that guide the teaching and learning process. Testing, regarded as a subset of assessment, must never be used to restrict access. Assessment should be used to facilitate student progress toward educational goals and, if administered properly, will increase the chances of student success.

A sound assessment process is necessary to assist faculty and staff in determining which educational interventions are most appropriate to ensure student success. Intervention is defined as any action that a college takes to participate in the progress of a student toward goal attainment. Developmental education is the most commonly practiced intervention strategy. Intervention is based on a "right to succeed" philosophy. It literally "comes between" the student and failure, and must be systematic and part of the ongoing functions of the college. In this context, the term intervention suggests directive and supportive efforts that will maximize the chances for student success.

The philosophy behind the sss Model makes the three elements—access, assessment, and intervention—integrally related. *Toward Mastery Leadership in Access, Assessment, and Developmental Education* has the same philosophic underpinnings as the sss Model (Keyser and Floyd 1987). These three elements must be viewed as equally vital factors in the equation of student success. For instance, strong and effective developmental education programs promote access by better preparing students for transfer and vocational courses. Such programs depend on judiciously administered assessment programs to clarify who will benefit from specialized support. Successful intervention strategies enhance academic standards, improve student retention and goal achievement, and provide important benefits for society as a whole.

The National Council on Student Development has produced several other handbooks. "The 1984 Traverse City Statement" made recommendations in the areas of contributing to quality reaffirmation and program accountability; strengthening partnerships with community constituencies; strengthening partnerships with campus constituencies; creatively managing resources; creatively managing enrollments and contributing to student persistence; using educational technology; and integrating student development into the educational experience (Keyser 1985). A year later, "The 1985 Traverse City Statement" made recommendations on developing the qualities of mastery leadership (Keyser 1986). Some of the more elusive dimensions of leadership are explored around the themes of managing vision, trust, meaning, and self. Both the 1984 and 1985 Traverse City Statements represent the assumptions of systems thinking and doing. Student development professionals are placed in a college-wide framework where their roles are defined, not separately, but in relationship to the roles of other college leaders.

In addition to the National Council on Student Development, several other networks for student success are noteworthy.

Since 1986, a coalition of Washington and Oregon deans have sponsored an annual Northwest Conference on Student Success Strategies (Green 1986, 1987, 1988). The first two conferences led to summary publications of ideas and techniques for creating student success systems developed around the themes of access, assessment, and intervention. The conferences were based on the assumption that interdisciplinary teams of faculty, staff, administrators, and students should represent each participating college. The team was intended to serve as an important catalyst for developing a coordinated, college-wide commitment to the implementation of student success systems. Boards and presidents were encouraged to identify retention as a major goal. It was recommended that the themes of student success should be reflected in the college mission statement, in written goals and objectives, and in proactive plans for intervention. The most recent conference focused on sharing implementation strategies and involving faculty members who have been successful in creating classroom strategies for student success.

Several years ago, the State of Alabama funded eight of its community colleges to pilot a major retention project. With the final goal of improving student retention, all aspects of the college environment were analyzed to determine their negative or positive impact on retention. Each college used interdisciplinary teams to evaluate and modify factors that hindered student success. Jo Beene, Dean of Students at John C. Calhoun State Community College and Director of the Retention Project, reported significant improvements in the retention rates of participating colleges. Her own college has experienced a 26 percent improvement in the retention rate (Beene 1985).

Organized in 1981, the Learning, Assessment, Retention Consortium (LARC) of California is a network of about 85 community colleges. The consortium now includes six regional groups, each of which is an autonomous consortium of colleges with its own officers, operating principles, and agenda. The common purpose of these groups is to translate issues and concerns about student learning into action. The original goal of the consortium was to examine assessment as a framework for improving learning and retention. Other goals are to maintain an information network among member colleges, conduct and coordinate research activities, refine a comprehensive assessment/placement/retention model for member colleges, and involve staff at all levels in college-wide action teams. Each LARC college has organized a team of faculty and staff to develop college plans related to learning, retention, assessment, placement, and guidance. Teams review LARC data and information to apply to their own college's needs.

The LARC Assessment/Placement Model describes what the consortium colleges believe should be included in a complete system designed to assist students to make progress toward their goals. The system includes not only testing and placement but also strong guidance, program planning, and research/evaluation components—all based on college-developed philosophy, goals, and objectives.

During the past several years, the LARC Consortium has focused considerable attention on student outcomes. The Statewide Outcomes Study in composition involved 8,000 students in 31 community colleges. The Outcomes Study is an example of how the LARC Consortium has become active in placing important issues before various policy-making bodies. LARC also has an active program of mutual assistance whereby colleges receive advice from colleagues through workshops, an annual state conference, and team visitations.

Susan Obler was one of the founders of the LARC Consortium. She and her colleagues developed an assessment model which has the goal of enabling students to define their personal goals and to plan an instructional program as quickly as possible (Obler and Ramer 1987). Figure 4.3 illustrates how the model functions with assessment and interpretation procedures that are completely customized for each student. The student's personal involvement helps the student "own" his or her goals and increases the student's motivation. Students participate in a full discussion of their strengths and liabilities. Implementing this model requires careful planning and budgeting. However, colleges can anticipate saving revenue ordinarily lost through the attrition of students who have ambiguous goals.

Other examples of student success networks include the Student Development Network of the League for Innovation and the Student Assessment Task Force of the Washington State Student Services Commission. All of the networks described in this section are evidence of the commitment of community colleges to student success. This movement is engaging others to participate, enabling many to be more effective, and giving clearer definition to future action.

IMPLICATIONS AND CONCLUSIONS

This chapter has traced the emergence of a new paradigm for conceptualizing and implementing programs and services that maximize the potential for student achievement of educational and career goals. Many professionals who have been placed in traditionally defined student services or student development roles have learned the systems approach. They have become, or are in the process of becoming, managers/leaders of student success systems. The SSS Model, although it has not been used to replace student services/student de-

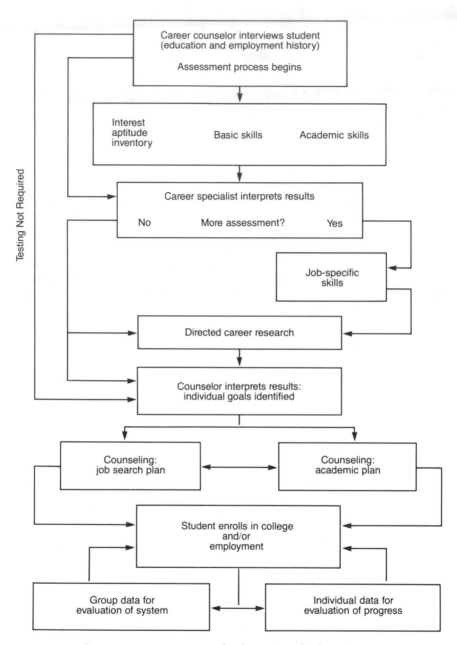

FIGURE 4.3. Career assessment and educational planning system.

velopment in the professional jargon, is, in reality, an accurate description of a major new direction for all community colleges. The new innovators in this field have merged their sensitivity to individual differences and their knowledge of developmental psychology with the systems perspective of thinking and doing.

Contrary to Elsner's discouraging comments, with which this chapter began, thousands of professionals are busy translating their vision of student success systems into practice. The breakthroughs achieved via the intelligent use of modern technologies have given new meaning to the goal of making a positive impact on students' lives. The understanding of the complexities of student behavior has never been greater, and the hope that this knowledge can be translated into systems for success has never been higher.

The profession is markedly different than it was 20 years ago. Student services/student development experts have moved into the mainstream to become architects of systems that maximize the chances for students to clarify and reach their goals. Computer technology and the greater power of the systems method made this transition possible. The challenges are the same, but it is now possible to confront them with greater sophistication. This has created a new excitement for making student success systems work on each campus.

Architects of student success systems work to design how various elements will best fit into a student flow blueprint. They clarify how resources will work in a complementary manner to achieve a common purpose and to nurture a continuing learning process that enables systems to become stronger over time. Rather than focusing narrowly on being student advocates, the staff can work with a student in the college-wide context where they are all working toward the same goal of facilitating student success. As such, they are much more than student services administrators who were, in many cases, concerned with regulating and maintaining a subset of a complex organization. These new innovators and architects of student success systems are holistic managers, leaders, and teachers. Their charge is much more ambitious!

This interpretation of what has happened is also a vision of what should occur. If the student success movement is to capture the minds and creative energies of more community college leaders, the following recommendations should be implemented:

First, presidents, deans and other institutional leaders should nurture organizational cultures in which student success is the primary purpose and where organizational values create productive effort toward this purpose. Clackamas Community College (Oregon) represents one approach to achieving this objective. The President's Council, representing students, faculty, classified staff, and the deans, set in motion a year-long, college-wide process to define the basic elements of institutional identity. The result was a staff handbook in which agreed-upon definitions were printed. The stated *purpose* was "Creating lifetime opportunities for success through responsive education." The *mission* was to provide high quality education and training opportunities within specified parameters (such as finite resources and state law). A *philosophic commitment* was made to be accessible, adaptable, and accountable. Values relating to the institution, students, faculty/staff relationships, and the decision-making process were specified. These values place all employees in a "culture" of problem solvers, idea originators, and collaborators in working toward the shared purpose.

The handbook and, more important, the continuing process that was set in motion to develop it, gives campus leaders the framework to enable and empower all staff to maximize their effectiveness in creating lifetime opportunities for student success. Part of the continuing process was the establishment of a student success task force representing all groups, with the charge of making recommendations in all areas of college–student interaction. A Title III grant application was funded with the theme of improving retention and the information base for analyzing student progress. The result is likely to be a redesign of the Clackamas student flow model. Any healthy organization depends on a dynamic process of ongoing self-assessment and improvement. Student success systems will never achieve their promise unless presidents, deans, and other institutional leaders constantly nurture a purposeful organizational citizenship.

Second, student services/student development professionals who are in the process of becoming implementers of student success systems, should assume a broad definition of their role. They should conceive of themselves as educators who work closely with faculty, staff, and instructional administrators to design, implement, and improve systems for student success. The entire college and community should be viewed as a classroom. And the same principles that are the basis for quality instruction should be the standards that guide the development of college/community-wide systems for student success. Generally, these principles are: unwavering belief in the student's capacity to learn; an enthusiasm for the teaching and learning process; the motivating nature of clearly defined goals and challenging expectations; a knowledge of the subject matter; presentation of material in an organized and sequential manner; and a sensitivity to individual differences.

The broad themes and recommendations developed at the Traverse City conferences (discussed earlier) are relevant not only to presidents, deans, and university professors. Initiative is needed from all professionals in the community college to design and implement student success systems.

Third, resources should be shifted to the "front end." This conclusion is based on research and experience which suggests that the first several weeks of a student's involvement with the college environment is the most critical part of a successful college/student relationship. Becoming "front-end loaded" includes aggressive efforts to reach disadvantaged, minority, and special populations and the necessary support services that will maximize their chances for survival. It also includes comprehensive advisement, assessment, course placement, and orientation programs, all of which aim to start each student with the appropriate match between program/career goals and readiness to pursue those goals.

This recommendation is based on the belief that few colleges will have access to new resources, but all will have the opportunity to shift resources if there is a strong rationale. Resource shifts will depend, to a significant extent, on community college cultures becoming more focused on student success. In any circumstance, shifting resources will be a difficult task, entailing a certain amount of risk. When Miami-Dade initiated its student success system, a precipitous enrollment decline occurred. This had significant implications for all staff, but especially decision makers who, in a time of perceived crisis, invariably have their credibility questioned.

With these caveats aside, a number of examples to guide resource shifts are in place. Miami-Dade, Mt. Hood, and other colleges have involved faculty, administrators, paraprofessionals, and students in advisement, orientation, outreach, and intervention efforts. All of these colleges have used the computer to multiply limited staff resources. Other colleges have strengthened partnerships with community constituencies. Clackamas Community College has developed an alternative schools program to reach the high school drop-out which comprises a partnership with the school district, business and industry, and the Private Industry Council. All share the burden of providing increased resources in an intensive support program that has impressive results. Many of the program completers continue their education at the college. Shifting resources and sharing resources are most likely to occur when not just the college, but the entire community is defined as a classroom.

Fourth, there should be less energy spent on organizational structure and more energy spent on purpose. A clear purpose is the key to a healthy organizational climate. Organizational theorists love to recite President Kennedy's charge to NASA: "A man on the moon by the end of the decade," as an example of the power of a vision which causes all parts of an organization to "align" toward a common purpose. Students of successful entrepreneurial organizations also point to the "champions" who, as a result of their expertise or commitment to a cause or product, emerge as leaders—regardless of their position or formal station.

The sss approach puts questions about organizational structure in a different context. The model suggests that the focus should not be so much on student services (student development, student affairs) or whether a dean of students reports directly to the president, as on how educational leaders should be trained and enabled to develop, monitor, and improve systems for student success. In recent years, it has become increasingly common for presidents to modify the traditionally accepted practice of having the dean of students report directly to them by integrating student services and instruction under a single, second-level manager who is usually called a dean or vice president of instruction/student services. The chief student services/development officer, usually titled a dean of students or associate dean of students, is relegated to third-level management. Some of these changes have been economically motivated by variations of California's Proposition 13. Others have undoubtedly been inspired by a "problem dean" or a misguided president.

The central question that should guide any such organizational change should be, "To what extent will this help the organization achieve a common focus on the student and improve the integration of systems to facilitate student success?" And the corollary to this is, "How can the organization encourage, inspire, develop, and promote champions of student success?"

Ultimately, however, integration between student services and instructional services (and the rest of the organization) will depend on leaders who are able to devise mechanisms for effective communication, cooperation, and coordination and to inspire people who have a strong commitment to make such mechanisms work. This commitment will be based on the shared goal of creating systems for student success. Simply stated, the right people are more important to this goal than the right lines and boxes. What works in any particular organizational environment depends on balancing the science of management and the art of leadership toward a common purpose.

REFERENCES

Armes, Nancy; J. S. Griffith; and Lee Trout, eds. 1984. *Guidelines for the Development of Computerized Student Information Systems.* Laguna Hills, Ca.: League for Innovation in the Community College.

Beene, J.N. 1985. *Focusing on Retention: A Commitment to Student Success. A Resource Manual for Alabama State Community, Junior and Technical Colleges.* A report of the Alabama State Task Force on Retention submitted to Charles Payne, Chancellor, Alabama State Department of Postsecondary Education. February.

ELLISON, NOLEN, and JANET SMITH. 1987. "Access and Excellence: The Articulation Challenge among Urban High Schools, Community Colleges, and Four-Year Institutions." In *Toward Mastery Leadersip in Access, Assessment, and Developmental Education*, edited by J. S. Keyser and D. L. Floyd. Iowa City: American College Testing Program.

ELSNER, PAUL, and W.C. AMES. 1983. "Redirecting Student Services." In *Issues for Community College Leaders in a New Era*, edited by George Vaughan. San Francisco: Jossey-Bass.

GREEN, CONNIE 1986. *The 1986 Student Success Strategies Conference*. Salem, Or.: Chemeketa Community College.

———. 1987. *The 1987 Student Success Strategies Conference*. Salem, Or.: Chemeketa Community College.

———. 1988. *The 1988 Student Success Strategies Conference*. Salem, Or.: Chemeketa Community College.

KEYSER, JOHN. 1980–81. "Cognitive Style Mapping at Mt. Hood Community College." *Community College Review* 8, no. 3 (Winter).

KEYSER, JOHN S. ed. 1985. "The 1984 Traverse City Statement." In *Toward The Future Vitality of Student Development Services*, edited by John S. Keyser. Iowa City: American College Testing Program.

———, ed.1986. "The 1985 Traverse City Statement." In *Toward Mastery Leadership in Student Development Services*, edited by John S. Keyser. Iowa City: American College Testing Program.

KEYSER, JOHN S., and D. L. FLOYD, eds 1987. *Toward Mastery Leadership in Access, Assessment, and Developmental Education*. Iowa City: American College Testing Program.

LEACH, ERNIE. 1985. "Student Development and College Services: A Consumer Perspective." In *Toward the Future Vitality of Student Development Services*, edited by John Keyser. Iowa City: American College Testing Program.

LEWIS, C.T., E.R. LEACH, and L.L. LUTZ. 1983. "A Marketing Model for Student Retention." *NASPA Journal* 20, no. 3 (Spring).

LINDEMANN, W.H.; A. W. DECABOOTER; and J. A. CORDOVA. 1987. *Student Success: The Common Goal*. Iowa City: American College Testing Program.

OBLER, S. and M.H. RAMER. 1987. "Is There Life After College? A Customized Assessment and Planning Model." In *Issues in Student Assessment*, New Directions for Community Colleges, edited by Dorothy Bray and M.J. Belcher, no. 59 (Fall). San Francisco: Jossey-Bass.

PARNELL, DALE. 1988. Letter sent to all college and university presidents regarding National TRIO Day, January 5.

ROWRAY, RICHARD D. 1986. *The Resource Notebook*. Iowa City: American College Testing Program.

5

Expanding Horizons
FOR
Learning and Technology

Kamala Anandam

In his book *Megatrends*, Naisbitt (1982) describes three stages of technological development. The first stage, he says, follows the line of least resistance, the second stage witnesses the use of technology to improve previous technologies, and the third stage discovers new forms of technology that grow out of technology itself. At present, a number of technological experimentations are being carried out in the community colleges; most of them are at the second stage of applying technology to improve prior practices, and a few are beginning to edge toward the third stage of creating new practices in the teaching/learning process. Collectively, the community colleges are at the threshold of a renaissance of innovation in educational technologies that will expand the horizons for teaching and technology. For the renaissance to come to full bloom, the educators need to recognize and nurture it. Nurturing the new technological practices will demand, no doubt, some substantial changes in institutional organization, administrative styles, teaching philosophy, and learning environments (Anandam 1986).

Those technocrats who lament that technological revolution in education is long overdue are not the ones who will bring about these changes; it is the faculty and the administrators in the educational institutions who will bring them about. The faculty who meet with the students day after day, stroking the students who succeed, prodding the students who slow down, reaching out to the students who drop out, can best judge which technologies will be broad-based and meaningful and consequently adopt them. The administrators who lead, direct, and guide the personnel will be the best change-agents for restructuring the teaching/learning environment in order for the uses of technology to become integral to the institutional practices. The examples cited in this chapter, without a single exception, trace their success to the commitment and dedication of such faculty and administrators.

Community colleges seem to follow three directions in their uses of technology. One direction is to determine the activities humans do not wish to pursue in teaching and delegate those activities to technology. Reflective of this decision are the management systems, test-scoring systems, drill- and-practice systems, and tutorials. Another direction is to introduce all the enhancements technology can provide to make the teacher a better teacher and the learner a better learner. Along this decision path appear electronically equipped classrooms, computerized tools such as word processors and calculators, and media production tools. Yet another direction is to use technology to perform the activities that humans wish they could do but find humanly impossible to do. In this category would fall simulations, adaptive testing, tailored tutoring, and expert systems.

In all three directions, educators' concerns seem to rest on the impact of technology on the educational process. The following four trends will be used in this chapter to illustrate the impact of the technologies:

- from technology-instigated education to education-instigated technology;
- from uniform information to customized information;
- from one-way communication to interactive communication; and
- from a focus on teaching to a focus on learning.

Each of these trends represents an important aspect of the yet-to-blossom renaissance of innovation in educational technologies. These have evolved over the last two decades, affected by the technological breakthroughs on the one hand and the educators' demands on the other. All four trends place the learners at the center of learning and expect them to be responsible for their own learning. The prospect for the renaissance of innovation in educational technologies rests on this conception of the learners as personally responsible for their learning. What follows is a discussion of each of the four trends.

FROM TECHNOLOGY-INSTIGATED EDUCATION TO EDUCATION-INSTIGATED TECHNOLOGY

The faddish, random love affair with technology of the early 1970s is giving way, slowly but steadily, to educational concerns that can be summarized in a single, short question: "Technology for what?" This question was battered around in the 1960s, and it is being resurrected again. A review of the research in the earlier period showed that the findings were inconsistent and inconclusive (Anandam and Kelly 1981). Continued research, however, is revealing some useful trends about computer-based education (Fisher 1983):

1. Information delivered by a teacher in a classroom during a semester can be delivered by computers in a matter of hours or minutes.

2. Computers are perceived as consistent, patient, and fair by minority students.

3. Computer-based instruction is more effective at raising achievement levels of low-or high-achieving students than it is those of students of average achievement.

4. Computer-based software that is integrated into the curriculum has a better chance of yielding positive results.

5. Computer-based education leads to improved attendance, increased motivation, longer attention span, and significant positive change in student attitudes.

The findings are at once encouraging and challenging. For example, while it is encouraging to know that technology helps students learn faster, it is challenging to determine what new learning activities in the classroom will enhance the students' capabilities to function effectively in a technological society. And, while it is encouraging to see that technology improves the affective attributes of the students, it is challenging to channel these positive changes toward improving students' learning. More important, it is encouraging that research has helped educators move from technology-instigated education to education-instigated technology.

Social concerns have also fostered the use of technology in education. For example, technology is being used to address the needs of (1) physically handicapped students, (2) adult students returning to college, (3) underprepared students, and (4) students who are not skillful in the use of the English language. Each of these groups requires special approaches to meet some of their special needs. At least four programs illustrate this point.

The *first* one is "Project Homebound" at Lewis and Clark College (Illinois). The faculty in data processing created a program designed to deliver their entire two-year program to homebound students. Although only four students are participating at this time, the originators claim that the system can handle any number of students from anywhere in the country. The students and the faculty dial the system at the scheduled hours, no matter where they are, and participate in a live discussion. They also communicate electronically on an individual basis and send assignments back and forth electronically. The ingenuity and persistence of the faculty in creating hardware and software modifications to accommodate the needs of the handicapped students are impressive.

The *second* illustration comes from the California community colleges system, which has established a High Tech Center for the Disabled. At this center, computer hardware and software have been adapted to meet the needs of the blind or visually impaired students, students with mild to severe orthopedic disabilities, and those with auditory deficits.

The *third* example comes from Central Piedmont Community College (North Carolina). To battle against the problem of growing adult illiteracy in the state, the college has developed Project ABLE (Adult Basic Literacy Education). With its array of microcomputers, sound/slide programs, videotapes, instructors, and volunteers, ABLE attracts an increasing number of students each year. The ABLE Center is located in a shopping mall and is busy day and night.

The *fourth* example comes from Itawamba Community College (Mississippi) which is responding to its state's request for adult basic education. Using IBM's SOFTWARE PAL (Principles of Alphabet Literacy), adult students are learning to write and read. PAL is an adaptation of the program "Writing to Read" for adult learners. This program illustrates how the use of technology has reversed a traditional concept from "reading before writing" to "writing to read."

Whether an institution adopts education-instigated technology or technology-instigated education is reflected in the guidelines it uses to introduce technology. Some of the guidelines that seem to operate in institutions are these:

- Buying the hardware and establishing computer labs;
- Buying off-the-shelf software;
- Buying state- of-the-art hardware;
- Concentrating on remedial education;
- Developing software to meet institutional goals;
- Focusing on support for handicapped students;

- Providing technological tools such as word processing;
- Providing technological support to the faculty;
- Using course-specific software;
- Using software applicable across disciplines; and
- Using software for testing.

All but the first three deal with educational concerns and choices—education-instigated technology. What is observed in most institutions is a combination of guidelines at work, sometimes in harmony and at other times in discord. If an institution were to develop a well-thought-out and explicitly stated set of guidelines, it would have a sensible way of allocating its resources and a systematic way of implementing educational technologies. Beyond this step, institutions need to examine the uses of technology in terms of students' learning. As a matter of fact, the movement toward understanding what learning is all about and understanding what kinds of research facilitate learning has begun. As this movement builds momentum, innovation in educational technologies is likely to develop more rapidly.

How can institutions get involved in the movement that focuses on students' learning and evaluation of their learning? *First,* educators need a better understanding of how students learn and, therefore, how teachers should teach. As Simon contends, "For every megabuck we spend in hardware and systems software, we will need to spend another megabuck for research on effective learning and development of modern learning environments" (1987, 5). While universities conduct research on learning, the findings seem to trickle down only to the elementary and secondary schools because the schools happen to be the focus of the studies most of the time. Consequently, the community colleges have to take their own initiative to review the existing research findings as well as conduct studies in their own settings. Partnerships with nearby universities might prove worthwhile to encourage graduate students to do their dissertations in a community college setting. Another quick source for research information is *Innovation Abstracts*, published monthly by the University of Texas at Austin.

Second, educators need to learn about what is appropriate for the students. Conventional beliefs about the computer's capability to provide immediate feedback or let the students progress independently at their own pace undermine the capabilities of the students and the computers. McKeachie (1983) points out that, in most cases, immediate feedback does not seem to make a great deal of difference for meaningful material. This is so because meaningful material calls for reflective learning, which is the process by which students contemplate their own thinking and responses and either confirm or correct them (Anandam and Kelly 1982). Also, the conventional belief that computers allow the students to progress at their own pace has been translated in practice to mean independent study at the computer. This practice ignores the merits of peer interaction along with computer interactions. One of the principles derived from cognitive psychology strongly suggests that peer interaction—when peers can challenge and contradict each other's ideas to create cognitive stress—is a great facilitator of learning. The magic number of three surfaces as the optimum number of students for such peer interactions. Educators need to apply this principle in using the interactive technologies for presentation of materials. Miami-Dade Community College has done so with an interactive videodisc on critical thinking.

Third, educators need to understand the nature of the cybernetic model for research to evaluate and refine the teaching/learning process. Cooley (1983) observes that reform efforts in education have tended to assume that the best way to improve educational practice is to adopt a new program that seems to address a particular problem, implement that innovative program, and then evaluate the program to determine its effectiveness in dealing with the problem (technological-experimental paradigm). An alternative to the experimental paradigm, according to Cooley, is the cybernetic paradigm, which involves monitoring indicators and tailoring practices. A fundamental feature of a cybernetic model is the notion of feedback to alter subsequent action. More recently, Cross (1986) proposes "classroom research" as a means of helping teachers evaluate the effectiveness of their own teaching. Classroom research, according to Cross, is a powerful, formative evaluation tool that holds promise for bridging the gap between research and practice.

FROM UNIFORM INFORMATION TO CUSTOMIZED INFORMATION

In the 1960s, technology was used well for classroom instruction. From a ditto machine to a photocopier to a copier/collator, from a chalkboard to a flip chart to a plastic board, from 35mm film to 8mm to videocassette, the technology improved in order to make it increasingly simple and convenient to use. Whatever use was made of whatever technology, it focused on enhancing the classroom instruction for a group of students. Sometimes, the group was as small as ten and at other times as large as a few hundred. The users of technology did not attempt to cater to individual needs. Rather, they used technology to assist them in delivering the same information at the same time to all the students in the class. In other words, the delivery of instruction through technology was content-specific, location-specific, and time-specific. It was not too long, however, before the idea of independent study was born, and resource centers were created with many study carrels. Gagne's ideas on task analysis, Skinner's principles of behavior modification, and Bloom's taxonomy of objectives were heavily relied upon in presenting the content to the students in this mode. Thus, what is significant in these innovations is their effect on the faculty in terms of organizing and presenting the information to their students in a systematic manner.

The 1970s saw the birth of telecourses—delivery of information at various locations through broadcast signals. Still content-specific, the technology delivered the information at scheduled times to the students wherever they might be. Very quickly, however, the problem of time dependence for telecourses was reduced by the introduction of videocassettes placed at local libraries and resource centers. More recently, videocassettes are available at video rental stores. In all these instances, the mode of delivery changed while the information remained the same for all the viewers. However, a new dimension was added to the educators' concept of the teaching/learning process by their having to design a course for students whom they would not see in a classroom. Some of the challenges in this regard included (1) planning far in advance; (2) allowing for late registration and submission of assignments at different times; (3) being specific and clear in written materials, besides having to write more; and (4) helping students not to procrastinate. These challenges created by the offering of telecourses have sensitized the faculty to the students' need for individual attention.

The 1980s introduced the idea of selectivity and interactivity for the learners in dealing with information. These features have taken off in two different directions, both of which seem necessary. One direction allows the student complete freedom in selecting the information and interacting with it at will. Databases of all sorts follow this direction. In this mode, the student has control over content, sequence, and pacing. The other direction allows the teacher/designer to tailor information for individual students and preprogram opportunities for students to interact with that information. In this mode, the student has control over pacing and, in some instances, sequence, but not over content.

Thus, from the 1960s to the 1980s, the focus of delivery is shifting from uniform information to customized information. While time and distance are becoming less restrictive in this shift, there are other implications that need to be considered by educators. For one thing, if delivery of information is delegated to technology, how will the activities in the classroom change to enhance students' learning? For another, if technology allows students to learn at their own pace, will the students be allowed to receive their grades as they finish and immediately enroll in a new course? In other words, will an institution permit continual enrollment and graduation? Will implications such as these challenge the institutions sufficiently to alter their ways, or will the promises of technology for customizing the delivery of information go unrealized?

An excellent example of altering the classroom activities comes from Brookdale Community College (New Jersey). After conducting their composition class in a computer lab for three hours one day a week, the faculty reported that their involvement was individualized and intense; their response to their students' writing was immediate and timely; and they liked the collaborative learning that was taking place naturally. Another example, equally innovative, comes from Johnson County Community College (Kansas), where the faculty in English and data processing jointly teach students how to write and how to use word processing as a writing tool. For the convenience of the students the word processing class follows immediately after the composition class. Such block scheduling makes the link between the two classes more meaningful to both the students and the faculty. Yet another example of integrating technology for the improvement of classroom instruction comes from Cuyahoga Community College (Ohio). For the past four years, this college has used word processing (Bank Street Writer) extensively in a network environment for teaching writing. From a modest beginning with two faculty members on one campus, the project now includes nearly 25 faculty on three campuses. According to the originators of this application, the faculty spend less time on the mechanics of writing and more time on the process of writing.

Attempts at addressing the issue of fixed-term boundaries are observed in technical colleges. Guilford Technical Community College (North Carolina) has reached the conclusion (after years of trying) that state funding procedures based on a student head count preclude the possibility of instituting variable time for entry and exit. On the other hand, Greenville Technical College (South Carolina), where state funding is based on credits completed, has succeeded in instituting continual registration that allows students to enroll in and complete a course any time. In this system, a course is equated to 11 weeks of instruction and students are given "time" credit if they finish earlier or charged extra fees if they take longer.

Removal of term boundaries will not be an overnight revolution. It will be a painstaking, time-consuming, nerve-wracking and horrendous undertaking. Nevertheless, major innovations in educational technologies can hardly be realized without questioning the current practices of admission, registration, end-of-term grades, and graduation. Many colleges have become flexible in their admission and registration policies to accommodate early and dual enrollment, but they have done very little or nothing to allow early completion. In a way, the technologies that help students finish their work faster are perceived as a threat to the sacred structures of education. This is a serious deterrent to the widespread use of technological innovations in education.

FROM ONE-WAY COMMUNICATION TO INTERACTIVE COMMUNICATION

Socrates had the right idea that one-on-one dialogues are the best way to educate (enlighten) students. He had a better idea when he insisted that the students should be responsible for raising questions and seeking answers. While some dialogues of this nature may occur in classrooms, they are more likely to be an exception to the rule. One-way communication, with the faculty conveying information to their students, has been the primary model of education for hundreds of years. This is not to say that the classroom is devoid of students' questions or discussions, but it will be hard to demonstrate that all students are equally interactive in a classroom situation.

Electronic and telephone conferences have managed to broaden the scope of classroom communication to include the students at different locations. Rio Salado Community College (Arizona) has used the telephone effectively for its telecourses for the past four years. It offers about 14 courses per semester in this mode with about 20 students enrolled in each. At scheduled times, students call in from wherever they are and participate in a live discussion with their instructor.

Phone and electronic mail systems remove the necessity to schedule class sessions electronically and allow the faculty and students to interact on a delayed time basis. Kalamazoo Community College (Michigan), is using electronic mail to facilitate two- way communication between the faculty and the students and among the students. This facility is currently limited to the business, math, and data processing programs. As students enroll in these programs, the computer system generates a unique password for each student and a distribution list for the faculty. By writing this front-end computer program locally, the college is able to use the VAX electronic mail system easily and effectively. Even though the interactions in this example are not taking place in real time, the system allows the faculty and students to communicate at a time when each is most ready to do so, regardless of the time of the day.

One of the oldest systems to provide interaction between the student and the information is the Plato system that originated at the University of Illinois and which operates on a mainframe computer. One substantial success story comes from the Bay de Noc Community College (Michigan). Plato materials have been used at this institution on a regular basis for science, English, and nursing for the past four years. Approximately 900 students of the 2,000 enrollees spend 30 hours each per week with Plato. The substantial amount of time students seem to be spending with the Plato system may very well contribute to the success of the program. With the advent of microcomputers, numerous other programs have been produced which provide increased access and interaction to the students. Other emerging technologies such as interactive videotape, interactive videodisc, Digital Video Interactive (DVI), and Compact Disc-Interactive (CD-I) hold great potential for increasing interaction.

Historically, the combination of audio and video in the same medium in the 1930s opened up a whole new set of possibilities for education. One can recall vividly the excitement over sound movies. The slide/tape combinations in the 1950s were lauded for their convenience of presenting information, and the multimedia projections involving multiple slide projectors and audiocassettes were acclaimed as sensational. The advent of the laser videodisc in the 1970s, with its high storage capacity (equivalent to 54,000 picture frames per side), random access, and durability, marked another milestone. In this medium, still pictures, motion video, and two channels of audio are combined. The two audio channels can be used to present the information in two different languages or explain the same information in two different ways. The durability of the disc and random access of the information make this medium attractive for repeated use. The power of the videodisc is increased greatly when connected to a computer that can be programmed to function as a super-manager of the medium. The computer's capabilities for graphics, branching, and record keeping have substantially improved the presentation quality of this medium. It can function, on the one hand, as a vehicle for storage and retrieval of information and, on the other hand, as a vehicle for sophisticated instructional delivery that is capable of tailoring the instruction to meet individual students' needs.

The CD-I and the DVI are the latest multimedia technologies that compact pictures, text, and data onto a 5" disc that has a tremendous storage capacity. Whereas the three channels (one video and two audio) of the laser videodisc are each limited to 30 minutes of playback, the CD-I and DVI technologies allow many different ways to play back the audio and visual signals for virtually unlimited time. In a way, these technologies represent a sophisticated version of the multimedia presentation, with some spectacular additions, including (1) with a single-band playback mechanism, one can introduce a number of audio interpretations for a visual; (2) rotations of the visuals introduce the three-dimensional effect; and (3) users' interaction with the content is integral to the medium.

Such a medium as CD-I or DVI stimulates educators to think anew about what learning is and to find ways to use the new medium according to their new conceptualizations of learning. More and more, the trend seems to be to move away from course-specific software to functional applications, and from the "presentation-test-feedback" model to simulations and games. In other words, the trend is to let the learners manipulate the technological programs to meet their own needs. These are desirable trends, and technologies such as DVI and CD-I help to develop products that reflect these trends. Unless educators respond to new technologies with some new conceptualizations about teaching and learning, the technologies may be underutilized.

Of course, none of the media by themselves have anything to offer until someone places the information on them. Developing technological programs for students is a major task. The skills and effort that a person needs to write on a blackboard are simple compared to what is required to place information on a CD-I disc. In its simplicity, the chalkboard offers users a great flexibility. Instructors can write on the board as and when they choose and erase what is on the board any time. Thus, the greatest strengths of the chalkboard are its spontaneity and erasability, both of which are sorely lacking in other technological media. This is not to say that the chalkboard alone will suffice, but rather to remind educators to examine closely the strengths of each medium and use them judiciously, singly or in combination.

The time and effort needed to produce quality technological programs are prompting individuals to seek the assistance of others. Collaboration, then, emerges as a significant aspect of innovation in educational technologies. Collaborators now include content specialists, educational psychologists, instructional designers, assessment specialists, media specialists, artists, writers, programmers, and researchers. Once again, the challenge of bringing about major changes remains with the people involved and not with the technologies. Success in meeting this challenge relies heavily on the willingness of educators to deviate from the "business as usual" path. Institutions should consider paying attention to, and providing support for, the development and delivery of technological education. This attention and support should find some tangible forms of expression. A department of educational technologies is such an expression, and it will go a long way to assist an institution to develop and/or deliver technological education in a meaningful way.

FROM FOCUS ON TEACHING TO FOCUS ON LEARNING

A discussion of innovation in educational technologies will not be complete without the mention of an emerging shift in focus from teaching to learning. This shift under the same name was acclaimed as a breakthrough in the 1960s. However, in practice, the focus on learning turned out to be merely *independent* study of the same materials and was dominated by the behaviorists' model of reinforcement and repetition. In the 1980s, the discussion of learning embodies the insights derived from cognitive psychology and proposes to use technology for *individualizing* the learning environment. This shift, just beginning to be acknowledged by educators, runs as a common thread through the other trends that have been discussed so far. The beginning of this shift can be observed in a number of electronic games that engage the students so intently. Learning through playing games seems quite appealing to the students. The students' motivational levels are persistently high and their involvement is intense until the game is over. The challenge for educators, then, is to present course content in such an engaging manner.

What is learning? When is one motivated to learn? What facilitates learning? What facilitates the transference of learning to other situations? How does one assess learning? These questions are being raised as educators shift their focus from teaching to learning. Focus on learning does not mean replacement of faculty or classrooms; it does mean, however, changes in what is done and how it is done.

For instance, inspiring speakers (faculty) can give lectures on certain topics to hundreds of students at once instead of having several "not-so-inspiring" faculty give lectures to smaller groups of students. If space is a problem, technology could deliver these lectures in many different forms—audio and video either in broadcast or cassette form. It would be the students' obligation to listen to these lectures. In the technological format, they could listen to them any number of times. The students could then bring to the classrooms their questions and concerns about the lectures and how to apply them to their own lives. The faculty could respond to the students' questions and concerns and, in addition, set the stage for discussion of larger issues affecting society in relation to the topics at hand. In other instances, faculty could be scheduled to spend time with fewer students to help them master skills that need close supervision and coaching. In other words, a focus on learning requires faculty, and it needs technology as well. The wisdom lies in designing the right mix of the two for the right students at the right time. The starting point for this to happen is to understand teaching and learning better.

An example to illustrate this starting point comes from Miami-Dade Community College. A five-year project was launched in 1987 under the title of the "Teaching/Learning Project." The college president, Robert H. McCabe (1986), announced the project in the following manner:

> Miami-Dade Community College has an educational system that monitors and directs the progress of students through their academic programs. The system is a comprehensive structure which encompasses the total flow of the educational program.
>
> The College has an excellent and committed faculty, and their work is the key to student success. The focus of our efforts must now be directed toward faculty development in order to strengthen teaching/learning and other functions where faculty and staff work directly with students. The following are important considerations in planning for advancement in teaching/learning:
>
> A. A common element contributing to the success of community college students is the relationship with caring faculty or staff who give them personal attention.
> B. There is a substantial body of research concerning the teaching/learning process, and much is known about successful practices; however, such knowledge is seldom utilized by faculty.
> C. Institutions put little effort into developing full faculty understanding of and commitment to institutional goals as they relate to students.
> D. The services colleges provide can be described as a combination of personal interaction and communications. However, despite the amazing advances in communications technology, faculty have, for the most part, utilized that capability only as an adjunct tool which is supplementary to the educational program.
> E. In the next five to seven years, nearly one-third of the faculty at Miami-Dade will retire. If the College is to continue to improve, the new faculty to be recruited must have the characteristics of our current successful faculty; they must also be prepared to apply knowledge gained from and through research in teaching/learning, and to fully utilize the capabilities of communications technology.

The project is organized in such a way that (1) student learning will become an institutional goal; (2) administrators, faculty, and support personnel will work as a team toward the institutional goal; (3) faculty and others will realize that the faculty are the key players in this effort; (4) productive technologies and strategies will be chosen to attain the institutional goals; and (5) administrative practices will be altered to meet the teaching/learning needs. Projects of this size are necessary for institutions to provide a contextual framework for a renaissance of technological innovations in education.

WILL THERE BE A RENAISSANCE?

Technological innovations in education have been evolving since the 1960s. Through the last two decades, educators have not accomplished breathtaking feats, nor have they stood still. What does the future hold for education? According to Naisbitt, "The gee-whiz futurists are always wrong because they believe technological innovation travels in a straight line. It doesn't. It weaves and bobs and lurches and sputters" (1982 41). In a similar vein, George Leonard wrote a decade ago that "anyone who tries to draw the future in hard lines and vivid hues is a fool. The future will never sit still for a portrait. It will come around a corner we never noticed and take us by surprise" (1968 139). He could not, however, resist the temptation to describe a scenario of the future. The crown jewel of his portrayal is ecstasy, the sheer joy of learning. To him it is education's most powerful ally.

At the 1987 annual League for Innovation national conference, Cross mentioned that educational reforms follow a spiral model which permits educators to alternate between action and reflection. Following the frenzied activities of the late 1970s with microcomputer technology, the mid-1980s has been a period of greater reflection. This reflective mood has placed the topic of students' learning as the focal point for considering technological innovations. It has also enlightened educators about the critical role of the faculty in selecting and implementing technological innovations that make sense. Consequently, during the next few years one of the primary concerns of educators will be faculty development. Unlike the 1970s, which attended to computer literacy, the 1980s will focus on "learning" literacy. Principles of cognitive psychology and cybernetic models of research will become integral to these "learning" literacy programs.

Attention to faculty development alone will not suffice to bring about the renaissance of innovation in educational technologies, although it is by far the largest contributing factor. What is additionally needed is an effort on the part of community colleges to develop some appropriate technological programs. If such development could be undertaken collaboratively, so much the better. If the collaboration expands to include the industries, it will be even better. The software development efforts should be directed toward four areas, namely, improving classroom activities, providing learning environments for individual students and peer groups, improving assessment tools, and improving communication between teacher and students and among students. The examples cited in this chapter indicate that community colleges as a whole are progressing in all four areas.

Faculty who are enlightened about learning will find it difficult to use technology productively if the institutional environment does not accommodate the demands of the new practices. Some of the demands that have emerged so far are time for faculty development, class schedules that allow half-day class sessions, other activities that account for faculty time besides class contact hours, and variable time for entering and completing a course. Once again, the examples cited in this chapter indicate that community colleges have begun to respond to these demands.

What is beginning to unfold in the late 1980s is a renaissance of innovation in education that will expand the horizon for learning and technology. Community colleges currently occupy an excellent and enviable position to create an environment (human and technological) in which students can experience the joy of learning. *That* future does not just happen; it must be made to happen.

REFERENCES

ANANDAM, KAMALA. 1986. "Technology for Education: Promises and Problems." In *Advances in Instructional Technology*. New Directions for Community Colleges, edited by G.H. Voegel, no. 55:65–74. San Francisco: Jossey-Bass.

ANANDAM, KAMALA, and J.T. KELLY. 1981. "Evaluating the Use of Technology in Education. *J. Educational Technology* 10:21–31.

———. 1982. "Teaching and Technology: Closing the Gap." *T.H.E. Journal* 10:84–90.

COOLEY, WILLIAM W. 1983. "Improving the Performance of an Educational System." *Educational Researcher* 12:4–12.

CROSS, K. PATRICIA. 1986. "A Proposal to Improve Teaching." *AAHE Bulletin* 39:9–14.

FISHER, GLENN. 1983. "Where CAI is Effective—A Summary of Research." *Electronic Learning* 3:82–84.

LEONARD, GEORGE B. 1968. *Education and Ecstasy*. New York: Delacorte Press.

MCCABE, ROBERT H. 1986. "Organizing Miami-Dade Community College to Emphasize Faculty/Student Performance." Miami-Dade Community College. Unpublished.

MCKEACHIE, WILBERT J. 1983. "A Dialogue on College Teaching." *Contemporary Education Review* 2, no. 3 (Winter):165–72.

NAISBITT, JOHN. 1982. *Megatrends*. New York: Warner Books.

SIMON, HERBERT A. 1987. The Steam Engine and the Computer: What Makes Technology Revolutionary." EDUCOM *Bulletin* 22:2–5.

6

Innovative Management

THROUGH THE USE OF

Communications Technology

Ronald D. Bleed

For many years, community colleges have been cited for their innovative approaches to serving the educational needs of their communities. Open-entry/open-exit programs, quick-start occupational programs for business and industry, and reentry programs for women and minorities are but a few examples of this dedication to finding better and newer ways to serve students.

Innovation in community colleges is not limited to educational programming, however. Innovative management has long been a characteristic of the community college movement, and nowhere is this seen more clearly than in the ways in which community colleges have begun to manage through the use of communication technologies.

HISTORICAL PERSPECTIVE

The use of computers for institutional management in community colleges has closely followed the development of the computer industry. Although computers were available for purchase earlier, it was not until the mid-1960s that computers became truly affordable.

Corporate America began purchasing computers in great numbers at that time, and larger community colleges followed suit. In the 1970s, as prices of computers declined, more community colleges acquired systems. During this period, many of the smaller community colleges obtained what were than called minicomputers, while larger community colleges purchased mainframe computers.

Computerization in two-year colleges was fairly widespread by 1980. The cost of a college's first computer was justified primarily as equipment for the direct support of instruction. Vocational and technical funding sources were often used to purchase these machines and courses in programming, operations, and systems analysis developed rapidly at many community colleges. Although instruction was always described as the major reason for the expenditure of funds for computers, administrative and student service applications were soon added. The computers' resources were often divided in half, with 50 percent of the resources devoted to instruction and 50 percent of the resources devoted to administrative applications.

In most colleges, the student records area became the focal point for administrative services on these computers. This use was closely followed by accounting and payroll systems. Most of the systems developed during the 1970s were of a batch processing mode. This mode required the data to be entered in punch card form and collected in batches. Computer runs were then made overnight or on a weekly basis.

It was not until the late 1970s that on-line processing began to develop at some of the colleges. In on-line processing, the data are entered through terminals directly into the computers. Terminals for on-line processing are located in the offices that control the data and the function. With the advent of on-line processing, on-line registration became the number one goal for new system development by most community colleges.

In the 1980s, a whole new revolution emerged with the introduction of the personal computer which was eagerly purchased by most community colleges. The computing resource for instruction was vastly expanded by these new lower cost, smaller systems. The magnitude of increase of computer power available to faculty and students was phenomenal. Computer literacy courses became the hottest course offerings at any college. Word processing, spreadsheets, and database management were taught as tools for the student. The demand was so heavy for these subjects that courses filled far in advance of each semester.

The colleges that were able to create laboratories of personal computers to support this demand were able to increase, or at least to maintain, their enrollment levels at this time. These courses were the underpinnings for much of the enrollment of the early 1980s and, as most community colleges have a large portion of enrollment-driven funding, these computer literacy courses became real money makers.

The personal computer revolution also had a major impact upon institutional management. First, the demand for instructional computing resources was somewhat offloaded from the mainframes or minicomputers to the personal computers, freeing the larger computer resource for administrative processing.

Second, more and more staff became computer literate and were eager to use some form of computing. The personal computer made computing ubiquitous. The success and publicity of the personal computer made all computing the "in thing," and thus a great demand for computing power was created. In addition, computing became omnipresent in American society. People expected to have the same benefits of computing in schools as they enjoyed in retail stores, banks, their homes, and their jobs.

Third, the same technical revolution that created the personal computer also generated tremendous improvement in mainframes and minicomputers. During this time, large-scale computing became more affordable and easier to use. All new processing efforts were designed for an on-line mode of data entry. The key punch disappeared from American life. The tub files of punched cards used during registration periods became extinct. By the mid-1980s, some of the larger community colleges moved into their third generation of computing, and most community colleges had a growing computing resource at a time when many other resources were declining.

During the early 1980s, another major technical revolution was also occurring. The divestiture of AT&T and deregulation of the telecommunications industry created a new world in which colleges had to manage their telephone and data communication services. The first impact was in the area of telephone service. Since divestiture in 1984, many community colleges have been forced to become, in effect, their own telephone companies. These colleges are expanding telephone service to their employees and students and saving operational dollars.

Another impact of divestiture and deregulation is the rapidly expanding use of communication lines. Telephone messages, computer data, and video images may now be carried over the same physical lines. During the mid-1980s, one of the biggest status symbols for a university was the amount of trenching taking place on campus. The trenching was done to install communication lines to support these newly integrated technologies, with integration of these technologies seen as the most appropriate way to serve the information technology needs of college users.

The past few years has also seen communication lines used to bring together larger computers and personal computers. It is no longer fashionable or productive to have a personal computer independent of any other computer. Personal computers are now viewed in two ways: first, as a stand-alone personal computer, and, second, as a workstation on the larger network that extends communication from the individual to the department, to the college, and to the vast external resources of the world.

OVERVIEW OF ADMINISTRATIVE SYSTEMS

Most of the attention paid to computing in community colleges has focused on instructional applications. While these applications are, indeed, important to community colleges, one of the best-kept secrets in higher education has been the successful use of computers for institutional management in many community colleges.

Variation in size and access to financial resources by community colleges make it difficult to generalize the degree to which computers and other forms of communication technology have been implemented for institutional management within community colleges. However, research done in this area by CAUSE, the professional association for computing and information technology in higher education, can be helpful in outlining the administrative functions in which major studies have been made.

The CAUSE research has been detailed by Charles R. Thomas and Dana S. van Hoesen (1986) in a monograph entitled *Administrative Information Systems: The 1985 Profile and Five-Year Trends.* This research was obtained from a 1985 survey of CAUSE member institutions with a total of 85 two-year institutions responding. The profile survey form listed nearly 160 administrative systems in 11 major categories.

Table 6.1 illustrates the most heavily used administrative applications within the two-year colleges responding. The table was prepared especially for this chapter by CAUSE staff who selected information for community colleges and projected 1986 data from the 1985 study (Thomas and van Hoesen 1986). Figures in the "Number" column reflect the number of institutions responding that had implemented a given application. Figures in the "Percent" column reflect the percentage of institutions responding. Findings are from a total of 85 two-year colleges.

It is not surprising that the highest ranking applications are in the Admissions and Records, Financial Management, and Planning Management areas. The heavy emphasis that many community colleges place upon student services and the nontraditional scheduling approach to course offerings (i.e., open entry/open-exit courses) requires community colleges to use sophisticated student information systems. In addition, sophisticated financial and planning systems are required because most community colleges must make rapid decisions at lower levels within the organization if they are to be truly responsive to community and student needs.

While the CAUSE research is valuable from a quantitative standpoint in revealing how community colleges are using computers in the management of institutions, much more can be gleaned from a careful examination of individual college applications. Of particular interest are examples of how individual community colleges have approached library automation, internal communications, student registration, student services, and human resources.

AN INNOVATIVE LIBRARY AUTOMATION SYSTEM

Community colleges have used several approaches to automate their libraries. There are a number of commercial library automation packages available on the market, and community colleges have used these quite successfully. In other cases, community colleges have formed consortia and have pooled resources or secured grants to develop a system that would apply to the participating institutions. In Illinois, for example, a consortium hosted by Elgin Community College has developed an automated library package that is used by a number of community colleges in the Chicago area. A third approach used by some community colleges is to develop software specifically designed for the institution using the internal programming staff.

Some community colleges have developed exemplary systems. Some are in the process of converting old systems to new ones. Some colleges are automating libraries for the first time, and others are beginning to plan for it. The more progressive plans for the future view library automation as a key to improving the instructional process and hold the most promise for restoring the library as a center of information dissemination and instruction at each community college.

Systems that are developed on very small, independent computers solve clerical needs for the libraries. They do not, however, promote this central role for the library. The role of information provider can be achieved only by making access to the library information available from any point within a college, not just inside the library. The same terminals that are used for instruction or are used as tools by faculty should have access to the library system. This is a networking or connectivity issue.

Networking is also essential for access to information outside the library. There is a tremendous revolution occurring in the late 1980s

Table 6.1
COMPUTER APPLICATIONS IN TWO-YEAR COLLEGES, 1986

Admissions and Records

	Number	Percent
Undergrad admissions processing	79	93
Course catalog records	68	80
Schedule of class preparation	73	86
Student class scheduling	68	80
Tuition and fees assessment	77	91
Student registration	84	99
Class rosters	83	98
Term student records and reports	80	94
Add and drop processing	83	98
Enrollment reporting	84	99
Grade reporting	83	98
Academic advisement records	43	51
Career planning	40	47
Student recruitment	33	39
Continuing education Units	47	55
Grade distributions	67	79
Veterans reporting	56	66
Honors program records	51	60
Student transcript	81	95

Financial Management

	Number	Percent
General fund ledger	74	87
General fund expenditures	75	88
Departmental expenditures	76	87
General accounts receivable	63	74
Student accounts receivable	69	81
Accounts payable	74	87
Payroll	72	85
Employee benefits accounting	49	58
Financial aid accounting	70	82
Tuition and fees accounting	73	86
Bank account reconciliation	49	58

Planning Management and Institutional Research

	Number	Percent
Budget forecasting	42	49
Budget preparation	69	81
Budget analysis	54	64
Budget position control	44	52
Institutional cost studies	45	53
Faculty salary analysis	48	56
Financial modeling	46	54

Administrative Services and Logistics

	Number	Percent
Facilities inventory	47	55
Classroom utilization analysis	38	45
Personnel records	58	68

Administrative Services and Logistics *(continued)*

	Number	Percent
Alumni records	35	41
Test scoring and analysis	43	51
Purchase order follow-up	29	34
Purchasing information	36	42
Vendor information	48	56
Equipment inventory	55	65
Automobile registration	17	20

Faculty/Staff/Student Services

	Number	Percent
Instructor evaluation	46	54
Financial aid evaluation	45	53
Financial aid awards	62	73
Student employment records	40	47
Work-study records	46	54
Teacher and job placement	18	21

Library

	Number	Percent
Acquisitions	37	44
Cataloging	42	49
Circulation	19	22
Bibliographic search	21	24
Media services	22	26
Card and materials preparations	55	65

with the development of external databases. These services are either accessed via phone lines through a terminal to a remote location or through the use of Compact Disk with Read-Only Memory (CD ROM) where the information is stored on a laser disk that can be read by a computer at a college. The amount of information made available in these two forms multiplies every day. Database information is a billion dollar business in this country. It is a true manifestation of the information age.

As deliverers of information, colleges need to have access to such databases. Some experts have suggested that the amount of knowledge in the world doubles every 20 months. This enormous increase makes it difficult for textbooks and faculty to remain up to date. Databases that can be updated daily at one point and then made available to an unlimited number of points are an answer to the information explosion.

Tarrant County Junior College (Texas) has been a national leader in the development of automated libraries. In the 1970s, the college developed systems in a batch mode to expedite the processing of information, and in 1980 automated the library system. Working closely with the computer center department, the library staff, under the direction of Kay Stansberry, designed the system.

The design and testing of the new system took less than two years with the on-line acquisition system first to be implemented because of the need for efficient financial tracking of book material purchases. Another major priority in the development of the system was the On-line Computerized Library Center (OCLC) interface. Information obtained from OCLC was used to streamline the cataloging process and thus save labor costs. After these two major modules, the other modules of authority control, circulation, serials, claiming, and on-line public access cataloging were implemented.

The Tarrant County Junior College (TCJC) system was designed based upon specific community college needs for libraries. Some of the advantages of the new system are the elimination of keyboarding requirements and elimination of errors in the technical services functions. The new system has also decreased redundancy of input effort.

More importantly, the TCJC library automation system has expanded the materials and holdings available to students in a three-college district. By use of a courier service, materials can be exchanged among the three libraries. All of the libraries have access to the same database which is kept updated on a daily basis. Instead of rapidly expanding the collections at three different sites, this shared approach has permitted a much more efficient management of the collections.

Because the system resides on a mainframe that is part of the other college administrative instructional services, any terminal in the system can access the library information. It is possible for students, faculty, or administrators to access the library information from their labs or their desks. They need not be in the library.

It has been proven that there is much greater student use of the libraries since the new automation system was put in place. In addition, the students work together to assist each other in the use of the public access catalog. There has been no adverse feedback from the student population regarding the use of automated terminals for library services. The community's image of the libraries has also significantly improved. Positive comments about the libraries from citizens are the kind of refreshing feedback needed for often overlooked libraries. Faculty have been very supportive of the entire process.

A key success factor is that the computer center has always been sensitive to the needs of the end users. The library and the computer center worked hand-in-hand in the development of this system. The TCJC computer center never attempted to lay down or impose their ideas of what a system should be.

With its major automation applications in place, TCJC District now interconnects to the regional offices of the Texas Association for Higher Education. Seventeen universities and colleges will be part of a network in which library information can be exchanged. The use of CD ROM for regional catalogs is being planned. The librarians believe the system has created an environment in which the libraries are partners in the educational process. They are a complete and total partner in educational activities, and they play a vital role in the instructional process in TCJC District.

The automation of the library/media centers in community colleges has been sporadic, yet there has been a growing concern that these functions need to be automated. In 1986, the League for Innovation in the Community College published a monograph *Guidelines for Library and Media Automated Systems* developed by a committee of representatives from League member colleges. Contained within this report are chapters that describe the components comprising a full library and media center. For each component, there is a description of the definition and purposes of that component, pertinent policy and procedural questions, as well as outputs and data elements. The guidelines also emphasize the use of an integrated system in which all components have interrelationships in common data elements. The suggested components of an on-line, integrated system as presented in this document are as follows:

1. acquisitions,
2. authority control,
3. cataloging,
4. serials,
5. public catalog,
6. circulation,
7. reserve,
8. reference,
9. interlibrary loan,
10. materials booking,
11. equipment inventory,
12. equipment scheduling and distribution,
13. equipment maintenance, and
14. media production.

AN INNOVATIVE COMMUNICATION SYSTEM

At Maricopa County Community College District (MCCCD, Arizona) a key computer strategy has been to decentralize computing from the district office to each of the colleges and at each of the colleges to the respective departments. A large network of Digital Equipment Corporation (DEC) VAX computers form the backbone of this network. This network is supplemented by many subnetworks of personal computers. Vast amounts of telecommunication capability exist to connect some 6,000 workstations.

At the time of the original decision to decentralize computing, office automation was considered a by-product of the instructional delivery systems and the basic administrative system. Therefore, in the point matrix that was developed to evaluate the alternative vendor proposals, office automation played only a minor role. However, office automation became the first system to be implemented with the new computers, and MCCCD became a nationwide leader in the use of an office automation network. Office automation is now considered to be more than a by-product. It is as important as any of the other major computing systems currently in use. The district is managed more effectively by this system, and it has become essential to the day-to-day operation of the seven colleges and two educational centers.

There are several reasons why MCCCD became interested in this electronic information system. First, the colleges within MCCCD are widely dispersed within the Phoenix metropolitan area. Second, faculty and staff are continually teaching classes or attending meetings so "telephone tag" can be a real problem. Third, the issue of computer literacy was considered to be important, and the strategy was to involve people with computers as soon as possible. It was hoped that hands-on experience would lead to a more computer-literate group. Fourth, the All-In-1 system from DEC could be delivered immediately whereas the other administrative systems had to be implemented in stages.

Once it was implemented, the importance of the new office automation system grew daily. The deliberate strategy of top-down approach was taken to put the executive network in the office of the chancellor, the vice chancellors, and the college presidents. These executives, who had never before had a terminal in their offices, were the first to receive terminals. The Chancellor, Paul Elsner, immediately issued a statement advocating paperless offices and made it clear that he would be willing to receive messages primarily in electronic form; he discouraged the use of paper memos.

Training sessions were held, and these executives began to use the network. Because of the success of the network, the executives were given systems for their homes as well as for their offices so they could communicate and extend their workday from their homes. In addition, their secretaries were given a word processor that had terminal capabilities with access to the same network. All of the executives were linked together on this network whether they were at home or in their offices. As additional equipment became available, the number of users began to spread through the organization. Today, it has reached almost all professional employees with over 1,000 users currently on the network.

MCCCD is governed by a locally elected five-member board of directors. It was decided after the successful executive implementation that all members of the governing board should also have access to the network from their homes, and they became members of this network. Each received a personal computer with terminal capability.

Individuals use the network for a variety of office automation applications, most notably, electronic mail. The network is organized so that the users are able to send messages to individuals or to groups of employees throughout the system.

Closely related to electronic mail is the electronic file cabinet where messages can be stored on a more permanent basis by subject, key word, and topic. Documents created on the word processor can be transferred into this system and filed. Another use of the system is the calendar management system. The greatest potential use for the office automation system is for accessing the administrative databases, reviewing the status of accounts, preparing the budget, and checking enrollments. The tools of spreadsheets, personal filing systems, and database systems are also used.

The DEC All-In-1 automation system is structured in a menu form that is relatively easy to use. This format is the model for all other systems because of its user acceptance. The All-In-1 system is now the operating system for most computer-based systems within Maricopa County Community Colleges. The electronic mail system is connected to Arizona State University, and administrators and staff from both organizations now communicate freely via electronic mail.

A study (Bleed 1984) of the executive network commissioned by MCCCD reported several major findings:

1. The executive's keyboarding skills do not play a major role in the level of use of the office information system or the length of messages.

2. Executives view the computer as a management tool. They become impatient if the response of the computer is not instantaneous. They resent reading messages that are frivolous or that are lengthy and technical.

3. Microcomputers in the home free the executives to work outside the office or without using the telephone to communicate with colleagues.

4. There was a noticeable reduction in the number of internal telephone calls and written messages among network users.

5. The use of the network did not reduce the number of scheduled meetings among the executives.
6. Executives view the creation of an electronic network as a personal way in which to communicate and develop a feeling of cohesiveness among colleagues.

AN INNOVATIVE REGISTRATION SYSTEM

One of the most innovative uses of computers is the touch-tone telephone registration system. This is a system in which students can register for courses from their home phones by keying in, through the touch-tone keys on a telephone, their course requests. The computer responds to these course requests with language from a dictionary of digitized words. The computer, in effect, talks to the student with a limited vocabulary and assists the student in the registration process.

This system was pioneered at Brigham Young University. Soon after their successful implementation, three community colleges implemented similar systems. These community colleges are the Maricopa County Community College District, Union County College (New Jersey), and Miami-Dade Community College (Florida). These three college systems have been examples that many universities are now attempting to follow.

Union County College has 7,000 students on four campuses in New Jersey. This community college views new technology as important for creation of a positive image for the college. UCC is located near New York City and must compete with many other colleges for student enrollment.

The touch-tone registration system created a positive image for the college and made registration easy and accessible to their students. UCC has a very efficient, on-line registration which means that walk-through registration lines are very small and there are absolutely no crowds. When added to the existing on-line system, touch-tone registration was able to save the college personnel costs because the computer, rather than a staff member, answered the phone and registered the students. The original capital outlay for the system was offset by the savings in personnel costs.

The UCC touch-tone registration system was installed in 1985. Since then, it has been proven to be very dependable, and the hardware has never failed. At the beginning of each registration cycle, 70 percent of the students choose this option.

Because New Jersey law now mandates placement for all college students, UCC has developed its own placement test. Completed tests are scanned and the results fed to college student information databases. As soon as that information is posted, any attempt to access courses that are inappropriate for that student by the touch-tone registration system are automatically blocked with the appropriate computerized message given to the student. The student cannot use the touch-tone system to circumvent any restrictions on enrollment or course selections.

UCC has implemented a full range of student information system features in addition to touch-tone registration. Admissions, grading, financial aid, and student receivables are major subsystems being used.

UCC believes, like many other progressive community colleges, that students are entitled to fast and effective services. Students of community colleges should not receive poorer services from the college than those they are now receiving from their bank or local retail store. Those colleges that can provide the convenience for their students are those that are going to be more successful in the recruitment and retention of students.

AN INNOVATIVE STUDENT SERVICES SYSTEM

Community colleges have always assigned priority to computerized student information systems. As measured by the number of transactions and documents processed, the largest paperwork activity of a college is within student systems. Thus, this function was a target for many of the first computerization efforts. Waiting in long lines to register for classes has been one of the traditions of higher education. It is also one of the traditions that is rapidly disappearing from the community college scene. With the advent of on-line terminals, registration is now an event with less pain than before. Registration is also not a process that occurs on a few days prior to the start of each semester. At many colleges, the registration office registers students daily throughout the year and often far in advance of the semester.

Because of the success in the automation of registration, many other activities in the student service function are now targets for automation. A national leader in the development of automated student systems has been Miami-Dade Community College (MDCC, Florida). This institution strongly believes in using the computer to monitor students at various checkpoints to ensure student success.

To accomplish the "one-stop" process, MDCC has designed an integrated student flow model. This overall system of student flow is designed in a marketing approach. All letters and communications that the student receives from the computer are personalized to his or her own specific situation. Within this flow, MDCC has designed several student support systems, or testing points.

The first of these testing points is a basic skills assessment program. This program is designed to identify basic skill deficiencies, potential honor students, or possible requirement waivers in English and math. In 1987, Miami-Dade moved this test from a paper and pencil mode to an on-line computerized mode at their South campus. A joint project with the college, IBM, the College Board, and the League for Innovation was developed to field-test this computerized assessment approach. The major advantage to the new on-line system was that students could be tested at their convenience and the results immediately known to the students.

A lab of 40 personal computers was created in the assessment center. The computer assessment software permits an adaptive testing mode. The computerized testing branches to different paths depending upon student responses. By having the computers available for students anytime between 8:30 a.m. and 9:00 p.m. months in advance of a semester, there are no lines or waiting for the assessment process.

Another student support system that is heavily used at MDCC is the advisement and graduation information system (AGIS). This particular system is renowned in higher education circles. AGIS is the system that most community colleges wish they had. It is also the system that many colleges are making plans to implement or acquire. The essence of AGIS is that it takes the student's transcript and current registration and matches them against curriculum requirements to determine the progress of the student toward a degree or certificate at that college, or the student's "transfer fit" to a four-year college. The system will also automatically graduate students and report graduation deficiencies. This system is particularly helpful to advisors who now spend less clerical time doing transcript matching and requirements for the student. Most important, the information they are giving to the students is now accurate and consistent across the district.

MDCC has recently added an additional module to the AGIS system called the course sequencing pathways (CSP). This on-line system tells the student what courses should be taken while enrolled at MDCC based upon major test scores or intended college transfer. What is very important to students is that it communicates course prerequisites and corequisites, some career information, and all registration holds. This system allows students to develop an appropriate plan of action for them to complete their educational program successfully.

Another important student system is the academic alert system. This system takes the mid-term grade and, through automated functions, combines that information with other demographic information about the student to prescribe personal intervention strategies to help the student. An individualized letter is generated by these data and then mailed to the students. Very specific prescriptive information is given the student to assist him or her in correcting weaknesses. For example, the letter to the student could indicate workshops and individual assistance programs that are available for that student. Often, information is given to the student regarding registration before the next term. Students who are making satisfactory progress are complimented and acknowledged for their efforts.

To facilitate the registration process at MDCC, a touch-tone computerized registration system has also been implemented. With this system, students can apply, be assessed, go through orientation and advisement, register, and pay for classes with one stop at a campus many months before the start of an academic semester.

The term "one-stop student services" is a key to the future for Miami Dade. All of their systems development centers around the creation of the one-stop student services function. A student will go to one location on the campus and meet with a college representative, complete an application, discuss career options and choices, be sent for career testing and basic skills assessment, take the results of the assessment to an advisor, set up a program of study, and register from a touch-tone telephone in one convenient stop. At this one-stop center will be large amounts of information about the college available to the student through the use of technology. In the future, the financial aid process will be added to this one-stop service.

Richard B. Schinoff, Dean at MDCC, has stated:

> The student support system, testing procedures, and registration gateway discussed above formed the basis of the integrated student flow model at Miami-Dade Community College. Although invisible to the student, there is a constant network utilizing computer technology, monitoring student progress, sending communication to students indicating how well they are doing or specifying areas for improvement and intervention strategies. Most important, advisors, counselors, and faculty use this information to provide the best possible assistance to students. (1987, 10)

At MDCC, this innovation occurred because of the creative leadership of a few key administrators. Technology was available and innovative leaders knew how to use it to help the college fulfill its mission.

AN INNOVATIVE HUMAN RESOURCE SYSTEM

In most community colleges, the operational budgets are composed of 70 percent or more for employee salaries and benefits. Education is a very labor-intensive operation. Most funds are spent on faculty salaries. Thus, it is strategically important to manage that human resource effectively.

One of the most important institutional computer management applications is the human resource system, which consists both of payroll and personnel processing. The magnitude and importance of this system can be best illustrated in the following way. Every time a community college hires a professional employee, it can be viewed as a million dollar decision because the college is likely to pay that individual a million dollars in salary and benefits before the person retires.

When a community college decides to purchase a $1 million computer, a lengthy and involved process takes place. Computers are compared, bids reviewed, facilities prepared, maintenance contracts signed, optional equipment purchased, staff operators assigned, and replacement costs calculated. Contrast that effort with the decision to hire one faculty member at a cost of $1 million and the minimal efforts that often follow for the recruitment, hiring, employment, and development of that individual.

This "people resource" needs to be successfully managed. In the stages of computer development, the payroll system was usually the third major system implemented in colleges after student and accounting information systems. Until recently, very little was done regarding personnel systems.

Dallas County Community College District (DCCCD, Texas) has been one of the innovators in the human resource area. The district developed a very traditional, batch-oriented payroll system during the early 1970s but recently has converted that payroll system to an on-line system with many new features. A very important complement to the system is the personnel function.

The human resource system at DCCCD was three years in development and has automated many of the features and functions of both the payroll and personnel operations. At DCCCD, the personnel office and the payroll office work under different management groups. However, the new system was developed as a joint effort of those two departments and computer services. With the development of the system, an excellent set of documentation and training materials was developed. In fact, for some employees there is a 40-hour training program for either personnel or payroll functions.

DCCCD utilized a language called NATURAL in the development of its new human resource system. NATURAL is a new fourth-generation language that accesses DCCCD's database structure. The use of this new language speeded the development and will make modification in the future much easier.

Within DCCCD, all the data about employees are kept in one common group of files so they will be easier to maintain and access. With this new system, the amount of data has been expanded for each employee and can be accessed on-line. This opens the door to the use of the human resource system as an effective management tool. The human resource system at DCCCD has been designed to be more comprehensive, easier to use, easier to maintain and modify, and serves as a valuable tool.

Within community colleges, there are a wide variety of pay scales, employment categories, and employment periods. To pay employees accurately requires some very sophisticated calculations. At DCCCD, all these calculations are now done automatically.

This human resource system interacts with the DCCCD student system to handle faculty payroll data automatically. From course information, the system automatically loads faculty data to establish a payroll distribution for faculty contracts. The new system creates more accurate distributions and accounting records. It is table-driven so that new coverage, rates, and amounts can be easily entered. The system also took advantage of the new technology and uses new, low-cost terminals for access and updates.

With some employers, there is a move toward an individualized benefits program. More and more employees are being permitted to select options in benefits. Also, various employee groups have differing levels of benefits. This creates a record-keeping nightmare. At DCCCD, the human resources system provides for individualized benefits for each employee with all record keeping done by the computer.

Another significant requirement that is being placed upon personnel offices in the 1980s is a more accurate tracking of employee applications because of federal guidelines for affirmative action and the increasing number of applicants for positions. This is another large paperwork burden. DCCCD has developed a sophisticated applicant tracking system to monitor the individuals who are applying for positions within the district. This database of applicants also becomes an excellent resource pool for future positions.

The existing employee group represents the greatest asset for a community college. To encourage growth, and innovation, employees need programs to further their training and development. Dallas County Community College District's human resource system can monitor career development information; enter codes and dates of awards and recognitions; update degree information, teaching experience, and professional licensing information; record all course work completed; maintain wellness participation and health risk profiles; and track the employee's job history through time.

TRENDS FOR THE FUTURE

There are several trends in the information technology industry that will have major impact on institutional management in community colleges. The first of these trends is networking.

Today, the computer is not the centerpiece of the new technology; the network is the key. The focus must be in developing systems that incorporate multimedia capability (i.e., voice, video, and data) for all users of the potential systems. It is important to understand that, in the future, information services can be delivered to users from anywhere on the campus, from their homes, or from their workplaces. The network will be the 12-lane highway that supports the instructional and institutional management processes. When the communications pipeline, or the network, becomes the focus, a different perspective is given to the end result. When systems are developed for mainframes, some very rigid protocols, dictated primarily by computer services, must be followed. When the network becomes the central point, innovative outputs such as voice response, graphics, laser printing, and video displays are possible.

It is important to note that, in the 1987 announcements of new families of personal computers, all the vendors stressed connectivity rather than the computing power of individual machines. Local area networks, wide area networks, metropolitan area networks, are the buzzwords of today. The freestanding computer is now considered an anachronism.

A second major trend is a blurring of the distinction between academic and administrative computing. All the systems previously described in this chapter, and the potential new ones, are increasingly in the gray area between those two traditional categories of computing.

For example, students and faculty need the advantages of electronic mail as much as administrators. Students need academic advisement to ensure success in their educational planning. The library should be a centerpiece of the instructional process. With the network capability, a student sitting at a personal computer or terminal can be routed to direct delivery of instructional software, or software that can be used as a tool in learning (such as word processing), or be connected to student information systems that deliver much valued advice.

There cannot be separate empires and strong barriers created that would prohibit this free communication among needed services. By viewing the computing resource as one larger picture, institutions can share resources more effectively. Recent experience at many colleges has shown how costly it is to buy individual software packages for every personal computer that exists. More and more colleges will be forced to move toward a time-sharing or library delivery system for software. The software of the future will also be more generic and less tied to a specific vendor's product.

Still another future trend is the development of systems for smaller computers. In the model innovations previously described, all of the applications are programmed for fairly large computers. The systems of the future may fit on smaller computers. Grace Hopper, one of the real pioneers of the computer world, describes the future reality with this analogy. She states that, when trees are cut down in Maine, the lumberjacks move them from the forest with an ox. When they encounter a very large tree that one ox cannot move, they don't attempt to grow a bigger ox and they don't attempt to create a dinosaur. They simply get two oxen to move the tree.

That is the view of future computing: multiple systems with which it is more effective to add additional units and modules rather than to create a dinosaur or a bigger computer. That analogy should be extended. When there are multiple oxen, they are still connected by yokes and lines that ensure they are all working in the same direction.

The move toward new management strategies for the organization of computing information technology is also a trend. Computing and networking are so pervasive and cross so many boundaries that new management strategies need to be implemented to manage the resources effectively. Increasing numbers of colleges are looking for, or have already created a position of, "computer czar" in the form of a vice president or vice chancellor for information services. In the corporate world, this position is called the CIO, chief information officer. This person is responsible for creating a viable college computing strategy across all of the departments.

This expertise will not come cheap to colleges. John Gantz has commented that these people will be difficult to find because they require technical, communications, and management skills.

> At this very moment, many community colleges are scouring the secret hiding places of the rock looking for likely candidates to turn into winged birds, for only a winged bird with the eyes of a hawk, the courage of an eagle, the persistence of a jay can soar above this tumultuous information processing scene existing today. (1985, 17).

Another alternative to the czar position is the creation of a high-powered executive committee that represents all interests of the institution. The formation of this type of executive council to make major policy decisions regarding both academic and administrative computing has worked well at the Maricopa Community College District. Maricopa has created the Information Technologies Executive Council (ITEC) which is not strictly an advisory group. It is an official body that takes direct action on information technologies, has line management responsibilities for the people who work in information technologies, and has final say on all hardware and software acquisitions. It determines priorities and controls all budget dollars allocated for computing. Within this framework, the council has created many planning opportunities for each college and each department.

The organizational structure for communication technologies should not only match general management philosophy but should be even more progressive in creating new structures. A strong influence on organizational structure is the risk-taking attitude of the management group. New structures are the opposite of tradition, and that automatically creates a risk. Community colleges are often less traditional than other institutions and this freedom encourages risk taking. This leads the way to implement a new structure without fear of having to redo it later.

Another attitude that influences the organizational structure is a philosophy of undermanagement. Unlike the philosophy that imposes strict management controls and that is often found in hierarchical organizations, a more relaxed and trusting approach that leaves room for innovation necessitates new structure.

KEYS TO SUCCESS

There are many reasons for the success of communications technology within organizations and colleges. Funds and people are obviously success factors. In the future, however, many other factors will come into play.

First, the organizational structure for communications technology will contribute greatly to computing success. The organizational structure of the future should include a blend of a centralized executive council and/or computer czar, a service-oriented information technologies group, and colleges and departments that plan and manage their own systems. This organizational structure will foster exciting new innovations at the college and departmental level. Many faculty and staff will be involved in creating new uses of computing. This large-scale involvement must be encouraged as a success factor for computing.

A second success factor for the future will be for community colleges to understand the value of information. The United States and much of the world have moved into the information society. Most careers and economic gains will be in the area of information processing. For people to succeed in the last part of this century, they will need to know how to access and manipulate information. The "knowledge worker" will need new skills. Colleges must develop programs that address these skill areas for staff as well as for students.

Very soon, progressive community colleges will have at the center of their instructional process the library, which will exist in a new form to provide vast amounts of information at students' fingertips.

This transformation of the library will hinge upon computing and telecommunications. This also leads to an important new literacy called "information access literacy." All people now have information overload. In most fields, professionals have a hard time keeping pace. They tend to treat many topics superficially and inefficiently because they are overwhelmed with this expansion of information.

The role of community college managers is to find and manage information rather than remember it. Students must be guided in a similar manner. An educated student has been said to be "one who gracefully interfaces with his areas of ignorance." Technology can now provide that interface in many situations. An integrated approach to information access by community colleges must use the professional training and human interface provided by the library professionals, the technology and software provided by computing services, and the new telecommunications capability provided by communication and media services. This integrated approach will provide information to the students and faculty when they need it and from any appropriate source—library, computer center, video studio, or external network. The user will expect information to be relevant and delivered quickly to his or her workstation, wherever that may be.

Another key to the future success of innovation in community colleges is the creation of partnerships among colleges, the technology vendors, and educational organizations. Development of the applications described earlier in this chapter required major efforts in many cases. Efforts of this type should certainly be shared and exchanged with other colleges. Technology vendors and educational organizations can also participate in these efforts through the sharing of expertise and hardware/software contributions.

The League for Innovation in the Community College is currently in the middle of a five-year plan to encourage these types of information technology partnerships. Working with the League member colleges on this partnership program are 11 leading computer vendors. It has been anticipated that there will be 15 to 20 major projects from this five-year commitment (O'Banion 1987).

The college arena is a profitable marketplace for the computer industry; community colleges should aggressively seek to form partnerships with commercial vendors. Community colleges can offer, in effect, some system development and "intellectual capital" in exchange for a reduction in hardware/software cost from these companies.

It is a well-established fact that students take hardware and software preferences with them into jobs after college and thus influence future purchasing decisions. This is an ongoing advantage to corporations working with colleges because students are "refreshable" in that there is a continuous flow of students moving into the market-place who are willing to instigate change and use the state-of-the-art equipment.

In addition, the computer marketplace has recognized that the college environment is a leading-edge indicator of the future. Computer companies look to colleges for direction on new hardware/software developments. Computer vendors are not interested in simply donating dollars for equipment to community colleges. They want community colleges to contribute something to the longrange profit pictures of their companies. The colleges must, therefore, bring something of value to the partnership, and they must also identify a unique niche from which they can attract a vendor. Community colleges must look at their location, their faculty, and their missions to find something that would be unique and attractive to a vendor. Truly innovative uses of computing for institutional management will interest the vendors of computers.

CONCLUSION

In his book *Innovation and Entrepreneurship,* Peter Drucker (1985) calls upon public service organizations to look upon social, technological, economic, and demographic shifts as opportunities in a period of rapid change. Otherwise, he states, they will become obstacles. Drucker is particularly concerned about colleges, which he believes will stick to programs and projects that cannot work in a changing environment. He accuses public institutions of not being able to rid themselves of any portion of their stated mission even though they cannot possibly accomplish these programs.

Drucker projects that colleges are endangered, but could adapt to the future. He sees innovation and consumer involvement as key issues.

> The knowledge is there. The need to innovate is clear. They now have to learn how to build innovation and entrepreneurship into their own system. Otherwise, they will find themselves superseded by outsiders who will create competing entrepreneurial public service institutions and so render the existing ones obsolete (1985, 185–186)

Innovations from only five community colleges have been featured in this chapter. As evidenced by the charts from the CAUSE monograph, many other community colleges as well have been innovative and successful in implementing computerized systems.

Some common threads run through each of the models featured. At Maricopa, the longstanding motto of the Information Technologies Services Department has been, "Assets make things possible; people make things happen." This saying also characterizes the innovation at each of the other colleges. Too often, administrative staff at community colleges have hidden behind the lack of dollars for computer hardware as an excuse not to use new technology effectively. This excuse has been overstated. People who want to make innovation happen will find the resources. In each of the previous examples, a few select staff members made things happen.

A second similarity is that systems do not remain in status quo once implemented. All of the colleges featured here implemented the system and realized it was not a one-time event. Innovations and improvements are continual in these systems. There is not a one-time quick fix that lasts for a long period of time. The technology changes rapidly, and innovations are needed to take advantage of the increased capacity and the cost-effectiveness of new technologies. This should not be viewed as a dilemma but as an opportunity to improve.

A third common thread is the fact that these systems were designed by, or in conjunction with, the users of the system. They were not directives from a technical guru, but each included participation by significant numbers of users.

Peter Drucker defines innovation as changing the value and satisfaction obtained from resources by the consumer. The key is the receptivity of the user. It is on the demand side rather than the supply side. The examples cited in this chapter were built upon user demands, not some technological breakthrough. This concept should give insight into strategies for innovation in community colleges. Seek ideas from students, faculty, and staff. Rather than seeking vendor-supplied hardware and software solutions, create systems for their needs.

REFERENCES

BLEED, RONALD. 1984. "Implementation of the Executive Network at the Maricopa Colleges." *CAUSE/EFFECT* 7, no. 5 (Sep.): 26–30.

BUNCH, CATHY, ed. 1986. *Guidelines for Library and Media Automated Systems.* Laguna Hills: League for Innovation in the Community College.

DRUCKER, PETER D. 1985. *Innovation and Entrepreneurship.* New York: Harper and Row.

GANTZ, JOHN. 1985. "Telecommunications Management: Who's in Charge?" *Telecommunications Products and Technology* (Oct.): 17–37.

O'BANION, TERRY. 1987. "Innovative Partnerships Assist Community College Computing Programs." *T.H.E. Journal* (June): 56–59.

SCHINOFF, RICHARD B. 1987. "Computerized Student Information System: The Miami-Dade Approach." Unpublished. Miami: Miami-Dade Community College (Aug.)

THOMAS, CHARLES R., and DANA S. VAN HOESEN. 1986. *Administrative Information Systems: The 1985 Profile and Five-Year Trends.* Boulder, Colo.: CAUSE Publications.

7

Initiatives

IN

International Education

Edmund J. Gleazer, Jr.

"Ten years ago I had to sneak out of town for international trips."
Those are the words of a community college president whose institution is recognized now as a leader in the field of international education. Did he exaggerate? Probably not very much, if at all. His
comment described a situation not unique to his college or community. Numerous obstacles slow the process of integrating into the
college program an international/intercultural perspective.

Close to the top of any list of problems would be money. Programs
of an international nature commonly rely on "soft" money. Administrators are quick to point out to board and community that no institutional or taxpayers' funds are involved. Why the evident sensitivity on this point? In a number of cases, the media have questioned
why a "community" college, a locally oriented institution, has any
business in extending its reach to global affairs. Further, faculty and
community may view the international field as the president's play-
ground and suggest that he or she would do better to spend more
time at home and on the job. And as the proportion of state financial
support has increased, frequently both legislative and executive officials have required the college to justify international interests.

Despite these problems, or perhaps because of them, a sector of
community college leaders committed to international/intercultural
learning experiences has been demonstrably effective. Their creative
initiatives reveal essential connections between global developments

136

and the communities served by the college. Validated by evident eco
nomic and social change, their efforts build upon contributions made
earlier in the evolution of community colleges.

DEVELOPMENT OF THE INTERNATIONAL DIMENSION

Prior to and during the dramatic growth period of the 1960s, independent and church-related junior colleges provided leadership in
international programs. Their activities largely emulated four-year
colleges with study-abroad experiences and recruitment of students
from other lands. On the other hand, the 500 community colleges
established in the 1960s directed their energies toward becoming authorized, organized, and operational. Studies of community needs,
which are acknowledged as fundamental to community college curriculum development, showed little interest in the international dimension.

However, the American Association of Junior Colleges (as it was
called until 1972) was involved in a series of activities related to political and technological world change. These included team exchanges with the *tekhnikums* of the Soviet Union, and educational
assistance to the newly independent nation of Kenya, followed by a
similar program with Nigeria a few years later.

The burgeoning of community colleges was observed with interest
in many countries where political and economic change required an
extension and diversification of educational opportunity. An increasing number of countries wanted information as well as opportunities
to see the colleges in action. In light of mounting activity, the AAJC
Board established a committee on international education in 1968.

A domestic development further raised the consciousness level
of the AAJC membership to ethnic and cultural factors. Many community colleges established in the 1960s served large cities and consequently drew heavily from minority populations attracted by college
proximity, low cost, and open admissions policies. Frequently cultural
characteristics and even languages were different from those of a majority of faculty and administrators.

The first international assembly of junior colleges was held at
the East-West Center in Honolulu in 1970 with financial assistance
from the Ford Foundation. Participants came from 18 countries, a
majority located in the Pacific Basin. A conference report urged continuance of communication and establishment by AAJC of an office
for that purpose.

A W.K. Kellogg Foundation grant to AAJC in 1972 enabled the
association to "explore and more fully develop the international di-

mensions and potential of junior and community colleges." In 1974 the association invited representatives of "short-cycle" institutions from other lands to a meeting in Washington where common interests could be explored. Participants agreed that they could learn from each other and expressed interest in forming an international organization.

Some 50 member institutions of what had now become the American Association of Community and Junior Colleges (AACJC) joined in the establishment of the International/Intercultural Consortium in 1976, to promote interinstitutional linkages which would facilitate access to the international expertise of the member colleges. Association leaders viewed the consortium approach as an opportunity to keep the national association involved and as a way to work with the leadership of those colleges particularly committed to the international field. There was an additional benefit to this arrangement. The association could avoid criticism by some of its members of using budgeted funds to promote international education. The consortium was to be self-supporting through membership dues.

Although still a minority movement, the pace of international activity quickened in the mid-1970s. The College Consortium for International Studies was founded in 1975 by three community colleges located in three adjacent states, Pennsylvania, New York, and New Jersey. Its primary function was to facilitate overseas study opportunities for students and staff. Another consortium, Community Colleges for International Development (CCID), was organized in 1976 "to implement international programs and projects which benefit countries as well as its own member institutions." CCID, in addition to providing opportunities for international exchange, was designed to assist other countries in mid-level manpower training and technical/vocational education.

In 1978 AACJC established the position of Director of International Services with the help of a grant from the Ford Foundation. That same year the association and the Johnson Foundation sponsored conferences on the topics of "International Education and the Community College," and "International Developments in Post-Secondary Education." The latter conference involved participants from other countries with "short-cycle" institutions.

The significant role community colleges could play was recognized at a national level in 1978 with the appointment of AACJC's President to President Jimmy Carter's Commission on Foreign Languages and International Studies. The 1979 report of the commission called for expansion of international education in the community college. In several states, the report of the President's commission coincided with stepped-up interest in international education. The State Board of Education in Florida adopted a resolution to support the concept of global education. At the national level, Congress passed Concurrent Resolution 301 which called for "strengthening the study of foreign languages and cultures; . . . the improvement of international studies in the curriculum at all levels of education; the encouragement of international exchange programs."

Perhaps the most influential factor in moving education toward a global perspective was not found in a plethora of reports and resolutions but in economic change in the 1980s. Newspaper headlines declared, "U.S. Faces Up to Erosion of Economic Supremacy." The nation was experiencing serious economic dislocation: the closing of steel mills and auto plants, the conversion of the industrial heartland into the Rust Belt, and a loss of millions of manufacturing jobs. For the first time since World War II, the United States in 1986 lost its position as the world's leading exporter, supplanted by West Germany, with Japan close by in third place. Other signs were troubling, for example, reduction in the U.S. share of the world gross national product from 40 percent in 1950 to 22 percent in 1980. Meanwhile the share of Japan and Europe rose markedly. Businessmen were heard to declare, "Global commerce is a reality." "We are in an international trade war." "We have to survive—education is the key."

In mid-1987, the nation's governors, through the National Governors' Association (1987), declared that the key to prosperity was the global view. They issued a report which emphasized steps necessary to improve America's competitive economic position. They urged that education place more emphasis on geography, foreign languages, and technology for students at all levels, as well as for business executives. The report further asserted that states and localities "must maintain an international perspective in all decisions, ranging from how we market our goods to how we educate our children." Of special interest to community colleges was one of the recommended major areas of action by the states, "helping local communities tailor their economies to global realities."

The report was in stark juxtaposition to the results of studies that revealed deficiencies in global understanding and charged that Americans' ignorance of their own country and of the world would have dire consequences for our nation's welfare, strength, and global interdependence (1979 President's Commission on Foreign Languages; 1981 Educational Testing Service; 1984 Joint Committee on Geographic Education; and the 1987 Study Commission on Global Education).

At the federal level, a Business and International Education Program was authorized under Title VI, Part B, of the amended Higher Education Act of 1965. The purpose of the program was "to promote institutional and noninstitutional educational and training activities that will contribute to the ability of United States business to prosper in an international economy." Clearly, the advancement of the economic well-being of the nation in a global marketplace was fast becoming a major reason for international education.

Another factor affected community colleges. Waves of immigration brought youth and adults from many parts of the world: Vietnam, Korea, Cambodia, Central America, South America, India, Ethiopia, and other areas. It became apparent that community colleges were utilized as means of access into the culture and institutions of the United States. An example is provided by Northern Virginia Community College which reported in 1986 that 22 percent of its full-time students were from 124 other countries. These included:

Vietnam	735
Iran	293
Korea	205
Ethiopia	159
Afghanistan	155

Northern Virginia officials announced that between 1982 and 1986 full-time international student population increased by about 19 percent. Other community colleges made similar reports. Clearly developments within the institutions and in their communities required consideration of the role of international education in the college mission. In the opinion of informed observers who were consulted for assistance in preparing this chapter, perhaps 20 percent of community and technical colleges have organized to implement the international dimension of their mission.

In 1982 the AACJC called for increased emphasis on international education to create a more competent citizenry who understand the diverse cultures of the world. Moreover, it encouraged its member institutions to

> establish clear institutional goals and policies regarding international/intercultural education that advocate the values of the international dimension throughout the total institutional program. (AACJC 1982)

For the first time, in 1987, the association's Public Policy Agenda included a priority specifically addressed to the international dimension. It is not surprising, considering the times, that it related to the economy.

> Work with the federal government, foundations, corporations, media, and other decision-making centers to enable community, technical,

and junior colleges to provide the training strategies and capabilities necessary to keep America working in an increasingly international economic environment. . . . (AACJC 1987)

Community colleges are now expressing their international interests in a variety of activities. Among these are:

1. education of students from other countries,
2. internationalization of the curriculum,
3. links between international education and business interests,
4. foreign language study,
5. overseas academic programs,
6. faculty exchange, and
7. technical assistance to other countries.

A number of institutions have advanced the concepts of global awareness, and through imaginative means they have stimulated other institutions to take appropriate initiatives. Illustrative of many exemplary programs are several described below.

EDUCATIONAL PARTNERSHIPS

A noteworthy development in international education has been the cooperative or consortium approach pioneered by the founding institutions of such organizations as the Community Colleges for International Development (CCID) and the College Consortium for International Studies (CCIS). CCIS was founded in 1975 by Rockland Community College (New York), Mercer Community College (New Jersey), and Harrisburg Area Community College (Pennsylvania). At its inception, it was made up of community colleges primarily from the eastern seaboard. Now it has a membership of almost 200 colleges and universities, two- and four-year, which cooperate to offer over 2,000 students annually the opportunity to study abroad for a semester or a year. It has become the largest consortium of its kind and has sent thousands of students to study abroad in its program in Europe, Asia, the Middle East, and Latin America. The major function of CCIS is providing the opportunity for overseas study for students and staff at member institutions.

Community Colleges for International Development (CCID) was created in 1976 "to implement international programs which benefit countries as well as its own member institutions." Now a consortium of 30 community colleges and technical colleges, it includes two institutions from Canada. Active in the organization of CCID was leadership from Brevard Community College (Florida),

Kirkwood Community College (Iowa), Bunker Hill Community College (Massachusetts), and Florida Community College at Jacksonville.

The founding institutions of CCIS and CCID were in the vanguard of a gathering movement which now totals more than 20 consortia—national, regional, and state. Many of these are solely for community colleges; others, including the Northwest International Education Association and the Florida Collegiate Consortium for International/Intercultural Education, include four-year colleges and universities.

At about the same time as CCIS and CCID were organized, a number of the participating leaders joined with AACJC in January 1976 to establish the association's International/Intercultural Consortium which now has a membership of 93: 66 U.S. community colleges and 27 international.

There were several benefits to a cooperative approach. In a time of financial austerity for many institutions, cost sharing was most welcome. Another value, not easily quantified, was the quality of personal interaction among presidents who had high regard for each other and who had worked together on earlier projects. Further advantages included the sharing of specialized resources, networking opportunities, and, without question, the added security in numbers. When the involvement in international education by community-oriented institutions was questioned, it was often helpful to tell critics that other respected colleges were participants.

CCID, Inc., is an excellent example of a creative educational response to a changing society. Max King, President of Brevard Community College and Chairman of the Board of Directors of CCID, reports that the idea for the organization came to him after a tour of higher educational facilities in Europe about ten years ago. Arranged by the U.S. Office of Education (USOE) for a number of college presidents, the purpose of the trip was to encourage U.S. colleges to internationalize their programs and promote student and faculty exchange.

Since USOE did not follow up, King turned to some of his friends, community college presidents with whom he had worked on other occasions, to form a new organization to develop further their common interests in international education. His colleagues included Bill F. Stewart, Kirkwood Community College (Iowa), Harold Shively, Bunker Hill Community College (Massachusetts), and Benjamin Wygal, Florida Junior College at Jacksonville.

The new organization was given impetus as a result of concurrent developments in Taiwan. Taiwan was seeking a relationship with educational institutions in the United States and was particularly interested in the community college. Further, governmental funds (Taiwanese) were available to support their efforts. Harold Shively had previously served as a consultant there. The result was an invitation for several presidents to go to Taiwan. Common interests quickly became apparent. The Taiwanese sought linkages with American community colleges. The American educators were interested in professional assignments overseas for their faculties.

The Coordination Council for North American Affairs and the Ministry for Education in Taiwan provided the organizational contacts for the Republic of China. CCID, at that time a fledgling entity, signed an agreement with the Ministry of Education in 1978. The program of activities that ensued served as a major building block for CCID and made possible subsequent activities in other parts of the world.

There were similarities between the American and Taiwanese institutions, particularly in the technical fields. Taiwanese educators wanted to learn how curricula are developed in the United States and how institutions are managed. They wanted to update the technical skills of their faculties. As a result of technological development in the Republic of China, institutions were required to become more proficient and better equipped for technical education. The Americans wanted faculty exchange and opportunities to learn more about Taiwan and other countries. It turned out to be a good match.

English was the major stumbling block. While commonly taught in schools, there was little opportunity to practice it. Presumed to be functional in English, the groups that came initially to the community colleges in the United States were not. Today faculty from CCID institutions are sent to Taiwan for a summer of concentrated ESL instruction for the educators who are to come to the United States in the fall. Now ten years old, the exchange program has involved more than 350 Taiwanese faculty. They have returned to their country with new textbooks, knowledge of new equipment, and sources of supplies. Their stay in this country is ordinarily for a semester, although sometimes for a year. A mentor is provided as well as office space. Experiences are made available in laboratories, classrooms, in development of curricula materials, and in other areas that will benefit the Taiwanese educator. Expenses are paid by their government or the educator's institution.

One semester is the usual stay for faculty from American institutions. Salaries and transportation are paid by the U.S. college and in-country expenses by the Taiwanese. More than 80 presidents and other staff have participated in the exchange programs which are usually for two weeks. Many of the institutions have established continuing sister relationships.

In the opinion of CCID leadership, there have been marked benefits to the American community colleges. The presence of Chinese faculty and administrators results often in new perceptions by American faculty of their own culture and greater appreciation of a different culture. At least one college was led to take a hard look at its expectations and practices when Chinese mathematics teachers observed that American students are "spoon-fed" and not encouraged to take enough responsibility for their learning.

Have the Chinese found the exchange agreement to be of value? The answer may be found in the fact that a new ten-year agreement was signed in 1986.

CCID has built other activities on the model agreement with the Taiwanese. These include a contract to help the South American country of Suriname (formerly Dutch Guiana) to develop vocational and technical programs. Recently an agreement was formalized with the Association of Colleges and Universities in Colombia to assist in developing a number of distance learning centers somewhat similar to community colleges. In 1986 a delegation of CCID presidents visited technical institutions in Eastern Europe and entered into an agreement with the Technical University of Budapest that will allow CCID faculty to teach in the international program which is conducted in English. The first exchanges took place in September 1987. Similar arrangements are under exploration with other technical institutions in the area.

Over a ten-year period, CCID has evolved into an experienced and proficient organization in international education as judged by the number of organizations in this and other countries that welcome working relationships. The objectives that shape its activities are:

- assistance to other countries in mid-level manpower training and technical/vocational education;
- opportunities for international study, exchange, and professional development for students and faculty of community colleges and cooperating overseas institutions;
- leadership and services in the development of international dimensions at community colleges.

LINKING INTERNATIONAL EDUCATION AND BUSINESS

It is a truism that community colleges look to the community for indications of educational need. In a time of unprecedented change in the international economic community, therefore, it should come as no surprise that these community-oriented institutions have built upon their experiences in working with local business and industry to develop services appropriate to international commerce. Trade deficits, export possibilities, state and national initiatives in economic development are among factors that have made international business education an area of substantial activity.

Prior to 1983, some institutions were responsive to mounting needs for information and training; however, without question, action that year by the federal government encouraged the creation of partnerships between higher education institutions and business and trade organizations. A program of grants was designed to promote education and training that will contribute to the ability of U.S. business to prosper in an international economy. The grants are awarded under the Department of Education's business and educational program authorized by Title VI, Part B, of the amended 1980 Higher Education Act. In grant competition, a number of community colleges have been successful. Among these are Central Piedmont, (North Carolina), Bunker Hill, Bergen, (New Jersey), and Loop, (Illinois), to mention only a few. Loop College, one of the eight city colleges in Chicago, is an excellent example of a community college that is contributing to the economic development of its community and state.

Loop College is located in downtown Chicago. Forty percent of the students are in business programs. Active advisory boards link the college and the business community. Students come from more than 50 countries; about 10 percent of the enrollees are from other lands. Twelve languages are offered, and college representatives declare that the world is their neighborhood.

A "structured internationalization" effort with a business emphasis was undertaken in 1984 with the assistance of a one-year Title VI grant. By the end of the first year, the college had introduced into courses 14 global modular units; created three new courses toward an international business degree; and engaged in other cooperative activities with the community to promote international and business awareness.

The college worked with members of the Chicago business community under a two-year renewal grant to develop and publish a directory of international database resources to assist in the expansion of international trade. The publication, *Resource Handbook for International Business*, (Loop College 1986), was designed to satisfy the basic information needs of those trying to identify new export or import markets, analyze their competition, ship or clear goods, or increase profitability through creative use of export finance programs. The handbook responded to the business community's stated needs for information and for training. Business leaders estimate that two-thirds of companies are capable of export although only one company in four is presently involved. The questions, particularly for smaller companies, were, "How do we get involved?" "Whom do we call?"

Following extensive surveys to identify information gaps, a second volume (Loop College 1987) was published. There was an apparent need for continual updating. As a result, Loop has entered into a collaborative arrangement with the University of Illinois at Chicago (UIC). The database has been conveyed to the UIC staff who will maintain and develop an electronic inquiry and delivery system, called the *Resources Directory*. Thus, there has been established a permanent international trade database which will enable Illinois users to access the most recent information on a continual basis. The *Resources Directory* has been welcomed by the international business community in Chicago and the State of Illinois. Loop College has assured continuance of a valued community service by utilizing the technological resources of a sister institution.

Another example of creativity is in the way Loop stabilized funding for its international business education program. About four years ago, the General Assembly of the State of Illinois mandated that every community college in the state have an office of economic development. Funds are appropriated by the State for that purpose. At Loop, until recently, there had been little connection between the office of economic development and the international business program. However, as a result of arrangements with the Illinois Community College Board and the chancellor's office of the Chicago City College, the economic development and international business interests now have been merged to create an office of international economic development. Consequently, continuity and stability are assured in a program begun largely on grant money. Loop College has established itself as an educational resource and functioning partner in the international business community of Chicago.

INTERNATIONALIZING THE CURRICULUM

Community colleges engage in a variety of activities to infuse international awareness into their programs, as suggested previously. None of these is as important in reaching the broadest segment of the college student population as what is done through the curriculum, hence the need to "internationalize" the curriculum. And yet, in the views of many observers, it is precisely this effort that has yielded the least success. Key players in any move to change the curriculum are, of course, the faculty, and faculty express some resistance for what they consider good reasons. One of these, faculty say, is the existing heavy load of teaching, advising, and committee work with little time or resources to develop new courses or revise existing courses. Released time for participation in curriculum projects has been made possible in a number of institutions as a result of federal grants. For example, at Mt. Hood Community College (Oregon), substantial development grants for internationalizing the curriculum were received from HEW, Title 601. President Paul Kreider reports that more than 60 professional staff participated in specific curriculum projects and that more faculty have done more research and curriculum development in the area of international and cultural issues than in any other. Among the results has been a published inventory of international teaching units.

Mt. Hood, Spokane Falls Community College (Washington), Pima Community College (Arizona), and Brevard Community College (Florida) have been among institutions that developed units or instructional packages designed to add an international perspective to courses. The efforts of Mt. Hood and Spokane Falls broadened to involve the Northwest International Education Association where Stanley Lauderbaugh directed a cooperative program to collect courses and units of study with an international focus. The program resulted in a catalog for consortium members that describes 190 courses and units developed under various grants to consortium colleges and universities.

Mt. Hood Community College developed a catalog that lists teaching modules available within its institution in some 17 subject areas. In a friendly and invitational manner, faculty are encouraged to use the modules developed by their colleagues.

> Here is material that could be used to add an international perspective to nearly any course on campus. The structure of the modules makes them easy for instructors to adapt to their own class formats, and a screening committee has worked on each module to make sure it is well-organized and clearly written. If you like the module, adapt it to your course. Take the best and leave the rest . . . let your colleagues know about any successes you have. Share the wealth! (Mt. Hood 1984)

Literature is one of the 17 subject areas. Following are examples of module topics:

- Voices from Around the World: The Literature of Social Protest
- The Polemics of Peace: Representative Essays from the World
- Fantasy, Magic, and Realism in the Short Stories of Contemporary Latin American Writers
- The Traditional and Modern Image of Woman As It Is Exemplified in Two Third World Novels.

Another approach to internationalizing the curriculum is suggested by Seymour Fersh, Coordinator of Curriculum Development at Brevard Community College. Fersh believes that faculty develop-ment is directly related to curriculum development. The approach at Brevard highlights the faculty in hopes of internationalizing general education. Instead of requiring specific content-centered courses, Brevard is having an effect on the curriculum (especially in non-social studies courses) by increasing the number of faculty members with meaningful transcultural study and experiences.

On the other hand, Broward Community College (Florida) has established a requirement to ensure that all of its students earning an Associate of Arts degree enroll in at least two courses that contain an international or intercultural emphasis. Broward is a large mul-ticampus institution serving the Fort Lauderdale, Hollywood, and Pompano Beach areas of southeast Florida. The college is strongly committed to international/intercultural education and has expressed its interests in many ways. Therefore, it came somewhat as a surprise in 1979 when research directed by William Greene, Director of In-ternational Education at Broward, revealed that large numbers of students received little or no exposure to courses of a global nature. More than one-third of the students surveyed who received an As-sociate of Arts degree did not earn credit in a single course that con-tained a major international content or emphasis. An additional 14 percent of the graduates completed successfully only one international course.

The case was made for changes in the general education require-ments that would ensure that students enroll in at least some courses that are international in scope. A proposal was approved by the Ac-ademic Affairs Committee that would require all A.A. degree students to complete successfully at least two international/intercultural courses prior to graduation. Students are not required to take addi-tional courses beyond the current general education requirements. They can choose from more than 80 designated courses.

The new requirement became effective in 1980. With the assis-tance of a grant received under the Undergraduate International Studies and Foreign Language Program for the period July 1, 1981, to June 30, 1983, faculty at Broward both developed a number of new courses of an international nature and modified existing courses. However, it was discovered that state-mandated degree requirements as well as budget constraints reduced the number of elective courses available to students. Broward found that course revision and the "infusion" method was more successful in "internationalizing" the curriculum than adding new courses.

The following criteria developed by the Council on Learning's (1981) National Task Force on Education and the World View have been adopted by the college to determine which courses to be certified satisfy the international/intercultural requirement:

1. *A fundamental understanding of the key elements of global and national interdependence,* as taught through the major fields of study in the humanities, the social sciences, the pure sciences, the applied sciences, and the professional disciplines. This understanding should equip college students to analyze and respond intelligently to domestic and international developments. Such competence should be evidenced by a student's independent analysis of the most important strands of the new global circumstances and comprehension of the United States' increased interdependence with other nations for its national survival and economic growth.

2. *A deeper knowledge and understanding of other cultures* as seen through their history, geography, language, literature, philosophy, economics, and politics. Students' perceptions of other cultures will substantially enhance their ability to understand the nation's needs and changing world position and enable intelligent consideration of highly complex developments on the world scene. The sensitivities learned about other cultures, the enhanced tolerance of differences, all contribute to a citizenry better able to cope with the 21st century problems and better able to approach conflict resolution.

3. *General competency in a second language* as a basis for the fuller comprehension of other cultures and of one's own culture in the global context. Skills in specific languages are becoming increasingly essential for meaningful communication in a wide range of contexts. Students' access to effective foreign language instruction is therefore a necessary requisite to the college experience in the 1980s and beyond.

REQUIRED ORIENTATION/ACCULTURATION COURSE FOR STUDENTS

More students from other lands are coming to American community colleges. In 1984 a national study by the Office of International Programs at Cuyahoga Community College (Ohio) found that 83 percent of the colleges replying indicated that foreign students were enrolled on their campuses. Generally the percentage was low, an average of 1 percent of the total student population. On some campuses, however, the foreign student enrollment was as high as 50 percent and at many colleges the numbers were in the hundreds, in a few cases in the thousands.

Enrollment of foreign students is growing for many reasons. Change from an agricultural to an industrial base in the economies of some Third World countries means pressing needs for training in technical fields. Students and their sponsors are thus motivated to look toward community colleges which specialize in programs at less than the baccalaureate level. Low tuition, availability of both academic and technological training in the same institution, and easy access to the community are among other reasons for the rising numbers. Government agencies, such as the Agency for International Development (AID), which generally used to limit aid to university programs, are less rigid and allow the student two years at a community college before going on to finish at a university. Moreover, AID is now funding short-term studies for A.A. degrees and certificate programs. Other reasons for greater numbers include active recruitment programs and the increased visibility of the American community college worldwide.

Many foreign students are from cultures markedly different from that of the community college. Most come from Asia, Latin America, and the Middle East—from such countries as Korea, Taiwan, Malaysia, India, and Japan. Obviously there are problems of cultural differences to deal with, meaning adjustments both for the institutions and the students. International students are often unprepared to cope with American culture and customs. Different languages, dating customs, dietary habits, attitudes toward study, problems with immigration regulations and authorities, and finances are among the difficulties to be dealt with. While community colleges have been busy developing international programs and linkages, there is some evidence that they have generally neglected to realign support systems to help the increased number of students coming to study in the United States. The problem is particularly critical in public community colleges which ordinarily do not have residential arrangements.

A novel program that responds to these needs has been developed by Pima Community College (PCC) in Arizona. Students learn about different lifestyles, customs, laws, and people as they pursue their academic objectives. Located only 60 miles from the Mexican border, PCC is a multicampus district. The college opened its doors in 1970. Three percent of the enrollment is international. More than 580 students representing 62 countries are reported with the majority coming from Mexico, although a sizable number come from Saudi Arabia, Venezuela, Iran, Libya, and Japan. Several years ago, PCC began a cross-cultural seminar for international business organizations in the community that were sending employees and their families abroad. When foreign students at PCC became aware of the program and expressed interest in participation, the seminar became the basis of a course now required for all entering full-time foreign students.

International Business Communications 120 was established as a 3-credit-hour cross-cultural seminar to examine cultural similarities and differences of the United States and selected foreign countries. Among the areas examined are the educational, social, political, and legal systems. Emphasis is given to the use of information to develop and improve the students' communication skills in the Tucson/PCC environment. Focus is on the academic system and "basic survival skills" for the Tucson area—how to find housing, deal with merchants, seek medical/legal advice, and find banking or child care services. The course has specific academic requirements and is based upon the stated objective that "the more quickly you adapt to your new environment, the more efficiently you can accomplish your primary goal—getting your education."

A Foreign Student Handbook has been prepared for the course and covers college, cultural, and governmental information. The Handbook begins with the fundamental question - "Where and What is Pima Community College?" (Pima Community College n.d.).

Following are just two examples of how different customs are examined:

> *Table Etiquette*—When you are at someone's home for dinner and are asked if you would like a serving of a particular dish, do not refuse out of politeness. You should accept if you want something. If you wait to be asked again, you may go hungry. After you have had enough, it is perfectly proper to politely decline additional servings. If you have dietary restrictions, it is acceptable, and in fact appreciated, if you inform your host.

> *Concepts of Dating*—In the United States today, relationships between men and women have become more informal and the range of shared activities more broad. You may find couples living together, maintaining one exclusive relationship, or individuals dating many people without commitment to any one person. The expectation that someone will be "faithful" after a date or two has caused many international students to become disillusioned about dating Americans. Going to social events together, even if this occurs several times, may not imply an emotional attachment but does indicate that someone's company is enjoyable.

Concepts of differences and similarities are dealt with in the course, not judgments of inferiority/superiority. In fact, students are advised:

> During your stay in America, you will be exposed to many values, customs of this country; do not lose or forget your own personal values and beliefs. If you are uncomfortable with an American custom or value, contact a friend or counselor and explain your discomfort to them.

THE JAPAN ADVENTURE—UNIQUE
ACADEMIC WORK-STUDY PROGRAM

Lansing Community College (LCC, Michigan), founded in 1957 and located just a few blocks from the Michigan State capitol building, has a working relationship with the Biwako Kisen Steamship Company in Japan. The company provides approximately 20 American students each year the opportunity to acquire proficiency in the Japanese language, employment in a Japanese company, and participation in studies of the Japanese business people and their society. Under a directed academic work-study program, Lansing Community College students earn the equivalent of one year of academic credit.

In cooperation with the Steamship Company, the college has a full-time project leader in residence with the students. Steamship employees and the college representative share in the development, supervision, and evaluation of the program. In addition, appropriate segments of the academic program are provided by several Japanese instructors. Instruction and work experience are integrated.

Work experience takes place aboard the cruise ship "Michigan" which sails on Lake Biwa, the largest freshwater lake in Japan. Students provide hospitality services on the three-decked cruise ship, which is a replica of the paddle wheel boats that once flourished on the Mississippi River and are ideally adapted to the environmental conditions of Lake Biwa. After five years of planning and construction work, the ship began operations in 1982 with 20 LCC students among the crew. By 1987, more than 150 students and a dozen LCC faculty members and administrators had participated in the program.

The present arrangement has its roots in a sister-state agreement formalized in 1968 between the State of Michigan and Shiga Prefecture in Japan. The two states have exchanged goodwill missions, government officials, health experts, economic missions, and a variety of other interest groups. Sister-city exchanges have been established as well as affiliations between educational institutions. Lansing Community College has a relationship with Shiga Prefecture Junior College.

While a member of the 1981 Goodwill Mission, Philip Gannon, President of LCC, and Tai Sung Kim, Director of International Programs at LCC, were approached by President Megumi Shigematsu of the Biwako Kisen Steamship Company to ascertain the feasibility of having Michigan college students work and study in Japan. The idea was not out of harmony with the LCC interests or those of President Gannon. In fact, he and Tai Sung Kim were at that time serving as consultants to the Ministry of Education in Korea, and the college had been involved in international activities for more than 20 years.

There was no available model for the proposed program. After numerous discussions, college personnel agreed that several conditions could be met: outstanding students could be recruited who were willing to study and work in Japan; a selection process could be designed; a project leader could be appointed; and an academic program could be developed. With assistance from the Arts and Science Division, the program was instituted in the Business Division. After six years of experience, evaluations of the program have been positive and supportive. The reaction of one parent is typical:

> The Japan Adventure is one of the most educational and enlightening programs available for young adults. It enables them to witness and partake of another nation's history, culture, language, customs and religion and to meet different people and form long-lasting . . . friendships with individuals and families.
>
> In Heather's case, it is going to enable her to further her career chance and ambitions for work in either the foreign service or the United Nations. It taught her discipline and gave her the ability to adjust and cope with strange, new, wonderful experiences. Lansing Community College and Biwako Kisen should be extremely proud of their courage and innovativeness allowing students insight to a world beyond Lansing, Michigan, or the United States, to widen their horizons.

Reportedly, the effects of the Japan adventure upon the college are numerous. One example is the fact that in 1985 LCC developed and instituted as its core course in humanities a three-course sequence on world civilizations, replacing Western civilization as the core course.

TECHNICAL TRAINING IN SPANISH—A DOORWAY INTO LATIN AMERICA

As a beginning point in the development of its curriculum, a community college assesses not only educational needs in the community but the resources available for college programs. El Paso Community College (EPCC, Texas) has made a careful study of its community and students. More than 60 percent of its students are of Hispanic origin, and one out of five instructors regularly use Spanish in the classroom. Forty percent of the instructors are bilingual, with the percentage higher in the technical areas. Many of the administrators provide technical assistance, counseling services, and intensive courses in both English and Spanish.

The College is well prepared to offer education to Spanish-speaking students and in 1979 conducted studies to determine ways of cooperating with technical institutes in Latin America. As a result, a binational cooperative agreement was formalized between EPCC and El Instituto Tecnologico Regional de Cd. Juarez, Chihuahua, Mexico. The *convenio* pledges both institutions to cooperate in the promotion of academic, administrative, cultural, and social interchange. A similar *convenio* was signed in 1983 with La Universidad Autonoma de Ciudad Juarez.

El Paso, a city of 500,000, is adjacent to Ciudad Juarez, Mexico, which is estimated to have a population of 800,000 to one million. These two cities, bound geographically, culturally, historically, and economically, comprise one of the largest bilingual/bicultural urban communities in the world. As such, the community is a major economic and transportation center for the southwestern United States, Mexico, and other Latin American markets. The rapid growth and increasing diversity of El Paso created a need for skilled technicians and mid-level managers in many fields. EPCC was established in 1971, largely in response to this need. Now the college has an enrollment of more than 20,000 students and provides technical training in 120 areas of business and technology through its division of Industrial Programs.

Building upon earlier efforts, the college is implementing a plan to blend its strengths in the technical and language/cultural areas as resources for a leadership role in the field of international technical education reaching beyond Mexico to Central America, South America, and the Caribbean.

Since the initial interinstitutional agreement of 1979, the college has engaged in a number of activities to further its aims of relating international cooperation and technical education. The following are examples of such programs:

- In 1979, 41 Panamanian professors participated in professional development and curriculum development workshops on the El Paso campus. The programs involved the U.S. Agency for International Development, the Instituto Politecnico de Panama, and the Ministry of Education in Panama.
- Between 1980 and 1982, a program was designed to exchange materials and technical assistance with the Dominican Republic, Mexico, and Venezuela. Special assistance was provided to the Dominican Republic to assess the capability of technical institutes.
- From 1982 to 1985, EPCC offered 15 different short-term programs (5–10 weeks) in Spanish to groups of mid-level technicians from Nicaragua and Panama (90 participants from private industry). Areas of training included electronics, industrial production, quality control, supervision, auto mechanics, and graphic arts.

- In 1986, EPCC participated in the Central American Scholarship Program which offered educational opportunities to economically and academically disadvantaged Central American youths. Two short term courses (4–6 months) have been offered in Spanish to 26 Central American participants. Other longer programs include participants from Belize, Guatemala, El Salvador, Honduras, and Costa Rica.

THE CONTEXT IS CHANGING—WHAT ABOUT THE INSTITUTION?

To one who is interested in international education, a study of community college initiatives is encouraging and provocative: encouraging because of an obvious growing commitment to the international dimension, and provocative because of a number of questions that emerge. Some questions are: How can change be brought about in the institution to match a community context increasingly affected by global factors? In the face of changing circumstances, are there guidelines to suggest particular roles for community colleges in international education? Where are further opportunities for innovation?

TO FACILITATE CHANGE

Circumstances are changing that frustrated earlier moves toward international efforts. The public itself is traveling more. There is a growing awareness of the effect upon local economies of developments in troubled areas such as the Persian Gulf, of trade balances, and of foreign investments. States are recognizing the economic efficacy of supporting international education. And many communities are now asking for more of a world view in college programs. For educational leaders, then, the key question may be, what can be done to facilitate appropriate change in institutions? Those colleges whose experience has been reported in this chapter engaged in a broad variety of activities that can be summarized for institutions desiring similar involvement.

- Involve the president through personal experience.
- Seek similar opportunities for board members.
- Through various means, encourage the active participation of those faculty members who show interest.
- Provide released time and funds for faculty for the developmental work required.

- Identify and utilize the resources of the community since the community may be ahead of the college in how life is becoming internationalized.
- Develop linkages with foreign institutions to encourage the exchange of teachers, students, technical expertise, and art work.
- Participate in sister-city and sister-state arrangements which now link many places in this country with counterparts in other lands.
- Encourage faculty to apply for Fulbright grants.
- Join one or more of the many consortia and participate.
- Participate in sponsoring international festivals and other community celebrations.
- Establish a college-wide international committee.
- Appoint a director of international education.
- Become acquainted with and utilize the resources of numerous organizations in the international field, such as the Citizen Exchange Council, the Institute for International Education, the Council for the International Exchange of Scholars, and the Council for International Visitors.
- Finally, and most important, relate new ventures to the existing resources, programs, and mission of the institution.

The latter factor appears consistently in the initiatives that have been described in this chapter. What was done was not out of character for the college but tied to existing circumstances in the institution. Programs were not created out of thin air; rather they often represented a new combination or new pattern of existing resources and relationships. In this respect, these initiatives represented what is often viewed as an expected result of intercultural experience, the capacity to achieve new perspectives, to see things differently. Two examples may clarify this point.

First, consider the events that led to the "Japan adventure." The meeting of President Philip Gannon with the President of the Steamship Company was not entirely by chance. Gannon was participating in a goodwill mission to Japan. As a result of earlier activities, he was ready when the question was asked about a work-study program for community college students who would come to Japan. Further, as a result of prior developments in Lansing Community College, he was able to elicit an immediate positive response from the faculty, staff, and board of the college. Both international and work-study programs were already a part of the college activities. What was new were the location and the circumstances. It was the combination that was the novel feature: work-study and Japan.

Loop College presents a similar case. Located in downtown Chicago, the college enrolls a large proportion of its students in business programs. The usual advisory committees draw upon the expertise and practical experience of the business community. Those same advisory committees keep the college aware of the growing "global marketplace." The partnerships of Loop College, the University of Illinois at Chicago, and the business community led not only to initial funding through federal grants but to the compilation of the *Resources Handbook.* Built upon this relationship, the handbook was then perpetuated through the electronic inquiry and delivery system of the university. The relationships were in place. The product of the relationships was new. Another new combination was created by the merging of the international business program into the office of economic development which resulted in an office for international economic development. Successful innovations appear to arise from the existing reality of the college. They are not patched on.

SPECIAL ROLES FOR COMMUNITY COLLEGES?

In much the same way that successful programs in international education are consonant with the mission, goals, and character of the individual institution, the opportunities for community colleges as a whole may be perceived by considering those special features that are usually associated with the community college. The distinctive characteristics that sometimes present problems of recognition and prestige, nationally as well as internationally, are really their greatest strength. So the solution is not to become more like other institutions, but to cultivate the unique features in recognition of their value. A case in point is technical/occupational programs. Education of technicians is of great interest to countries in the Far East, Latin America, and the Middle East for reasons already observed. Increasing numbers of students are coming to the United States for training at the same time that nations are requesting assistance to establish such programs.

Economic and social change in many parts of the world, and particularly in the Third World, is requiring education to be extended and diversified. In this process, several features of the community college are of interest, in addition to technical education. Among these are:

- The ways in which community colleges handle the range of students now coming to study at all academic levels.
- The comprehensive nature of the institution that results in keeping open educational and occupational options as the student clarifies goals. (In many countries there is an early division between the presumed academically gifted and those

thought to be occupationally inclined. The hope of finding a confluence for change of program and objective is slim.)

- The primacy of the teaching function. In scores of countries, there is a strident outcry—"the examination system is archaic, the syllabi are out of date, our professors do not teach," hence the relevance of an educational institution (such as the community college) in which student and teacher are actively engaged in the learning process.
- The "remedial" or "developmental" function providing an opportunity for improving basic literary skills for adults whose earlier educational experiences may have been inadequate.
- The concept of community-based and community-serving institutions that utilize public and private community resources in the learning process and that adapt to changing community conditions, demands, and circumstances.

Within such common interests, there are possibilities of productive relationships that up to this point have been limited largely to the field of technical education. Further, there is a value base to these considerations, a point of view about education and the potential of people. This could place community colleges on common ground with a large proportion of the world's population who see education as empowerment in the fulfillment of individual potential and in the development of their communities. Community colleges, functioning as "peoples' colleges," have "connective" possibilities, beyond many other American institutions, with that large part of the developing world's population whose destiny holds such importance for the shape of future world society. Here is an area for innovation.

REFERENCES

American Association of Community and Junior Colleges (AACJC). 1982. Statement of Board of Directors. Washington, D.C.: AACJC.

———. 1987. 1987 Public Policy Agenda. Washington, D.C.: AACJC.

Council on Learning. 1981. National Task Force Statement on Education and the World View. New Rochelle, N.Y.: Change Magazine Press.

Loop College, City Colleges of Chicago. 1986. Resource Handbook for International Business. Chicago, Ill.

———. 1987. Resource Handbook for International Business. 2nd ed. Chicago, Ill.

Mt. Hood Community College. 1984. International/Intercultural Teaching Units Catalog. Gresham, Or.

National Governors' Association. 1987. Jobs, Growth, and Competitiveness. Washington, D.C.: National Governors' Association.

Pima Community College. N.d. International Student Handbook. Tucson, Az.

8

The College/Private Sector Connection

BOOM OR BUST?

James P. Long

For decades, companies and communities have depended on their local two-year colleges to supply technicians and other workers with the advanced training needed to contribute productively to work and society. Business and industry, in particular, have looked to the community, junior, and technical colleges to provide preservice education for new employees, as well as upgrading of skills for veteran employees.

With the changing economy of the 1980s, two-year colleges recognized the opportunity—indeed, the necessity—to expand their roles and partnerships with business and industry. These connections (1) speak to the new emphasis on human resource development in the private sector, and (2) involve the colleges directly in local economic development. In many cases, the outcomes are striking.

This chapter examines a number of innovative types of cooperation between two-year colleges and the private sector, and critiques their strengths, weaknesses, and future potential. It begins by placing them in historical perspective.

AN EMERGING CYCLE

Historically, the major involvement a community, junior, or technical college had with local companies was to provide on-campus education, preemployment and occupational in nature. Such education followed established college curricula and conventional teach-

159

ing methodologies. Program graduates then went to work for the companies.

These firms typically had little input into what was taught, or how. Curricula were established by the college faculty. At most colleges, faculty consulted an advisory committee, whose members usually included business and industry representatives, but academic customs and values held sway. Too often, advisory committees merely "rubber-stamped" the faculty's curricula.

Similarly, traditional academic instructional methodologies prevailed. Teaching entailed on-campus lectures and hands-on technical training provided by full-time college faculty, many of whom had little recent business or industry experience. No one thought of this approach as human resource development. It was simply good general or technical education upon which employers relied as the foundation upon which to build their own human resource development programs.

Beginning in the late 1970s, changing attitudes brought two-year colleges and employers into closer cooperation to help develop workers who could "work smarter." Human resource development became a watchword, one of sudden, new importance, and colleges assumed new roles in its achievement. Some of the results of the new partnerships included:

- college-run assessment centers for persons who apply for jobs with business and industry;
- college career guidance programs for employees of local companies;
- college testing services to place employee-students in appropriate programs and courses;
- college courses customized to fit employer needs, frequently offered at the worksite;
- college instructional programs and courses developed by employers but offered on campus, sometimes for certificates or degrees;
- sharing of equipment between the college (for training) and the employer (for production);
- upgrading or retraining courses offered for employees, frequently with fees paid or reimbursed by the company;
- special college programs to retrain workers about to be (or already) displaced from their jobs.

These kinds of activities involve full partnerships between the colleges and employers—an innovation of the 1980s.

In addition to these changes in human resource development, the

1980s brought other changes to the campus. Before this decade, few two-year colleges collaborated with business and industry for economic development. Economic development was the task of chambers of commerce, regional development authorities, planning districts, corporate directors of economic development, and other persons and organizations that functioned mainly as creatures of business, industry, labor, and government.

Educators served faithfully on the boards of these organizations as good citizens and as deliverers of the educational services needed to attract and retain business in the area. Rarely did a two-year college take leadership in this arena. In fact, more than one college was told to "stay out of my way" by economic development executives from government or the private sector.

All of this changed in the 1980s. First "Putting America Back to Work," then "Keep America Working," major initiatives of the American Association of Community and Junior Colleges (AACJC), became the bywords at both the national and local levels. Many two-year colleges took up these challenges. These initiatives provided leadership for a wide range of activities that included:

- retraining displaced workers,
- technology transfer,
- business incubators,
- partnerships with employers to upgrade employees,
- high technology centers and parks, and
- customized training.

As a result, it is commonplace for two-year colleges to work with other local and state entities—including the private sector—to attract, develop, and retain business and industry in their areas. These efforts constitute a major amplification of the mission of community, junior, and technical colleges—another innovation of the 1980s.

What happened to bring about these innovations? Did employers change? Did the colleges change? Are college/private sector partnerships for human resource and economic development totally new phenomena? And are these activities substantive and effective enough to be called innovations, or are most of them little more than public relations rhetoric?

HAVE EMPLOYERS CHANGED?

Chances are, employers themselves have not changed. All things being equal, most still feel more comfortable handling their own personnel and economic development programs without the participation of two-year colleges. They would prefer that the colleges continue to prepare people for employment with a broad-based education, upon which the firms can then build company-specific training after hiring.

What *has* changed is the economic climate. With simultaneous increases in foreign competition and the aging of the "baby boom" generation, business and industry face the dual problems of a dwindling workforce along with the need to operate more efficiently and productively. This double bind sparked the need to "do more with less"—including human resources. Using public postsecondary occupational education to take over some of the task of human resource development offers attractive cost savings to companies.

Profit-making companies usually cannot operate productively in economically distressed locations, and most economic development initiatives require more resources than companies are willing or able to devote. Funding for economic development initiatives is often available from state and federal governments, and partnerships with two-year colleges can provide important leverage to obtain these funds. Private sector involvement in such partnerships is probably a reluctant one, however. Should economic development funding conditions change, two-year colleges are likely to find themselves on the outside again, looking in.

HAVE THE COLLEGES CHANGED?

The priorities of colleges apparently have evolved to include serious involvement in both human resource and economic development activities. Earlier generations of two-year college leaders were less interested in the business/industry connection than they are today. During the growth years of the 1960s and 1970s, colleges devoted themselves to expanding facilities and programs to serve the burgeoning numbers of students, mostly youth, who wanted pre-employment education and training.

As enrollment growth curves flattened or declined in the early 1980s, the colleges naturally turned more attention to retraining and upgrading the skills of adults. This change seems to be a true conversion; no evidence emerges to suggest that the colleges would prefer to go back to serving only pre-employment students, should enough of them become available.

The jury is still out, however, on the commitment of two-year colleges to full partnerships with business and industry for economic development. It may be that colleges are willing to collaborate in these efforts only so long as someone else is footing the bill. If future demands require colleges to commit significant portions of their own resources, they could readily withdraw from the economic development arena.

ARE THE INNOVATIONS REAL?

Many of the kinds of cooperative arrangements in which two-year colleges join with business and industry for human resource or economic development are rooted in early efforts of the 1960s and 1970s. Isolated examples exist of close college/private sector connections from the very start of the community college movement. What is new in the current decade is the abundance of such examples.

But are these abundant, new cooperative programs truly effective, or are many of them little more than "window dressing"? Two-year colleges have become adept at public relations, and instances do exist of glowing media coverage for what are essentially cosmetically altered pre-employment programs or glossy "high-tech" programs with short lifespans and weak impact. Fortunately, in most cases, the substance lives up to the image, with valuable outcomes for students, companies, the college, and the community.

PARTNERSHIPS FOR HUMAN RESOURCE DEVELOPMENT

According to Gold and Charner, "Human resource development can be interpreted in either the more narrow, utilitarian, economic development sense of investing in people to make the most productive use of their talents or in the broader humanistic sense of enabling people to develop their individual talents for their own sake" (1986, 5).

For the most part, human resource development partnerships between colleges and the private sector fit the first category. They address employee or job application assessment, customized training and retraining, occupational skill development and maintenance, and outplacement and preretirement services. These efforts can range from a one-day seminar to a two-year program resulting in award of an associate degree.

JOINT TECHNICAL TRAINING

A good example of an innovative college/private sector connection for human resource development is the Special Technician Training Program operated at Arizona's Rio Salado Community College for production line workers of Motorola, Inc. Workers receive paid leave for one year to attend the program, and Motorola pays all tuition expenses. Program graduates are then placed in suitable positions within the company. The college/company agreement provides for a training center as well as necessary technical equipment and cooperative education for the students.

Similar partnerships exist between two major U.S. automobile manufacturers and two-year college automotive technician programs around the country. General Motors (GM) has established 38 (some sources give a different number) Automotive Service Education Programs (ASEP) at the colleges, which include Bessemer State Technical College (Alabama), Catonsville Community College (Maryland), Delta College (Michigan), and Triton College (Illinois).

The college/GM partnerships were formed because training became too much for the company to handle. Under the agreement, each ASEP student must be sponsored by a GM dealership and be accepted into the two-year associate degree program. The sponsoring dealership serves as the on-site training location for the future GM mechanic. The company provides additional GM-specific training for faculty and donates GM products on which students practice. According to John Walstrum of Catonsville Community College, a college must have a history of excellence in automotive training before it is accepted as a partner in the ASEP program.

The Ford Motor Company has parallel partnerships with 12 community colleges. Ford's Automotive Student Service Educational Training (ASSET) program also trains automotive technicians through a cooperative associate degree program at the colleges. In ASSET, students alternate between learning in a college classroom/laboratory setting and applying the learning to real work in a local Ford dealership. Some Ford ASSET partners include the University of Akron's Community and Technical College (Ohio) and Guilford Technical College (North Carolina).

The Nissan Company and Gateway Community College (Arizona) operate a much briefer in-service program to upgrade worker skills. The program, which requires only four days to complete, is the first satellite training program for dealership automotive technicians. Nissan provides the instructors, and the college furnishes the facility and equipment.

APPRENTICESHIP TRAINING

Partnerships with labor organizations often address apprenticeship training. Such training spans a fixed time period, entails on-the-job training along with classroom instruction, and produces highly skilled graduates—usually with jobs already waiting for them. Arrangements such as these avoid investment by the college in expensive equipment while supplying the in-depth academic foundation that the industry or labor organization could not provide.

Numerous successful apprenticeship partnerships exist. For example, Alabama Technical College offers apprenticeship training in cooperation with a local steel corporation; Bainbridge Junior College (Georgia) trains apprentices for a local electrical/mechanical maintenance company; and the Community College of Rhode Island joins with the Rhode Island/Southeastern Massachusetts Chapter of the National Tooling and Machining Association to produce apprentice-trained workers for that industry. In the Rhode Island program (Liston 1986), graduate machinists receive a Journeyman's Certificate at the same time as they earn college credit toward an associate degree in Machine Processes.

CUSTOMIZED, ON-SITE TRAINING

Many two-year colleges conduct training programs for companies or industries at the worksite. For instance, the Community Colleges of Spokane (Washington) offer customized, on-site training through their Workshop on Wheels. In one of these workshops, the colleges assigned an electronics faculty member to a full-time teaching assignment at the Kaiser Aluminum Corporation until all Kaiser electronics maintenance workers had received the training they needed.

Brevard Community College (Florida) provides on-site, customized training for a number of local companies, including the McDonnell Douglas Astronautics Company and the Defense Communication Division of ITT. The initial funding for these partnerships is provided by the state's Sunshine State Skills program. Employers who benefit must match the state funding.

Another example of on-site training takes place at the Aluminum Company of America Tennessee (ALOOA), where the State Technical Institute (Tennessee) prepares industrial electric maintenance and industrial mechanical maintenance apprentices as well as machinist specialists. The college also offers a "train the trainer" program to prepare ALCOA personnel to be in-house instructors. According to ALCOA, this partnership with the college has paid off with fewer employee layoffs, more jobs, and a rosier economic future for the company in the area.

EQUIPMENT SHARING

A special kind of partnership between a two-year college and the private sector occurs when a company offers to share equipment with a college to use during off-hours for training. Such a relationship exists between Bessemer State Technical College (Alabama) and Fluid Power Systems, distributor of Rexroth hydraulic equipment. Relevant college programs have use of state-of-the-art Rexroth hydraulic equipment during off-hours when the equipment is not in use by company employees.

Similarly, Orangeburg-Calhoun Technical College (South Carolina) provides training for Case I.H. (International Harvester) dealer mechanics. Students use college facilities for classroom instruction and have access to Case I.H. tractors for their hands-on training.

PARTNERSHIPS WITH GOVERNMENT

Some human resource development partnerships involve government units. A good example exists between Cochise College (Arizona) and the U.S. Army Information Systems Command at Fort Huachucs. The college saves the Army—and taxpayers—considerable money by offering a three-phase computer literacy program for Army personnel at the post.

AN INTERINSTITUTIONAL TRAINING CENTER

The Community Colleges of Spokane have a unique partnership with Gonzaga University, a private institution. They have established the SPOCAD Educational Center, an instructional facility specializing in computer-aided design (CAD). To help cover the cost of this venture, the schools sold SPOCAD memberships ($100–3,000) to local businesses. As members, the businesses are entitled to use the CAD equipment—devices much more sophisticated than most of the companies could otherwise afford. The same advanced equipment is also used for training of students from both educational institutions.

ADULT LITERACY AND BASIC SKILLS TRAINING

Some human resource development partnerships address adult literacy and basic skills needs, often offered to workers at the company site. At the request of GM, Dundalk Community College (Maryland) provides members of the United Auto Workers labor union with the skills and knowledge necessary to complete the General Education Development (GED) examination. Participating GM workers are excused from their jobs with full pay for the length of time it takes them to complete preparation for the exam. The college reports a 98 percent passing rate on the GED for these GM employees.

The R.J. Reynolds Tobacco Company initiated an arrangement with Forsyth Technical Institute (North Carolina) to conduct basic skills courses for its employees. Company workers needed advanced technical training to operate and maintain equipment in the new computerized manufacturing plant, but many employees lacked the literacy skills necessary for technical training. The college provided basic skills courses at plant sites, and the company paid the tuition costs.

Along the same lines, the Texas Instruments Company asked Austin Community College (Texas) to provide remedial math, English, English-as-a-Second-Language, and GED preparation courses, primarily for new employees. These were offered through the company training program as part of its human resource development program. Texas Instruments determined the need for such training because of a lack of qualified entry-level workers.

EMPLOYEE SELECTION SERVICES

Helping companies select workers is an unusual task for a two-year college, but Fox Valley Technical Institute (Wisconsin) operates a Business Assessment Service that helps local employers identify candidates for hiring or promotion. At other locations around the country, two-year colleges have recently begun to offer similar services for a fee. Typically, these colleges serve small- to medium-sized businesses (50–500 employees). Services include use of pre-existing, carefully tested assessment instruments to help pinpoint likely candidates for specified positions. In the process, the colleges also discover opportunities to provide education and training to companies or to the general public.

DUAL-PURPOSE PARTNERSHIPS

A number of collaborations serve both human resource and economic development purposes. This is especially evident in relationships that involve training for international corporations or for displaced workers of companies or industries.

TRAINING FOR AMERICAN WORKERS OF INTERNATIONAL CORPORATIONS

It is difficult to determine whether the partnership between Durham Technical Institute (North Carolina) and the Mitsubishi Company, for example, should be classified as an economic development or human resource development effort. It is probably both.

One reason why Mitsubishi chose to build a plant in Durham was because of the college's strong reputation for training in microelectronics skills. Before building the plant, meetings were held between the partners to discuss the training needs and the college's ability to meet those needs. College officials also visited Mitsubishi headquarters in Japan to receive hands-on experience in plant operations, using the required equipment. The resulting program at Durham Tech provides new workers with training in semiconductor testing procedures as well as information about Japanese history, culture, and management style.

DISPLACED WORKER PROGRAMS

Growing problems in several sectors of the economy include how to redirect and retrain dislocated workers and who should take responsibility for these services. Some college/private sector partnerships have been formed to address these problems. For example, in cooperation with affected firms, Brevard Community College (Florida) provides assessment, educational planning, and career counseling for skilled engineers and technicians laid off after the space shuttle accident in 1986. The college also helps the workers evaluate the pros and cons of transferring their highly specialized, nontraditional space technology skills to more traditional occupations.

A partnership with much the same purpose has been formed by the Los Angeles Community College District (California), the Lockheed California Company, the International Association of Machinists and Aerospace Workers, and the Engineers and Scientists Guild. This partnership provides retraining for laid-off or soon-to-be-displaced aerospace workers in Southern California.

In Pittsburgh, the Community College of Allegheny County (Pennsylvania) and the county commissioners have joined forces to help an estimated 100,000 employees laid off due to the closing of the steel mills. The Dislocated Worker Educational Training Program provides career counseling, job search workshops, communication and math skills training, and technical skills training to help participants understand and exercise some control over the options available to them. Participants can earn one-year certificates or two-year associate degrees.

St. Louis Community College (Missouri) provided leadership to another dislocated worker program conducted by St. Louis Labor/Management Committees and the St. Louis Regional Commerce Growth Association. This Metropolitan Reemployment Project provides counseling, job information, retraining, and methods for changing careers. The program also brings together program participants (displaced workers) and potential employers.

A program designed to work with employees even before the layoffs begin is being conducted by Metropolitan Technical Community College (Nebraska), Northwestern Bell Telephone Company, and the Communication Workers of America. About 7,000 jobs will be eliminated at Northwestern Bell over the next few years. To address the needs of these workers, the college offers a three-year Career Development/Retraining program, which provides career assessment, counseling, and educational services for all nonmanagement personnel. It is available to 12,000 Northwestern Bell employees in five states and involves 42 other postsecondary institutions. Metropolitan Technical Community College designed the comprehensive program and manages it for all 42 colleges.

ADMINISTRATION OF PARTNERSHIPS

Many colleges have established a separate division or department devoted specifically to developing and managing human resource development partnerships with business, industry, and government. The unit at Tennessee's State Technical Institute is called the Business, Industry, and Government (B.I.G.) Division and is concerned with cross-training and upgrading area workers. At the Dallas County Community College District (Texas), the unit is called the Business and Professional Institute. Florida Community College at Jacksonville calls its unit the Center for Economic Development. Similar units can be found at nearly every two-year college.

PARTNERSHIPS FOR ECONOMIC DEVELOPMENT

The entry of two-year colleges into the economic development arena is a significant event in the evolution of economic development activities. College partnerships with business, industry, labor, and government working for economic development might involve community development, institutional development, or business development.

COMMUNITY DEVELOPMENT

Gold and Charner define community development as "planning and implementing projects and programs to improve the economic and social qualities of life in a whole community or geographic area" (1986, 10).

A prime state-wide community development program is Iowa's special tax incentive, which funds customized training for private sector employees at the state's 15 community colleges. Through the use of funding certificates sold like general obligation bonds, the program pays up to 50 percent of the trainees' salaries during on-the-job training. For example, Des Moines Area Community College developed a training program for Greyhound Lines, Inc., to facilitate the relocation of the company accounting center to west Des Moines. As part of this service, the college accepted and reviewed job applications and trained 700 new employees. Other Iowa community colleges have trained new employees for Sara Lee and the Wal Mart Corporation.

South Carolina's well-known state-wide Technical Education System (TEC) provides customized technical training for business and industry through its community and technical colleges. TEC's Division of Industrial and Economic Development offers free training for new and expanding companies in the state. Such preemployment training ensures for companies a supply of fully trained, productive personnel from their first day on the job.

INSTITUTIONAL DEVELOPMENT

Institutional development "involves new ways of identifying the tangible and intangible assets of the institution and finding ways to capitalize those assets and market them to potential partners" (Gold and Charner 1986, 11).

The model CAD/CAM Training Center at Milwaukee Area Technical College (Wisconsin) illustrates one kind of partnership for institutional development. The center offers software, materials, and training in computer-integrated manufacturing for retraining industrial workers. A microcomputer-based CAD system was developed for the center, which has since sold the system to other educational institutions and set up a dealership network.

Two-year colleges have also begun helping business and industry learn about, select, and use advanced technologies. Wisconsin's Fox Valley Technical Research Incubator Park, associated with Fox Valley Technical Institute, attracts private sector firms using new technologies that are compatible with the college's technical, education, and business support services. A Technical Innovation Center, also a part of the park, will soon include a technical library, economic development center, product development service center, flexography laboratory, customized concepts laboratory, and classrooms. The park, planned and funded cooperatively, is the offspring of a consortium of the college, the University of Wisconsin Center-Fox Valley, Lawrence University, the Institute of Paper Chemistry, area high school districts, and the local JTPA organization.

In South Carolina, Greenville Technical College, in partnership with Michelin Tire Corporation, has built a 16,000-sq-ft. training facility on campus for mutual use. Michelin will use the building for its own training courses during the day, and the college will offer continuing education courses there at night.

Chemeketa Community College (Oregon) uses the Service Corps of Retired Volunteers and the volunteer services of other professional and business people to work with small business owners, prospective or established. The city of Salem funds the salary of a volunteer coordinator who matches volunteers with entrepreneurs needing advice. The program also refers business people to sources of venture capital and to relevant workshops, courses, and short-term training.

Another Oregon college, Mt. Hood Community College in Gresham, operates a nationally recognized small business management program that has already provided specialized services to more than

40 local firms, including General Telephone, local banks, Fire District 10, Boeing, and Rango Wagner Mining Equipment. The college has also set up international programs and currently has a grant to expand its Business and International Education Program.

Along similar lines, Greenville Technical College and the U.S. Department of Commerce have joined forces to introduce South Carolina business and industry to international markets. The effort involves an export training program at the college to encourage and assist small- and mid-sized businesses in exporting their products globally.

Milwaukee Area Technical College's Partners in Progress consortium joins this Wisconsin college with more than 15 companies and 6 educational institutions or professional groups to provide education and training in advanced technologies. Those partners who make financial contributions constitute the Advanced Technology Council, which establishes priorities for funding advanced technology training and technology transfer projects.

All 38 community college districts in Illinois have business assistance centers that provide economic development assistance, customized job training, entrepreneurship training, contract procurement assistance, small business incubator activities (in which small, independent businesses actually operate on campus), and job search services. The centers receive funding from the state, JTPA, federal small business development center funds, foundation grants, local donations, and college operating funds. In FY 1986, these centers assisted in creating or retaining nearly 18,000 jobs in the state (Illinois Community College Board 1986).

The Mid-Florida Research and Business Center of Daytona Beach Community College maintains a database for local industry that includes information about taxes, new business starts, economic growth trends, labor market conditions, and available training. Requests for information come from the Volusia County Business Development Center, local chambers of commerce, companies, state officials, accountants, and lawyers.

BUSINESS DEVELOPMENT

The third type of economic development, business development, includes elements of both community and institutional development. The goal is to develop new enterprises or assist older ones through incubator centers, loans or grants of venture capital, and small business assistance centers, often using state or federal funds.

For example, Niagara County Community College (New York) supports small business with management advice, a small business incubator, and loan fund management through its Technical Assistance Center funded by special state appropriations. The incubator approach provides facilities, telephone and clerical help, and computer access for new small businesses. Incubator tenants are considered students and may use college facilities and consult staff at no cost.

The Business Development Center at Kirtland Community College (Michigan), a rural college, offers microcomputer networking, access to local and regional economic data systems, and help in developing business leads for the local private sector. The center also maintains local industrial files.

Incubator projects at 17 community colleges in the Illinois Community College Educational Development Association provided services to 19 businesses in 1986 and created 100 jobs. The colleges' roles ranged from providing employer training and management assistance to helping organize and even operate the incubators.

Portland Community College (Oregon) also uses the incubator concept to assist small businesses for the first two years with low-cost space, support services, classes, seminars, and professional consultation. After two years, the college assists the company with relocation.

North Central Technical Institute (Wisconsin) operates an incubator mall at a shopping center as part of its small business management program. The college provides technical assistance to these new businesses in several ways, including facilitating technology transfer through its laser technology program to cooperating firms. The college Applied Technology Center will also purchase special equipment cooperatively with these firms. In these partnerships, the center acquires the equipment for training, and the companies use it during off-hours.

Umpqua Community College (Oregon) houses two full-time staff members with the Tri-county Economic Development Organization. Umpqua provides business counseling and classroom instruction for local industry and also serves as a broker for free consulting services. The college is a member of a state network of 15 community colleges and 3 universities, all of which receive state lottery monies for small business development.

Pueblo Community College (Colorado) opened its Myers Center for Small Business in 1983 in response to local layoffs and high unemployment. Since then, the center has contributed directly to the creation of 57 new small businesses and the survival of 71 others representing a combined workforce of 194 full-time and 87 part-time employees (Zeiss 1987).

ASSESSING THE TRENDS

What can be said about the value, weaknesses, and future of these many joint ventures between two-year colleges and business, industry, labor, and government? Are they worthwhile for the colleges? For employers? What changes, if any, are likely to—or should—take place?

If value is in the mind of the customer, recent college/private sector partnerships for human resource development have a built-in measure. As long as the customers—business and industry—turn to the colleges for assistance, and pay for it, its value to them is clearly positive. An issue of fairness has been raised, however.

Is it "fair" for profit-making companies to use tax-supported institutions to complement or replace their own training departments? If so, is it fair to help some companies and not others? Such questions seldom arose in earlier decades when the mission of two-year colleges was primarily pre-employment in nature. The innovations of the 1980s raise many such questions about fairness. The answers differ, depending on one's assessment of the proper role of government in meeting private sector needs and how those needs relate to local or national economic priorities.

On the other hand, the value of human resource development partnerships to the two-year colleges themselves is indisputable: enrollments increase; influence expands; and facilities, equipment, and personnel are complemented by those of the private sector partners. The few higher education "purists" who decry the long-range risks of such close entanglements with the private sector attract a scant following. To most college leaders, the immediate value overshadows the potential risks.

The value of partnerships for economic development is less clear. No reliable data report the number of jobs created as a result of the involvement of two-year colleges. What many term "economic development" is frequently little more than cosmetically altered education or training activities. Even the business incubator concept involves a great deal of training and consultation services—traditional educational institution activities. The "value added" to economic development activities by two-year college involvement does not appear, on close examination, to be very great.

Most current college/private sector partnerships, whether for human resource or economic development, do have visible weaknesses. These need only to be listed to see that most are not fatal; taken collectively, however, they should give the forgers of such partnerships reason to ponder where the best-laid plans might go wrong. Some of these weaknesses are as follows:

- Colleges that rely on the private sector to inflate enrollments, at a time when traditional-age students (recent high school graduates) are less numerous, risk unpredictable enrollment drops (and increases) with all the consequent problems.
- Academic standards might be lowered in response to corporate pressure for less rigor.
- Customized training might fit students for employment in one company only, rather than for careers in an industry.
- Tax dollars voted for education can be channeled to make individual business enterprises more profitable.
- Most educators do not have the background of experiences and education to become effective economic development specialists.

For the future, it seems likely that trends in human resource development partnerships will continue along current lines until the turn of the century. At that time, traditional-age enrollments will begin an upswing as the "baby boomlet" generation graduates from high school. Two-year colleges might then focus more attention on this primary market, with consequently fewer resources available to devote to college/private sector collaborations.

For business and industry, interest in, and use of, two-year colleges for human resource development can be expected to rise and fall somewhat in response to normal boom/recession cycles. It seems likely that the pace of the nation's industrial "retooling" will eventually slow. In addition, there will be times when some employers—motivated by improved profit margins and/or dissatisfaction with training provided by the colleges—will return to high levels of in-house training. A realistic view of the future allows for the possibility that employers' demands for college-based retraining might decrease significantly from the current levels.

Overall, the forecast for college/private sector economic development partnerships is also somewhat pessimistic. Evidence strongly suggests that most current activities called "economic development" by two-year colleges are not really worthy of the name. Few jobs are created as a result of such activities. With the passage of time, a more appropriate term will probably emerge for what the colleges are now doing to assist other groups involved in economic development. Colleges have become genuine "good corporate citizens" of the nation, states, and communities in which they reside. As such, they have a great deal to contribute to the economic health of their service areas. Doing so effectively should perhaps be called "civic responsibility," rather than economic development.

THE BOTTOM LINE

There are far more benefits than shortcomings in college/private sector partnerships, for all participants. If nothing else, the "ivory tower" approach to what is truly feasible through cooperative efforts has largely faded. Two-year colleges are already in the world of business and industry in very real ways. The products sold to business and industry by community colleges (e.g., education and training) must be sufficiently high in quality to satisfy their customers, yet inexpensive enough to capture a market share from other potential suppliers. Colleges will lose market share if excellence wanes or if the price is not competitive. These same threats face all businesses. This dose of reality is seldom available to tax-supported institutions.

A final benefit often observed to result from college/private sector partnerships are the changes in teaching practices, methodology, and technology that have carried over from the private sector to the colleges and often vice-versa. Computers, television, measurable learning objectives, and outcomes assessment are but a few of the valuable educational innovations borrowed by colleges from business and industry training departments.

As a result of such benefits, American two-year colleges are vastly enriched by their connections with business, industry, labor, and government. Partnerships involve the colleges in a variety of activities—both for human resource and economic development—in settings more professional and demanding than any since the community college movement began. The college/private sector connection is a boon, whether it booms or busts.

REFERENCES

BERNSTEIN, MELVIN H. 1986. *Higher Education and the State: New Linkages for Economic Development.* Washington, D.C.: National Institute for Work and Learning.

GOLD, G.G., and I. CHARNER. 1986. *Higher Education Partnerships: Practices, Policies, and Problems.* Washington, D.C.: National Institute for Work and Learning.

Illinois Community College Board. 1986. *Fiscal Year 1986 Economic Development Grant Report.* Springfield: Illinois Community College Board.

KALAMAS, DAVID J., and CATHARINE P. WARMBROD. 1987. *Options: Linking with Employers.* Columbus: National Center for Research in Vocational Education, Ohio State University.

Keeping America Working through Partnerships with Major Business/Industry Employers and Labor Unions. 1986. Washington, D.C.: American Association of Community and Junior Colleges and Association of Community College Trustees.

LISTON, E.J. 1986. "A Partnership for Progress in Economic Development." A presentation to the National Council for Occupational Education, San Diego, Ca., October.

LONG, JAMES P., ROBERT A. GORDON; CHARLES SPENCE; and GARY MOHR. 1984. *Economic Development and the Community College*. Columbus: National Center for Research in Vocational Education, Ohio State University.

MCNETT, IAN. 1986. *The Development Triangle: Community College Assistance for Economic Growth*. Washington, D.C.: Center for Regional Policy, Northeast-Midwest Institute.

WARMBROD, CATHARINE P., and ROXI A. LIMING. 1987. *Case Studies of Programs Serving Adults*. Columbus: National Center for Research in Vocational Education, Ohio State University.

ZEISS, P. ANTHONY, and RICHARD G. HALLOCK. 1987. *A 4-Year Study of the Myers Center for Small Business*. Pueblo, Co.: Pueblo Community College.

9

Innovations
IN
Staff Development
Al Smith

A book or series of books could be written on the innovations that have occurred in the area of community college staff development programs since the 1960s. Staff development (SD) has become one of the most important programs in the two-year college movement because of the central role it plays in almost all aspects of college life. Staff development today can be viewed as the "heart" of the community college body. It is the organ that pumps life-giving blood and new vitality into the individuals and programs that make up this institution of higher learning.

Staff development has not always been viewed in such a positive light. Prior to the 1970s, most college staff development programs consisted primarily of a series of faculty orientation days that may or may not have addressed the needs of the faculty or the needs of other staff members, that is, administrators, academic support staff, part-time faculty, clerical staff, counselors, librarians, and so forth. How is it that this innovation has achieved such a prominent place in the two-year college?

THE EARLY BEGINNINGS

It all began when some key people (O'Banion 1972; Cohen 1973) noted that there was a need for in- service staff development programs in two-year colleges. These individuals observed that while the 1960s and early 1970s had been a time of expansion and growth for two-year colleges, the later 1970s and the next decade promised to be a time when far fewer faculty and staff would be added to the college payrolls. While preservice faculty development programs were important to the rapid growth of the two-year college in the 1960s, well-planned and organized in-service training programs were what was needed for the 150,000 faculty already on the job in the 1970s. These prophets proved to be correct in their projections; the years from 1975 to 1985 became a time of reduced resources, fewer new faculty, stabilized enrollments, and faculty/staff retrenchment.

This author believes that the need for even more expansion and innovation in the area of in-service education will be needed in the 1990s. Recent U.S. Department of Education statistics indicate that the number of higher education faculty will decline by 8 percent from 1985 to 1995 (Center for Education Statistics 1987). If these projections hold up, one might expect to find only 193,200 teaching staff in 1995, reduced from the 210,000 in 1985. This projected decline of staff is anticipated because of a predicted 3 percent decline in students in two-year colleges from 1985 to 1995. It is projected that the community college student body will drop from its current figure of 4,531,000 students to 4,403,000 students in 1995–96. With few new hires, an aging faculty and staff are going to need expanded opportunities to remain current and up-to-date in their teaching and related areas of responsibility.

Few individuals, colleges, or states saw the need for the improvement of professional competencies prior to the 1970s. One state, however, took the lead in this area. In 1967 the Florida legislature passed community college staff and program development legislation (hereafter referred to as SPD). The original funding base for this SPD program was an additional budget allocation to each of Florida's 28 colleges of 3 percent of the institution's instructional salaries budget. In July of 1973, a new funding plan was established for SPD. The new plan required SPD expenditures of at least 2 percent of the operational budget of the college (Kastner 1973). This state plan is still in existence today and has been promoted as a model for other states. Nearly $50 million has been spent on SPD activities in Florida's 28 community colleges since 1968. Individuals in other states have proposed similar pieces of SPD legislation; however, to date, the Florida community college system remains the only state system of community colleges with this unique and well-funded program of staff development.

EARLY WRITINGS SET THE STAGE

In the 1970s a number of publications stressed the need for faculty and staff development programs in both two-year and four-year colleges. The Group for Human Development in Higher Education (1974) made seven key recommendations for instituting or continuing quality faculty development programs in a time of higher education retrenchment. One of the key suggestions, particularly applicable to two-year colleges, was that colleges and universities should organize regular campus programs on teaching, coordinated by an institute supported by the general college budget, and sustained primarily by the faculty themselves. As a result of this publication, in the latter half of the 1970s, hundreds of new teaching improvement programs and centers were established in two-year and four-year colleges around the country. Substantial funding was provided for these new programs and centers by such funding agencies as the Fund for the Improvement of Postsecondary Education, the W.K. Kellogg Foundation, and the Lilly Foundation.

Also in 1974, the American Association of Community and Junior Colleges (AACJC) provided support for the staff development movement through its publication *New Staff for New Students*. This publication emphasized the magnitude of the institutional investment in faculty:

> The staff of a college is its single greatest resource. In economic terms, the staff is the college's most significant and largest capital investment. In these terms alone, we affirm that it is only good sense that the investment should be helped to appreciate in value and not be allowed to wear itself out or slide into obsolescence by inattention or neglect. (Yarrington 1974, 139)

Of particular interest in this statement was the use of the terms "staff development." While the emphasis in four-year colleges has been primarily on faculty development programs, most community colleges have taken the position that all staff should be included in the professional development program of the college.

Another pivotal piece of literature during this period was Gaff's (1975) book on faculty renewal. Gaff condensed the various professional development activities he studied into three general categories: The designing of new courses, redesigning of current courses, and updating of instructional materials he labeled "instructional development" activities. Programs that focused on reorganizing the institution itself or units within the institution in order to create a better environment for teaching he described as "organizational development" in nature. Activities that focused on helping faculty members develop their talents and teaching skills he called "faculty development" activities. This conceptual scheme for thinking about staff development activities was very helpful at that time and still is today. The most effective staff development programs today are performing all of these activities under the umbrella term of staff development. However, there is still a considerable amount of debate as to how much emphasis should be given to each of these three areas in any one staff development effort.

EARLY GUIDELINES FOR SUCCESS

Numerous sets of guidelines and suggestions for organizing staff development programs were published in the latter part of the 1970s (Hammons, Wallace- Smith, and Watts 1978; O'Banion 1978). Basically these publications have stressed the following guidelines for establishing effective staff development programs in the two-year college.

1. An assessment should first be conducted to determine the level of presidential and administrative support for a new or revised program. This support is considered essential to the success of any program. Further assessments should be made of the availability of funds and personnel to operate the program.

2. A statement of philosophy for the program is critical to its success. Involvement by all staff members in the development of this statement is essential along with their full endorsement of the finished product. A program without this involvement and support from the college staff will surely fail.

3. The most effective staff development program will always be one that is coordinated with a staff development person. Ideally this should be a person who is full-time, knowledgeable about the staff development field, and enthusiastic and interested in his or her assignment. An advisory committee of faculty, administrators, and noncontractual staff is always desirable. Such a committee can provide direction and valuable contacts, but without a coordinator who is clearly in charge, the program is likely to flounder.

4. The program planned must be related to the mission, needs, and priorities of the institution. The program must also be designed to offer a wide variety of activities to meet the various needs of all of the constituencies represented in the institution. Comprehensive programs have included such activities as faculty grants, travel funds, summer and year-long institutes, short-term workshops, graduate study, staff retreats, sabbaticals, faculty exchange programs, visitations, packaged programs, in-house continuing seminars, a professional library, professional reading, and released time for project work.

5. There must also be appropriate incentives and rewards for the participants. These can take the form of both monetary

and nonmonetary rewards. Some examples of incentives that have been used with success include promotions, direct stipends, salary increase, institutional recognition, certificates, released time, teaching awards, recognition dinners, and paid travel. In many cases it has been found that the incentive of personal and professional growth is all that is needed to attract high levels of staff involvement and growth.

6. While large amounts of funds may not be necessary to run a highly successful staff development effort, adequate funding must be made available to achieve the program's objective. The level of funding will be determined to a great extent by the objectives set for the program and the amount of current resources already available at the college. The allocation of at least 2 percent of the college's budget to staff development has proven to be a very good guideline for administrators and faculty over the last 20 years in Florida.

7. All programs must be evaluated on a regular basis; in most cases, this means yearly. Some methods of evaluation that are currently being used include attendance figures; followup questionnaires; self-evaluations; supervisor, peer, and student evaluations; and improvements in student achievement and development.

These guidelines, when followed, have led to the development of some very successful and innovative staff development programs around the country. Before looking at some of these programs, a review of some of the other innovations that have occurred in the community college SD field will provide perspective.

NEW LEADERSHIP

New leadership and research emerged in the late 1970s and first half of this decade in the staff development movement. This leadership and research continue to provide direction and assistance to community college staff developers and staff development programs today.

An innovation in and of itself was the establishment of the National Council for Staff, Program, and Organization Development (NCSPOD). This national organization, which serves as the national network for over 500 community college staff developers, was formally organized in October of 1977. In January 1978 it was approved as an affiliate council of the American Association of Community and Junior Colleges. The purposes of this council are to:

1. foster staff, program, and organizational development activities in public and private two-year community, junior, and technical colleges;

2. develop innovative and effective approaches to staff, program, and organizational development;

3. generate means for staff development of persons interested in staff, program, and organizational development;

4. maintain communications among offices and organizations concerned with staff, program, and organizational development; and

5. foster research and evaluation in the field of staff, program, and organizational development (Lukenbill 1982, 10).

NCSPOD provides a wide range of services and opportunities, including a national newsletter, *Network;* a national conference held every fall; regional skill-building workshops; research and dissemination; a human resources referral directory; recognition for outstanding service; and assistance to state organizations. One of the real values of this organization has been its identification each year of model and innovative staff, program, and organizational development programs in the two-year college field. Each year NCSPOD has presented "Outstanding Program Awards" to some of the most innovative single- and multicampus staff development programs in the country. Some of the recent winners of these awards will be described later in this chapter.

New forms of leadership have also developed from a number of universities with community college leadership programs. At the University of Texas, under the direction of John Roueche, a National Institute for Staff and Organizational Development (NISOD) was created in 1978. NISOD is now a consortium of nearly 500 two-year colleges and universities which share a commitment to supporting teaching excellence in higher education. It is housed in the Community College Leadership Program at the University of Texas at Austin and offers an annual National Conference on Teaching Excellence and Conference of Administrators each May in Austin. NISOD staff also publish *Innovation Abstracts*, a practical guidesheet which offers tips on successful teaching and administrative practices from across the country and summaries of relevant, current research in this same area. Over 40,000 professionals are now weekly readers of this publication. Six annual issues of NISOD's newsletter, *Linkages*, provide members of this consortium with information regarding innovative programs, practices, and teaching techniques. Finally, NISOD provides a wide array of workshops and consulting services for two-year colleges committed to the concept of institutional development.

The Journal of Staff, Program, and Organization Development, a quarterly journal started in the Spring of 1983, provides some of the most current information and research on staff, program, and organization development programs in the country (Dollar 1987). This journal provides information about resource development and personnel practices that facilitate and support staff, program, or organizational development. Topics covered include: faculty and staff development, administrative development, administrator evaluation, personnel practices, part-time faculty development, instructional program evaluation, organization development, resource development, institutionalizing professional development, faculty evaluation, descriptions of award-winning staff development programs, organization development techniques, evaluating staff development programs, and legal aspects of personnel development and evaluation.

Leadership has also emerged at the state level in a number of cases. Starting with Florida, a number of state associations have been formed to provide leadership in the area of two-year college professional development programs. In 1975, the Florida Committee for Staff and Program Development was formed. Under the leadership of Roland Terrell, then Florida Junior College's Director of Staff, Program, and Organization Development, the Committee became the nucleus for the Florida Association for Staff and Program Development in 1976. This organization, along with similar associations in other states, continues to provide leadership at the state level through an annual conference and newsletter for colleges and staff developers.

INNOVATIVE MODELS

As mentioned earlier, the National Council For Staff, Program, and Organizational Development makes "Outstanding Program Awards" to colleges with particularly innovative and successful staff, program, and organizational development programs. In this section, some of the programs of the more recent recipients of these awards will be described. The purpose of these descriptions will be to highlight some of the more innovative staff development practices in community colleges today, both in small, medium, and large colleges.

MULTICAMPUS—EASTERN IOWA COMMUNITY COLLEGE DISTRICT, DAVENPORT, IOWA

The Eastern Iowa Community College District (EICCD) has a well-organized staff development program. Each of the three colleges in the district has its own staff development coordinator and plan. These activities are enhanced and coordinated by a District Staff Development Council. Council activities include a mentor program, technical updating grants, cooperative projects, an all-district workshop held once a year. Each college has an in-house grants program, computer- literacy program, and other activities unique to its institution.

In 1983–84, the Clinton campus of this district conducted 46 different staff development activities. These activities ranged from a "New Teachers Workshop" in August to "Part-time Faculty Orientation" in December to "A Staff Breakfast (for all)" in May. Similarly the Muscatine campus conducted 50 staff development activities in 1983–84 ranging from an "Administrative Off-Campus Retreat for Deans" in August to a "Wellness Program (all staff)" in February to a "Great Teachers Workshop" in May. During the same year on the Scott campus, activities ranged from "IBM-PC Classes" in November to "Juggling Life's Priorities" (all staff) in February to "Office Education" for all faculty in May. Clearly this is a college that is trying to meet in a variety of ways the needs of each and every staff member.

While the workshops and short-term programs at EICCD are pretty standard in colleges that have developed a comprehensive staff development program, some of the other programs are not. For example an innovative program at this college is its "Mentor Program." Under this program, a structured mentor relationship is developed that involves a contract to complete a project that addresses the career development of an employee and/or analyzed need of EICCD. Under this program the employee may apply as a candidate to: (1) investigate, through a special project, career paths compatible with his or her potential development needs and goals, (2) investigate job-related opportunities in other departments and areas of the college, or (3) pursue field experiences internally and/or externally that could enhance development in his or her career, that is, internal or external retraining. This particular program is an innovation that has not been tried to any great extent in two-year colleges, yet it would appear to be a needed program at a time when the demands for retraining of faculty are increasing.

Another more recent innovation on the Scott Community College campus of the EICCD is the "Floating Staff Development Day." Under this new program, all staff and faculty at the college are responsible for planning three Floating Staff Development Days. The guidelines for this program are as follows:

1. The activity must be considered beneficial to a department, work area, special interest group, , or individual in enhancing work performance, curriculum development, subject matter knowledge, and/or instructional delivery (i.e., professional development).

2. The Floating Staff Development Day (FSDD) proposal must be submitted and approved by the immediate supervisor and/or associate dean, if applicable, two weeks prior to the activity.

3. Expenses incurred for the activity must be approved in advance through the appropriate department, the Staff Development Committee, or obtained through a Project Improvement Grant.

4. An evaluation form for the activity must be submitted to the Staff Development Coordinator within two weeks of the date of the activity's completion. Each participant in a "group activity" must complete an evaluation form. (Baker 1987)

The Floating Staff Development Day is an innovative way of providing some flexibility for professional development experiences.

SINGLE CAMPUS—RANCHO SANTIAGO COLLEGE IN SANTA ANA, CALIFORNIA

In 1984–85 Rancho Santiago College (RSC) received the single-campus achievement award for an outstanding staff development program from NCSPOD. The objectives of the RSC Staff Development Program in that year were:

1. to provide opportunities for faculty to develop educational materials they can not normally complete as a part of their regular contractual obligation due to a lack of time and resources;

2. to provide opportunities for interaction between full-time and part-time faculty;

3. to provide intellectual renewal for faculty to be obtained by study, research, travel, work experience, or creative activity; and

4. to provide opportunities for professional development among both certificated and classified staff. (Mills 1987)

This set of objectives illustrates how important objectives are to a college's staff development efforts. These objectives clearly shaped the staff development programs at RSC for 1984–85. They also provided a more concrete basis for evaluation at the end of the academic year.

Rancho Santiago is another good example of a comprehensive staff development program. It includes a faculty committee of 27 members which surveys the faculty each year regarding their needs. This committee also identifies institutional goals for staff development each year. The flex calendar program at RSC allows all faculty to participate in staff development activities during the academic year in lieu of teaching. In recent years, as many as 19 staff development days have been scheduled, of which faculty have been able to select 13. Much of the work the staff does on flex days includes curriculum development, revision of courses, updating of skills in the high technology areas, independent research, on-site visits to business and industry as well as other campuses, and conferences between full-time and part-time staff. A comprehensive evaluation program is completed each year.

The newest and most innovative program at RSC is its "Profiles in Excellence Program." Started in May 1987, this program provides a publication from the Chancellor, honoring the most outstanding faculty and sharing their accomplishments with the rest of the faculty (Jensen 1987). In this very attractive program publication, 13 faculty are singled out for the following awards: (1) Annual Faculty Lecturer Award, (2) Curriculum Development Award, (3) Professional Achievement Awards, (4) Publications Awards, (5) Sabbatical Leave Award, and (6) Staff Development Awards. The rewarded faculty member's picture appears on one page of the publication along with a one-page description of his or her accomplishments for that year. This is a good example of how a college can use a nonmonetary reward for recognizing faculty contributions which also provides incentives for others who are involved in improvement activities.

MULTICAMPUS—JEFFERSON COMMUNITY COLLEGE, LOUISVILLE, KENTUCKY

One of the two most recent 1985–86 NCSPOD outstanding program awards was given to Jefferson Community College (JCC). What makes the JCC program unique is the diversity of workshops offered. The first part of the program is the *Faculty/Staff Development Program.* The Faculty/Staff Development Committee, in conjunction with the half-time Professional Development Coordinator, uses a needs assessment survey filled out by the faculty and staff to plan workshops, seminars, and conferences that the faculty and staff feel are necessary for their professional development. The workshops and conferences are presented by both internal and external people with the majority of the workshops being led by in-house faculty and staff. This has increased attendance because faculty and staff come to "share" with their peers.

In 1985–86, the Faculty/Staff Development Committee offered over 60 workshops, seminars, and conferences in five general areas. The areas were: teacher improvement, administrative concerns, intellectual development, physical and mental well-being, and classified staff concerns. Three classified staff members sit on the committee, and that year they helped plan such workshops as "Travel Forms," "Bulk Mailing Simplified," and an all-day conference on "Institutional Values." By offering different workshops and seminars two or three times a week, this college has achieved a very high participation rate in its staff development programs. Approximately 90 percent of the faculty and 96 percent of the staff attended at least one professional development sponsored program in 1985–86. What makes this program all the more amazing is that it is managed on an annual budget of less than $5,000.

A second part of the program is the Teacher Improvement Program (TIP). In this part of the program, a faculty member can request a TIP consultant to videotape and visit his or her classroom. The consultant then gives the faculty member advice to improve and reinforce teaching skills. Consultants are current faculty members who have been selected by the faculty for their outstanding teaching. The administration is not privy to any information about the TIP process.

Evaluation is an important component in JCC's professional development program. The primary evaluation used by Jefferson is a 15-question instrument distributed after each workshop and then sent to the coordinator. The evaluator completes the instrument, rating each question 1 to 5—5 being the highest. Questions such as these are asked: value of the conference to you, level of clarity of presentation, degree of usefulness of the information and techniques presented to your work setting, clarity of objectives of workshop, level of sufficiency of information presented. The evaluator also asks if the respondent would want the particular program repeated again next year. In 1985–86, all but one of the 60 workshops had an average evaluation score of 3 or above, and 46 of the workshops had scores of 4.5 or above. Another innovation, then, in this program is its emphasis on systematic evaluation, something not always found in two-year college staff development programs.

SINGLE CAMPUS—ELIZABETHTOWN COMMUNITY COLLEGE, ELIZABETHTOWN, KENTUCKY

An innovative aspect of this staff development program is its planning committee. The program, which began in 1975, modified its structure in 1985 to invite any employee who wished to join the planning group. This innovation encouraged over 30 people to participate in the planning meetings and resulted in 90 percent of the employees participating in the activities. This college received the 1985–86 NCSPOD outstanding single-campus program award.

Near the end of the 1986–87 academic year, a formal evaluation of the staff development program was distributed to all personnel. A key element in the success of this program has been the open committee. Such negative comments as "The administration controls the committee," "The same people always do the programs," and "I'm not interested in any of those topics" no longer appear. Follow-up sessions on programs have also been very effective. A follow-up on Myers-Briggs personality types reinforced what the committee had learned about recognizing and understanding differences. In looking at the college profiles on this type indicator, the committee found that the college staff had a large number of "introverted-sensing-feeling-judging" types (ISFJ), introverted feelers who had to deal with facts. The ability to deal with change was not this group's strong point. To try to combat some obvious communication problems related to a large number of staff with this type, the committee scheduled programs on stress awareness, causes of burnout, and conflict resolution. Here is another case where an innovative, multifaceted approach to evaluation is paying off for a college.

SINGLE CAMPUS—TRI-COUNTY TECHNICAL COLLEGE, PENDLETON, SOUTH CAROLINA

While Tri-County Technical College has not been a recent recipient of a NCSPOD award, it still provides a good illustration of another innovation in staff development programs in two-year colleges. That innovation is the preparation of a professional development plan for each faculty member in the college. A faculty member's development plan may include the following types of activities:

1. Membership in professional organizations. The college can reimburse a faculty or staff member up to $40 for professional dues.
2. Periodic review of professional literature. The Learning Resource Center and the ACCTION Consortium Resource Center subscribe to a large number of professional education journals and discipline-related journals which are available to faculty and staff.
3. Participation in workshops, conferences, seminars, and institutes sponsored by professional organizations, educational institutions, and industries.
4. Participation in on-campus in-service activities.
5. Return-to-industry/business through internships with industry/business.
6. Exemplary-site visits to other colleges, to industries using advanced technology, or to training sites for business and industry.
7. Participation in seminars in South Carolina Technical Innovative Centers.

8. Enrollment in courses for credit or no credit at Tri County Technical College through regular curriculum programs or Continuing Education.

9. Enrollment in courses for credit or no credit at other institutions.

10. Educational leave without pay for exchange programs, full-time internships in business/industry or at other institutions, or full-time college study.

11. Networking and peer group meetings to increase awareness of professional development or discipline-related developments.

12. Practice and application of upgraded or new skills on the job.

The college provides financial assistance within budget limitations and other assistance within the parameters of state policy toward an individual's development program.

This college has also used the DACUM (*Developing A Curriculum*) process as a very effective staff development and program development process at the college. The DACUM process is a modified brainstorming process, facilitated by an impartial third party. It has proven to be a low-cost, high-yield way of determining skill profiles for jobs, bringing together experienced people to identify job skills needed for intelligent curriculum planning. An *Implementation Manual* was developed by the Instructional Development Office at Tri-County to assist faculty in implementing the planning, managing, and evaluating (PEM) model for instructional programs (Watkins and McCombs 1984).

MULTICAMPUS—FLORIDA COMMUNITY COLLEGE AT JACKSONVILLE, FLORIDA

Some of the most numerous and varied innovations have come from two-year colleges that have had well-funded staff development programs. Florida Community College at Jacksonville (FCCJ) falls in this category.

Staff and Program Development (SPD) in the Human Resources Department at FCCJ has provided funds for eight major staff and program development activities. These programs are as follows:

1. *In-service Development Programs (IDPs).* In-service development programs are available to all college employees—administrators, full-time and part-time faculty, and full and part-time career employees. The programs are designed to assist employees in professional and human development while

in their present jobs and geared to helping develop new job skills and competencies to meet the growing educational needs of the college and the community. Most programs are offered during regular work hours and employees may attend them as part of their regular work activities.

2. *Graduate and Undergraduate Course Program.* Full-time and permanent part-time employees are eligible for course reimbursement not to exceed $960 per fiscal year in tuition fees only. Coursework may be either undergraduate or graduate level.

3. *Educational Leave Program.* Any full-time employee who has completed five years of satisfactory service is eligible for an educational leave of absence. Leave may be approved for up to 12 months. Employees will receive 70 percent of their base salary plus benefits for the number of days of their educational leave.

4. *Master's-Plus-Thirty Certification Program.* Faculty members are encouraged to upgrade their skills and competencies in their area of expertise or related areas. A master's-plus-thirty certification places faculty members in a higher-level classification and pay rank.

5. *Professional Development Travel Program.* Professional Development Travel supports the professional improvement of knowledge and skills of the college employee within his or her area of responsibility and includes transportation, lodging, meals, registration fees, and other related expenses.

6. *Program Development Projects.* Program development is limited to the evaluation and improvement of existing programs, including the design of evaluation instruments to establish bases for improvements as well as the designing of new programs. It is program initiation or improvement rather than maintenance or expansion of an existing program. Program development includes: researching, planning, designing, and evaluating; salary payment for staff; and purchasing of instructional equipment and supplies.

7. *Staff Exchanges.* Staff exchanges provide opportunities for professional and institutional growth by allowing college employees to exchange positions with individuals at other colleges for a period of one month to one year.

8. *Workshop Grant Program.* Full-time college employees are eligible to receive one workshop grant per fiscal year either within or outside of the district. Travel, lodging, meals, and registration fees can be funded, not to exceed $800. (Cotroneo 1987)

The 1988 fiscal year budget to support these programs amounted to $671,149. This is a good example of how important some colleges view their staff and program development activities. The purpose of staff development at FCCJ is to provide professional, career, and personal development support to all college employees.

SOUTH CAMPUS—MIAMI-DADE COMMUNITY COLLEGE, MIAMI, FLORIDA

The Faculty, Staff, and Program Development Office (FSPD) on the South Campus of Miami-Dade Community College (MDCC) is a part of the Division of Training and Development. This division is part of the staff of the campus Vice President's Office. The FSPD Office provides all faculty, administrators, and staff with consultation and assistance in planning in-service training, professional growth opportunities, and program development. The staff at the office includes the director, the coordinator of academic computing, a secretary, and a part-time clerk typist. The three major programs of this office are (1) Workshops/Seminars, (2) Travel Opportunities, and (3) New Technology Training. Many new and innovative approaches have developed out of this program.

One of the newest innovations, however, at MDCC is also housed in this Division of Training and Development. This program is the division's Center for Professional Development. For those colleges seeking ways to develop new ties between their faculties and business and industry in the 1990s, this center offers an excellent model to achieve such a goal. The center is designed to meet the educational and training needs of business, government, labor, and industry. Its primary goal is to link the college's resources with the needs of the public and private sectors and, through collaborative effort, offer flexible training programs which should provide productivity benefits for employers and career growth for employees. The center is responsible for developing and coordinating a broad range of educational programs in both credit and noncredit areas. Instructors for the modules in this program are the faculty from Miami-Dade Community College. The modules are designed in three-hour segments, or multiples thereof. Arrangements can be made by individuals or business or other groups in the community to take these modules one at a time or in a series. At the present time, the Miami-Dade faculty has developed modules in the following areas: (1) communication skills, (2) leadership/management, (3) preparing for change, (4) managing and utilizing conflict, (5) corporate wellness, (6) microcomputer institute, and (7) special seminars. Fees are established at a standard rate for each module and are dependent on the content and number of participants (Nock 1987).

RESEARCH ON STAFF DEVELOPMENT

One of the first research studies or critiques of community college staff development programs came from Centra (1976). Of the 721 two-year colleges that responded to his initial survey, 456, or 63 percent, indicated that their institution had an organized program or set of practices for faculty development and improving instruction. Three years later in 1979, Smith (1980) surveyed all 1,315 two- year colleges to determine the nature and effectiveness of some staff development programs in two-year colleges. In his survey, 687 colleges responded and 413, or 60 percent indicated they had a staff development program. Assuming that the nonrespondents did not have an organized program or set of practices in these two studies, one can see that there was still room for growth and expansion in at least 40 percent of the nation's two-year colleges in the late 1970s.

Smith (1980) found that the following staff development practices in two-year colleges were considered to be the most effective activities by the directors of SD programs:

1. travel funds available to attend professional meetings;
2. use of grants by faculty members for developing new or different approaches to courses or teaching;
3. summer grants for projects to improve instruction or courses;
4. faculty visitations to other institutions (or to other parts of the home institution) to review educational programs or innovative projects;
5. travel grants to refresh or update knowledge in a particular field; and
6. specialists on campus to assist faculty in use of audiovisual aids in instruction including closed-circuit television.

Smith also discovered that 56 percent of the colleges responding to his survey reported having a unit or person responsible for staff development. This reflected an increase from a 49 percent figure found in Centra's review of two-year colleges. It would appear that in the 1970s some progress had been made on the "institutionalization" of staff development programs in community colleges.

Some concerns expressed in Smith's study were in the areas of staff involvement, funding, and evaluation. He found that a higher proportion of his responding colleges were reporting declines in funding for staff development as compared with the respondents in Centra's 1976 study. Also, he discovered that fairly large proportions of certain two-year college staff were described as having "very few" individuals involved in development activities. These groups were part-time faculty, clerical staff, and other nonacademic staff. Finally, both Smith and Centra found that a large proportion of the colleges with programs were not evaluating their efforts. Both studies found that 42 percent of the responding two-year institutions had not evaluated their staff development programs or activities.

A number of studies of two-year college staff development programs have been conducted in the 1980s. These studies shed additional light on the nature of two-year college staff development programs and some of the problems and concerns they are facing. First, Hausen (1983) surveyed the chief academic officer of each of the 52 community college campuses in Illinois. In this study he concluded that the traditional in-service type of SD activities may not be the "one best way" to deliver faculty development programs that have as their major goal the improvement of teaching. He feels that the frequently used workshop/seminar approach is often weak because it is constructed in general terms and usually only meets the needs of a few instructors. Hausen argues for more personalized, individualized staff development services for community college faculty, that is, more one-on-one discussions, more opportunities for faculty initiative in designing courses, and more reallocation of funds to support advanced graduate study and faculty attendance at professional meetings. Finally, Hausen found that a disproportionate number of institutions were relying entirely or very heavily on verbal feedback and questionnaires as their only source of information for evaluating activities, verifying the effectiveness of current programs, and planning for future activities. He recommends that staff development directors and colleges design and use more creative and imaginative evaluation techniques that go beyond the recording of participant reactions and the simple counting of participants.

A follow-up of Hausen's study was conducted in Texas in the Fall of 1985 (Richardson and Moor 1987). The purpose of this study was to determine the status of faculty development activities in Texas community colleges. Responses were received from 56 of the 62 two-year colleges in Texas for a response rate of 90 percent. Of the 56 questionnaires returned, only 4 (7%) reported not having a staff or faculty development program. Of the 52 colleges with some type of activity, 93 percent indicated they had some form of "organized" faculty development activities. This study clearly showed that at least one state has a higher percentage of two-year colleges involved in faculty development activities than Centra (1976) or Smith (1980) found in their previous studies. If this trend has occurred in other states, then one might conclude that the community college movement is reaching a point where there may be a formally organized staff development program on every community college campus in the near future. The data gathered in this study also revealed that most programs were group as opposed to individually oriented and were perceived as effective. However, in this research Richardson and Moore conclude that there is little evidence that SD programs are "being used as a major instrument for institutional change and improvement that is linked to the accomplishment of college goals and the establishment of accountability" (1987, 29). These investigators go on to conclude that development activities in Texas seem to be "mixed" in traditional "hit-or-miss" schemes that are evaluated primarily on the basis of audience reaction. In this respect, their findings confirm the continuing concern in this field that there is a need for evaluation plans that will show a more direct link between staff development programs and activities and student or faculty/staff change and development.

Richardson and Moore (1987) also reported that the activities offered by more than 10 Texas colleges that were perceived by most program directors as the most useful were all-day workshops for full-time faculty, personal enrichment programs, multisession workshops, and released time to develop instructional projects. Interestingly enough, on-campus activities were perceived by the respondents to be more useful than off-campus activities. The most commonly employed approaches for evaluation activities were verbal feedback, open-ended written statements, and questionnaires. Pre-test/post-test activity, testing of student outcomes, and colleague or administrator classroom observations were seldom used. This research documents the wide range of staff development activities found in Texas community colleges today. It becomes clear from reading this and other research studies that there is not "one best way" to organize a staff development program. However, this lack of consensus may be due to the relative newness of this innovation and apparent lack to date of effective evaluation of programs that are being offered.

One of the most valuable studies on professional development activities of community college faculty was conducted by Miller and Ratcliff (1986). These researchers analyzed the self-reported behavior of faculty with regard to their involvement in faculty development activities. Most previous studies have included only the program director's views on faculty involvement and the effectiveness of selected development practices. In this study, the influence of selected variables on the hours of faculty participation in development activities was assessed using a stratified random sample of 187 full-time Arts and Sciences and Vocational-Technical faculty in 15 Iowa community colleges. Miller and Ratcliff found that faculty with doctoral degrees reported the greatest number of hours spent in professional development activities. Faculty with high school diplomas participated the least. Most of the other variables such as the teaching field of the faculty member, the faculty member's total years of teaching experience, and whether or not the faculty member paid for the development activities out of his or her own pocket were variables found not to be associated with the level of participation in faculty development activities.

What Miller and Ratcliff (1986) found that should be particularly useful to staff developers was that on the average, individual faculty spent 161 hours in development activities over a year's time. A significant portion of those hours were outside normal working time and were personally financed. This is an impressive statistic, particularly if it can be validated for community college faculty in other institutions. If faculty are indeed putting this much time into their own personal development activities, then there is potential for great change and impact both at a personal and organizational level.

With the exception of enrollment in coursework and special projects, however, faculty participation in single SD activities averaged fewer than seven hours. Therefore this investigation found that most faculty development activities were of "insufficient duration" to constitute an adult learning project. Current college efforts to promote the greater use of computers and/or other instructional technology, reform in the quality of educational programs, or the development of high technology programs may require a more substantial devotion of an individual's time to learning skills than staff development programs have provided. The findings of this study suggest that a greater devotion of time to single development activities may prove more beneficial to faculty and to college renewal than encouraging faculty to participate in a variety of different short-term activities.

The investigators also offer some new ideas for evaluating staff development programs. They recommend that colleges consider finding out how faculty are using their development time both inside and outside the college's normal working hours. Their findings that faculty tended not to choose activities that lead to salary increases or advancement also have implications for how an institution might reward or promote more faculty development activity. If faculty are willing to pay some of the cost of their development, then programs may not become all that more expensive to operate.

SPECIAL PROBLEMS

At least three major problems seem to have developed in the field of community college staff development over the last 15 to 20 years. The first problem relates to whether or not colleges should focus on faculty or personal development, instructional development, or organization development. The innovations reviewed earlier in this chapter show that the best approach to staff development is a varied one, an approach that allows for programs in all three of these areas. The emphasis a program gives to any one of these areas will depend on the needs of the college and its staff at any given time. It does appear, however, that in the next decade the emphasis will need to be more on organization development activities than it has been in the past. As colleges reexamine their missions and decide on a new or revised course to follow in the 1990s, staff development funds and staff time will be needed to help the college move in new directions. There will have to be a closer match between college goals and staff development goals than has been true in the past.

A second problem exists in the area of the relationship between faculty development and faculty evaluation. Should faculty evaluation and faculty development be organized as one program, or should they be viewed as two separate programs? Certainly at the college-wide level it is desirable to separate the two programs, with the dean or vice-president responsible for both programs. However, at the division or department level, the department head or chair must perform both responsibilities. The problem has been that most chairs have focused on their evaluation role rather than their faculty development role.

The University of Florida's National Faculty Evaluation Project for Two-Year Colleges, offered through its Institute of Higher Education from 1980 to 1986, demonstrated that colleges could revise their staff evaluation procedures and strengthen their staff development efforts at the same time. In the case of this particular project, 12 two-year colleges found that, in order to have an effective staff development program, a college first needed to assess carefully the strengths and weaknesses of its staff. With this type of data, the colleges were then able to expand and strengthen their staff development efforts at both the college and department levels.

The third major problem facing the staff development movement in two-year colleges is in the area of program evaluation. This is the most frequently mentioned problem in community college staff development programs today. To date, most of the evaluation of staff development programs has been done by participant questionnaires. Evaluation of these programs in the future must focus more on the achievement of specific staff development goals and objectives and on program outcomes. Directors of staff development programs have not usually been trained in the area of evaluation techniques and strategies. Instead, they and their advisory committees have tended to focus on program development as opposed to program evaluation.

Now is the time to assess the impact of their innovations in terms of changes in faculty, staff, or student behavior or in terms of organizational changes in the colleges. The question now is, "Which of the many staff development programs has had the greatest or most favorable impact on staff, organizations, and students?" In seeking answers to this question in the 1990s, staff development directors will probably want to turn to other administrators, directors of institutional research offices, and universities for assistance in developing appropriate evaluation models and techniques.

SOME SUGGESTIONS FOR THE FUTURE

Tremendous innovation has occurred in community college staff development programs over the last two decades. This innovation has helped to maintain the two-year college as a growing and vital segment in American higher education during a time of declining resources, stabilizing enrollments, and rapid technological change. College presidents, boards of trustees, deans, department chairs, faculty and nonacademic support staff have come to realize the importance of this innovation to the survival and growth of the two-year college. Continued innovation and support of staff development is most important if problems facing the two-year college today and in the future are to be appropriately addressed.

At a workshop on staff development prior to the 1986 AACJC annual meeting, two-year college presidents, SPOD practitioners, and pioneers in the staff development movement met to discuss "what should be the priorities of institutional staff, program, and organizational development during the next five years?" Their responses provide a good set of guidelines for improving staff development programs. These responses were:

1. Expand focus on total organizational development.
2. Involve CEOs and other major managers in the design and development of SPOD programs.
3. Provide support and leadership for institutional management development programs.
4. Provide incentives for innovation and entrepreneurial activities.
5. Educate faculty and staff as change-agents and organizational developers.
6. Promote student success through SPOD programs.
7. Promote commitment to community college philosophy by all faculty and staff.
8. Develop programs that emphasize individualized, personal, and professional development activities.

9. Develop internal and external accountability measures for "service" programs.

10. Provide leadership in coping with managing and shaping change (in cooperation with management). (Betts 1987).

The community college that attempts to implement these guidelines should be successful in its staff development efforts over the next five to ten years.

There is perhaps one additional priority that colleges should set for their staff development programs in the 1990s. Colleges must focus on the development of the whole staff member. The focus must be on the staff member's cognitive, affective, and physical development, not only on the cognitive. Much of the staff development movement to date has focused on cognitive or skill development of staff members, particularly in relationship to the teaching function. For growth to occur in individuals and organizations of the future, the staff development movement will have to expand its services to meet the multifaceted professional and personal needs of staff members.

It is unlikely that colleges can expect students to develop new knowledge, skills, values, and attitudes if the same development is not occurring in its staff. Perhaps education has focused too much on the development of the "whole" student in the past few decades and not enough on the development of the "whole" faculty or staff member. Certainly a broader view of staff development, similar to this one, is needed if staff development programs are to continue as the lifeblood of the of the community college movement.

REFERENCES

BAKER, J. 1987. "Floating Staff Development Day: Guidelines." Scott Community College: Davenport, Iowa.

BETTS, L.J. 1987. "Revitalizing Our Colleges Through SPOD." *Journal of Staff, Program, and Organizational Development* 5 (Spring):19–20.

Center for Education Statistics. 1987. *Trends in Education, 1975–76 to 1995–96.* Washington, D.C.: Office of Educational Research and Improvement, U.S. Department of Education, March.

CENTRA, J. 1976. *Faculty Development Practices in U.S. Colleges and Universities.* Princeton, N.J.: Educational Testing Service, November.

COHEN, A.M. ed. 1973. *Toward a Professional Faculty.* New Directions for Community Colleges Series, no. 1. San Francisco: Jossey-Bass. (Spring).

COTRONEO, K. 1987. *Staff and Program Development* (SPD). Jacksonville, Fl.: Florida Community College-Jacksonville.

DOLLAR, D. 1987."A Letter From the New Editor." *Journal of Staff, Program, and Organizational Development* 5, no. 1 (Spring):3–4.

GAFF, J.G. 1975. *Toward Faculty Renewal.* San Francisco: Jossey-Bass.

Group for Human Development in Higher Education. 1974. *Faculty Development in a Time of Retrenchment.* New Rochelle, NY: *Change Magazine.*

HAMMONS, J.; T. H. WALLACE-SMITH; and G. WATTS. 1978. *Staff Development in the Community College: A Handbook.* Topical paper no. 66. Los Angeles: ERIC Clearinghouse for Junior Colleges, June.

HAUSEN, D.W. 1983. "Faculty Development Activities in Illinois Community College System." *Community/Junior College Quarterly* 7 (April/June):207–230.

JENSEN, R.D. 1987. *Profiles in Excellence.* Santa Ana, Calif.: Rancho Santiago Community College District, May.

KASTNER, H.H., JR. 1973. "A System-Wide Approach." *Community and Junior College Journal* 44, no. 3 (November):14–15.

LUKENBILL, M. 1982. "Outlook: National Council for Staff, Program, and Organizational Development." *Community and Junior College Journal* 52, no. 6 (March):10

MILLER, D.J. and J. L. RATCLIFF. 1986. "Analysis of Professional Development Activities of Iowa Community College Faculty." *Community/Junior College Quarterly* 10, no. 4:317–43.

MILLS, B. J. 1987. Personal correspondence, August 26

NOCK, M. 1987. *Organization Development Series.* Miami, Fl.: Center for Professional Development, Miami-Dade Community College, South Campus.

O'BANION, T. 1972. *Teachers for Tomorrow: Staff Development Programs in the Community Junior College.* Tuscon: University of Arizona Press.

———. 1978. *Organizing Staff Development Programs That Work.* Washington, D.C.: American Association of Community and Junior Colleges.

RICHARDSON, R. and W. MOORE. 1987. "Faculty Development and Evaluation in Texas Community Colleges." *Community/Junior College Quarterly* 11:19–32.

SMITH, A. 1980. *Staff Development Practices in U.S. Community Colleges.* Lexington, Ky.: Publications Commission, AACJC National Council for Staff, Program, and Organizational Development (NCSPOD), January.

WATKINS, B., and C. McCOMBS. 1984. *Implementation Manual.* Pendleton, S.C.: Tri-County Technical College, March.

YARRINGTON, R. (ed.) 1974. *New Staff for New Students: Educational Opportunity for All.* Washington, D.C.: American Association of Community and Junior Colleges.

10

Entrepreneurial Management

A FOURTH CONCEPT OF COLLEGE MANAGEMENT FOR THE DECADE AHEAD

William L. Deegan

American community colleges enroll over one-third of the total enrollment in higher education. The over 1,200 community colleges have enjoyed an 85 year history of enormous growth and development. The period from the late 1950s to the mid-1970s was a period of special growth when bigger was often equated with better. Colleges grew in size; some community colleges districts became "multicampus"; and organizational units within colleges became larger. Most of what was undertaken in community colleges during that period was a result of governance and management models that were some combination of collegial, political, and bureaucratic. The bureaucratic model (Merton 1963) is based on principles of rationality and involves such concepts as hierarchical structure, formal communication and authority systems, and avoidance of conflict. The collegial model (Millett 1962) is based on the concept of a community of scholars, which suggests that consensus and participation, rather than hierarchy and authority, are the guiding principles for decision making and policy formulation. The political model (Baldridge 1971) assumes conflict as a factor at the heart of decision making; decisions are made in a context that is neither hierarchical nor collegial, but rather one in which conflict is normal as different interest groups compete to influence decisions and policies. Decisions are arrived at through negotiation and compromise.

Despite the literature, in reality, colleges involve aspects of all these general models. Some observers feel that colleges are best understood when viewed as "organized anarchies" (Cohen and March 1974). The unique organizational characteristics of colleges and universities as "organized anarchies" consist of ambiguous and diverse goals, unclear organization processes, and fluid participation by decision makers who wander in and out of the decision-making process. According to Cohen and March, "The American college or university is a prototypic organized anarchy. It does not know what it is doing" (1974, 3).

Challenges to the comprehensive mission of community colleges, issues of student and staff development, demands of a rapidly changing society, and projected fiscal problems of the decade ahead all call for the development of effective mechanisms to facilitate governance and management processes. Rather than accepting the inevitability of an organized anarchy, there is a need to develop more effective frameworks and concepts that can assist leaders in the difficult period ahead.

A fourth concept of management and leadership is now emerging in many community colleges—entrepreneurship. Entrepreneurship has enjoyed a resurgence in American society generally, from large corporations to small individual businesses. In the business sector, new business creations are reflecting an entrepreneurial explosion. Americans were creating new businesses at the rate of 93,000 per year in 1950. Today 700,000 new businesses are created annually. The entrepreneurial spirit has also spilled over into the public service sector and is reflected in a growing number of proposals and calls for the use of more entrepreneurial activities as a supplement to other processes. As Peter Drucker writes: "The need for innovation and entrepreneurship is clear. Public service institutions now have to learn how to build those qualities into their own systems" (1985, 186).

During the past few years, primarily because of changing fiscal and demographic circumstances, there has been a growing interest in supplementing community college collegial, political, and bureaucratic processes with some entrepreneurial and intrepreneurial approaches to solving problems and creating opportunities. Entrepreneurial activities are defined as those that help generate resources (such as contract training programs with corporations or the creation of private foundations to raise funds). Intrepreneurial activities (see Pinchot 1985) are activities that help reduce costs or increase productivity within the organization. But, while the interest in entrepreneurship has gained great acceptance in American society generally, the term "entrepreneur" remains controversial in education.

Advocates claim that the concept can lead to programs that will help generate resources from external sources while benefiting the community and the college, and it can also lead to programs that can help reduce costs and improve quality and productivity internally. Opponents warn of the danger of leading the college into the wrong kinds of programs, of the potential for divisiveness, and of the potential to change community college value systems in ways that might have negative long-term consequences. In view of these challenges, the objectives of this chapter are to review a number of emerging forces and trends that will influence the future of community colleges, to review the concept of entrepreneurship in theory, and to present research findings about, and suggest guidelines for, the use of entrepreneurial management concepts in community colleges.

THE NEW TERRAIN OF HIGHER EDUCATION

America has just emerged from two decades of social ferment which have had profound influence on the course of development in society generally and on education in particular. In the 1960s, the dominant themes were freedom and participation, and these themes brought about major value shifts in American society and in education. There were significant changes in curriculum, in faculty and student participation in governance, and a general opening-up of American society and its values.

In the 1970s, the predominant theme became accountability, and American society again shifted. There were increased governmental reviews of programs and passage of taxpayer initiatives such as Proposition 13 in California. General disillusionment occurred as educational institutions foundered and corporations lost ground to international competition.

Now, in the 1980s, the dominant themes of quality and productivity will set a new climate for much of the foreseeable future. The emergence of these themes is abundantly clear in both the renewed emphasis on standards in education and the advertising campaigns of major corporations. In addition to these general themes, there are a number of specific issues emerging which will have significant implications for American higher education in the decade ahead. These issues include the following.

INCREASING COMPETITION WITHIN HIGHER EDUCATION. Competition has not been absent from American higher education in the past, but competition among colleges has begun to intensify and will increase significantly in the period ahead, requiring new campus modes of operation and management. Competition will increase for students and faculty among all segments of higher education. The military and other providers of education and training, such as corporations and other nonprofit educational providers, will also compete for students and faculty.

FUNDING AND MANAGING TECHNOLOGICAL DEVELOPMENTS. The rapid growth of electronic technology in the past two decades presents colleges with the first major transformation in the transmission and storage of ideas and information since the introduction of printing. It is a development requiring rethinking of nearly every aspect of higher education. Community colleges need to keep up more effectively with new technology and delivery systems, but some faculty resistance, scarce resources, and aging facilities will make this even more difficult in the decade ahead. A recent survey in California found that 67% of the equipment used in occupational education was "somewhat or seriously" out of date (Chancellor's Office 1985). Colleges cannot produce the best students without qualified teachers and state-of-the-art equipment, and they must develop new linkages and consortia to help meet the demands and the cost of technology in the decade ahead.

CHANGING STUDENT CLIENTELE. American campuses face a demographic revolution. Not only will there be one million fewer 18-year-olds in 1994 than there were in 1979; the composition of the 18-year-old cohort will be quite different. There will be fewer white students and more blacks because white births have dropped sharply since 1960. There will be many more Hispanic students, and there will be a much larger number of Asians.

In addition to the change in students' ethnic backgrounds, a second major change is in the age of those enrolled. Not too long ago, nearly all students in American colleges and universities were between the ages of 17 and 24. In 1979, the National Center for Education Statistics estimated that 36 percent of the students were 25 years old or older. That same center now projects that 49 percent of all students will be over 25 in 1993, and that large numbers of these students will prefer to attend college on a part-time basis. These changes in student age, background, and attendance patterns will present profound challenges to colleges in the decade ahead—challenges that will require new programs and management skills.

INCREASING FACULTY SHORTAGES. College faculties are getting older, and fewer new members are being hired as higher education cuts back. But, while there is currently a surplus of teachers in many areas, toward the end of the decade ahead large numbers of faculty will retire. For example, in California in 1983, close to 40 percent of the full-time faculty were 50 or older and 21 percent were over 55. A large percentage of faculty will have to be replaced over the next ten years, and colleges need to plan for that now through more attention to staffing patterns, staff development, and new roles and the use of technology.

GROWING STATE CONTROL. As Keller (1983) has written, state budget officials, the courts, Federal legislation and guidelines, and new state agencies of higher education have become much more active in trying to manage colleges and universities. Over 70 percent of all public institutions now cannot start a new academic program without elaborate application and approval procedures from their state coordinating boards. To some extent the new restraints are proper. Some colleges have been slow in accepting full racial and sexual equality. Others have tolerated poor fiscal management or unrealistic and expensive academic ambitions. But just as often the restraints derive from zealous government officials for political reasons. They have often been overly ambitious. If educational institutions are to reverse, or at least slow down, the trend toward outside interventions in their affairs in the decade ahead, they must shape their own destinies in ways that are acceptable to the public and its elected leaders. This will require greater management skill and creativity as new demands and issues clash with a relative scarcity of resources.

COMMUNITY COLLEGE ISSUES

In addition to the issues bearing on American society and higher education in general, a number of trends are emerging that have implications which will influence the future of community colleges in particular (Deegan and Tillery 1985). These trends include the following:

1. The emphasis of community colleges will shift from providing access to one of a greater emphasis on improving quality and productivity. These themes will dominate funding, planning, and evaluation by outside agencies.
2. Regional and community variations in demography, economics, and occupational characteristics will become even more pronounced. Consequently, community colleges, whether in

state systems or under local control, will need to offer programs and services that fit the needs of their local communities. This need will conflict with state agency needs for conformity.

3. Adults will have increasing needs for recurring education. Among the implications for community colleges is the fact that most suppliers of education will respond to adult needs for occupational retraining, academic remediation, and life-long learning. This competition will require the colleges to offer cost-effective programs falling within their mission and with verifiable learner outcomes.

4. New information and learning technologies will change why, how, and where people learn. As a result, much more formal learning will take place outside traditional educational institutions—in industry, the military, community agencies, and through the media. Community colleges, therefore, will need to redesign their curricula and methods of instruction. They must be much more effective in assessing the prior preparation of entering students, placing them in appropriate courses of study, and measuring learning outcomes. Faculty training in the new technologies of learning and instruction will be essential.

5. The American economy, in spite of fluctuations, will be strong enough to provide resources for the improvement and expansion of education. However, competition from other social institutions does not ensure increased funds from either federal or state governments. This means that competition for both public and private resources will demand greater public accountability as a result of good institutional planning, efficient management, and clear evidence of achieving college objectives.

6. Aging facilities and equipment will become an increasing problem in providing education of high quality. This trend will be exacerbated by needs for new technologies for management and instruction. Regional cooperation among the colleges and with high-technology industries will be essential for access to state-of-the-art equipment and facilities in some areas of instruction and management. Furthermore, state appropriations for maintaining the infrastructure of the colleges will be based on evidence of efficient management and public accountability.

All these issues point to the need for more creativity and management effectiveness than has been the case in the past. New demands for services, a changing clientele, and new competition from other educational providers may require more entrepreneurial management strategies to complement collegial, bureaucratic, and political processes. The next section of this chapter will briefly review the concept of entrepreneurial management and offer a synthesis of thought that begins to constitute a theory of entrepreneurship for colleges.

ENTREPRENEURSHIP IN THEORY

A number of writers have proposed that entrepreneurship will be a dominant management concept in the decade ahead. Peter Drucker (1985) has said that ideas need champions, and George Keller (1983) has written that the best-laid plans go to waste without entrepreneurial leadership. A good deal of the current literature on organizations emphasizes the importance of unleashing the power of entrepreneurship to solve problems.

American institutions may be coming to the end of a 25-year trend toward building bigger organizations. A movement is underway to "deinstitutionalize" America—both in the creation of smaller and more specialized businesses and in the search for ways to incorporate entrepreneurship in larger ones. Entrepreneurial management for large organizations is a concept in its infancy. While no generally accepted theory of entrepreneurial management in large organizations exists, a number of concepts are emerging which constitute a basis for building a theory of entrepreneurship for large organizations. First among these is focusing managerial vision on opportunity. Managers tend to see what is presented to them; what is not presented tends to be overlooked. What is usually presented to most managers are "problems," especially in the areas where performance falls below expectations, which means that managers often tend not to see the opportunities.

A fundamental basis of entrepreneurial management is the need to create a proper climate, or organizational culture, conducive to developing an awareness of opportunities for entrepreneurship. This means attention to organizational structure, funding, rewards and incentives, and the proper balance between control and freedom. Drucker (1985) suggests that once decisions are made to encourage entrepreneurial management, a key first step is to build a systematic search for sources of opportunity. He sees seven sources of opportunity:

The first four sources lie within the enterprise, whether business or public service institutions. These four sources are:

- the unexpected—the unexpected success, the unexpected failure, the unexpected outside event;

- the incongruity—between reality as it actually is and reality as it is assumed to be or as it "ought to be";
- innovation based on process need; and
- changes in industry structure or market structure that catch everyone unaware.

The second set of sources for innovative opportunity involves changes outside the enterprise or industry:

- demographics (population changes);
- changes in perception, mood, and meaning; and
- new knowledge, both scientific and nonscientific.

So building an organizational climate and an active awareness of, and search for, opportunities are critical first steps in the development of entrepreneurship in colleges.

A second key concept is that entrepreneurial activities, as much as possible, should be organized separately. Policies, practices, and measurements make possible entrepreneurship and innovation. They remove or reduce possible impediments, and they create the proper attitude and provide the proper tools. But innovation is done by people, and people work within a structure. For an organization to be capable of innovation, it has to create a structure that allows people to be entrepreneurial. It has to devise relationships that center on entrepreneurship, and it has to make sure that its rewards and incentives, personnel decisions, and policies all reward the right entrepreneurial behavior and do not penalize it. This means that the entrepreneurial, the new, has to be organized separately from the old and existing. It also means that someone in the top levels of administration should be responsible for providing support and guidance for entrepreneurial initiatives in order to break down barriers and ensure a fair chance for new ventures.

A third concept essential to promoting entrepreneurship is the creation of a "venture capital" fund. Colleges should set aside a small percentage of their budgets (even if it means small cuts in some area budgets) to provide seed money for new ideas. Colleges often talk about developing new ideas, but it is surprising how few have been willing to provide even small amounts of seed money to help get projects translated from theory into actions. Colleges need to consider the place and priority of entrepreneurial projects within the total college plan as well as the kinds of "risk capital" that the college is willing to allocate to support these programs during the early stages when costs exceed returns. Agreement on target results expected after one, three, and five years (and provision of adequate resources to meet those targets) will help in the development and management of effective entrepreneurial programs, and it will also foster a critical analysis of the role these programs will play in the future of the college.

Related to the concept of a venture capital fund is a fourth concept—the need to consider what rewards and incentives will be provided to encourage and motivate staff to undertake new initiatives. This is a complex issue because the college does not want to encourage a rash of wild initiatives or reward people for failure, but neither does it want to penalize them or discourage them from trying. Each college will need to develop policies on rewards and compensation based on its unique traditions and culture, but the development of such policies is a key ingredient for a successful entrepreneurial program.

A fifth key concept to help encourage entrepreneurship is a long-term emphasis. Too often, projects are not given a fair chance to develop. The American "quick fix" often does not permit much time to pass before new projects are discarded. As with the venture capital fund, clarifications and agreement on project objectives and results to be expected after specified periods of time will help prevent unsuccessful projects from continuing, and it will also allow new projects sufficient development time to demonstrate their value to the long-term interests of the college.

A final concept is the need to ensure that projects are systematically evaluated. Too often innovation and entrepreneurship are described only on the "up" side—that is, as projects are developing. Educators need to hear more about what works, what did not work, and why. There is much to be gained from sharing information about both successes and failures, and colleges should develop systematic evaluation programs to ensure that people learn from the past to help improve the future.

While there is no absolutely agreed-upon theory of entrepreneurship in large organizations, a review of the literature indicates that the development of an organizational climate, an active search for opportunities, a separate organizational structure, a venture capital fund, an agreement on rewards and incentives, a long-term emphasis, and a systematic evaluation program are key concepts in helping to ensure the success of an entrepreneurial program. The final section of this chapter will examine the use and impact of these concepts (and others) in community colleges.

ENTREPRENEURIAL MANAGEMENT IN COMMUNITY COLLEGES

Community colleges will need to be much more entrepreneurial and innovative in the decade ahead. The rapid changes in today's society, technology, and economy will present greater problems, opportunities, and competition.

But public service institutions, such as community colleges, often find it more difficult to innovate than many "bureaucratic" companies. Resistance to change may be even more of an obstacle in service institutions. Every service institution likes to get bigger, and, in the absence of a profit test, size and growth often become the criteria of success. Stopping what has "always been done" and doing something new are both difficult for these kinds of institutions. There are several barriers to innovation and entrepreneurship in public service institutions in general, and community college administrators should recognize them before starting new programs or projects. Drucker (1985) identifies three critical barriers that proponents of entrepreneurial management should consider before taking action. First, the public service institution is based on a budget and not paid for results; moreover, it is paid for its efforts out of funds somebody else has earned. The more efforts the public service institution engages in, the greater its budget will be. Success in the public service institution is often defined by building a larger budget rather than obtaining results, and efforts to reform policies and practices may take a back seat to the politics of bureaucracy.

A second barrier to implementing entrepreneurial management practices is that a service institution is dependent on a multitude of constituents. In a business that sells its products on the market, one constituent, the consumer, eventually overrides all the others. A public service institution has to satisfy everyone; it cannot afford to alienate anyone. The moment a service institution starts an activity, it acquires a "constituency," which then usually refuses to have the program abolished or even significantly modified. But anything new, such as entrepreneurial projects, is always controversial. This means that new enterprises are often opposed by existing constituencies before the new ventures have formed a constituency of their own.

A final barrier is that staff of many public service institutions tend to see their mission as "doing good works" which they often view as not subject to improvement, reductions in cost, or understanding and analysis by anyone but themselves.

Given these barriers and the increasing interest in entrepreneurship in society in general, a survey of entrepreneurial management practices in community colleges was developed and mailed to a random sample of 400 community college presidents as part of a larger study of the use and perceived impact of various management concepts. The survey was conducted in Spring 1987, with funds provided through the Institute for Studies in Higher Education at Florida State University. Returns were received from 105 community college presidents (26.2%). The colleges were generally representative of community colleges nationally in terms of enrollment and geographic distribution.

The study had two objectives: to try to develop some baseline data on the kinds of management concepts being used in community colleges, and to try to gain insights about the impact of the various management concepts as perceived by community college presidents. The presidents were asked to respond to a checklist of management concepts organized around the functions of planning, organizing, budgeting, staffing, and evaluating. They also had the opportunity to write in responses or concepts not included in the checklist. The baseline data gathered in this study will be used to develop case studies of selected institutions as a second part of this project.

Table 10.1 shows the kinds and the range of use of the entrepreneurial concepts identified in the study.

Eighteen concepts were identified as entrepreneurial—either primarily designed to generate funds from external sources or to re-

Table 10.1
A FRAMEWORK OF ENTREPRENEURIAL CONCEPTS

	Percent of Community Colleges
I) Most Used (> 66%)	
1. Creating a college foundation	76
2. Strategic planning (institution-wide)	72
3. Establishing a contract training program	68
4. Using of business leaders as a primary planning advisory group	67
II) Used (> 32%)	
5. Creating a special unit/facilitator for innovation and entrepreneurship	46
6. Creating a special fund for internal innovation	45
7. Creating new reward systems to encourage staff initiative	41
8. Creating futures task forces (college)	40
9. Contracting with vendors from outside the college	38
10. Strategic planning (departments)	33
11. Creating a merit pay system	40
III) Used in 20–30%	
12. Hiring more staff to write grants on a full-time basis	26
13. Creating futures task forces (departments)	26
IV) 19% or less	
14. Using matrix organization (college-wide)	18
15. Rotating jobs (within units)	13
16. Quality circles	11
17. Using matrix organization (within units)	8
18. Rotating jobs (between units)	7

duce costs and increase productivity within the college. The data clustered into four categories. The most used entrepreneurial concepts were: creating a college foundation, strategic planning (institution-wide), establishing a contract training program, and using business leaders as a primary planning advisory group. Three of these four concepts are primarily geared toward raising funds, while the fourth, strategic planning, is geared toward generating a more focused institutional direction both internally and externally.

The second, third, and fourth levels of use of entrepreneurial concepts shown in Table 10.1 consist of concepts primarily focused on internal activities, with the exceptions of contracting with vendors from outside the college, hiring more staff to write grants, and some of the activities of futures task forces.

It is interesting to note that the top three internal entrepreneurial activities—creating a special unit or facilitator for innovation and entrepreneurship, creating a special fund for internal innovation, and creating new reward systems to encourage staff initiative—are concepts highly recommended in the literature about entrepreneurial management. The least used concepts—matrix organization, job rotation, and quality circles—all have been highly touted in recent literature about Japanese management theory.

One of the interesting questions that these data suggest concerns the gap between the amount of strategic planning taking place institution-wide (72%), and the amount of strategic planning at the department level (33%). These data suggest that much strategic planning may not be translated into action beyond top management levels, an issue that will be examined in the case study aspect of this project.

Given this perspective on the extent of use of entrepreneurial concepts, a second part of the questionnaire asked the community college presidents to rate the impact of the various concepts on their institution. They were given a 4-point rating scale with choices that included very successful, moderately successful, no impact, or negative impact. As might be expected, many presidents rated concepts as moderately successful. For purposes of this chapter, only responses marked *very successful* are included.

Table 10.2 shows the percentage of presidents rating the various entrepreneurial concepts as very successful.

Table 10.2 shows four levels of success ratings that emerged from the study. The two concepts with the highest rating were establishing a contract training program and creating a college foundation, both rated very successful by more than 50 percent of the presidents. The second category of success rating (33–42%) contains several of the concepts suggested in the literature about entrepreneurial manage-

Table 10.2
THE PERCEIVED IMPACT OF ENTREPRENEURIAL CONCEPTS

I) > 50%	% Very Successful	
1) Establishing a contract training program	55	
2) Creating a college foundation	51	
II) 33–50%		
3) Use of business leaders as a primary planning advisory group	42	
4) Creating a special unit/facilitator for innovation and entrepreneurship	39	
5) Strategic planning (institution wide)	36	
6) Creating a special fund for internal innovation	36	
7) Rotating jobs (within units)	33	
III) 20–32%		
8) Creating a futures task force (college)	29	
9) Hiring more staff to write grants on a full-time basis	27	
10) Creating a futures task force (departments)	26	
11) Creating new reward systems to encourage staff initiative	22	
IV) 19% or less		
12) Rotating jobs (between units)	17	
13) Contracting with vendors from outside the college	16	
14) Strategic planning (departments)	16	
15) Creating a merit pay system	15	*(41)
16) Quality circles	13	*(30)
17) Matrix organization (college-wide)	9	*(34)
18) Matrix organization (within units)	6	*(25)

*Indicates negative impact. These concepts were rated as unsuccessful by the percentage of presidents shown in parentheses.

ment, including creating special units and funds for innovations and strategic planning institution-wide.

The other two categories (20–32% and 19% or less) raise some interesting issues. First, contracting with vendors from outside the college for certain services, a concept that has received a great deal of attention in both education and business management literature recently, received a relatively low rating as a very successful concept. Second, much of what has emerged from Japanese management theory—matrix organization, quality circles, and job rotation between units—also received low ratings of success. An interesting fact is that job rotation *within* units was rated fairly well and over twice as high as the other Japaneses management concepts.

Finally, four concepts showed high negative ratings—the most unsuccessful impacts as perceived by the presidents. These were merit pay, quality circles, and matrix organization (both college-wide and within units).

SOME CONCLUSIONS AND ISSUES FOR DISCUSSION

Ultimately, management is an art. Success and use of various concepts will vary depending on the history, traditions, and financial status of an organization. The goal of the study cited above was to develop some baseline data about the use and impact of various entrepreneurial management concepts. The data present a broad perspective on these concepts—on what is being tried and with what success. While the survey data need to be analyzed further through in-depth case studies, they do suggest some issues that might serve as a focus for analysis by community college administrators.

First, entrepreneurship has emerged as a fourth force and complement to collegial, political, and bureaucratic concepts of management and leadership. This emergence of entrepreneurship may reflect the new "deinstitutionalization" of large organizations that is taking place in many sectors of American society.

Second, the most used and most successful entrepreneurial activity is primarily geared externally. Concepts such as contract training, creating a college foundation, or the use of business leaders in planning and developing programs have both high use and high ratings of success.

There is also a good deal of use of entrepreneurial management concepts taking place internally in community colleges. From strategic planning to the development of innovation funds and the use of facilitators for innovation and entrepreneurship, many community colleges are creative and systematic in their pursuit of quality and productivity. While no comparable data are available on entrepreneurship in other organizations such as hospitals or other nonprofit organizations, community colleges would probable fare well in any comparison made.

There is also, for a change, a good fit between theory and practice. There is some consensus in the works of Drucker (1985), Pascale and Athos (1981), Peters and Waterman (1982), Keller (1983), and Pinchot (1985) that entrepreneurship is facilitated by strategic planning and the development of an organizational climate, an active search for opportunities, a separate organizational structure, a venture capital fund, an agreement on rewards and incentives, a long-term emphasis, and a systematic evaluation program. The survey data on the use of these concepts suggest that many colleges are practicing what theory advocates, and a good deal of it is leading to successful ventures.

Finally, in regard to external entrepreneurial projects such as the development of college foundations or contract training programs, community college staffs should consider whether those programs are part of a plan with goals and limits, or whether they are just growing in an ad hoc and piecemeal manner. These kinds of external ventures need goals for one, three, and five years; quality control; venture capital; and a realistic sense of potentials and limits. This is especially true in programs such as contract training where colleges may be setting up separate "management institutes" to market these programs and where there may be high use of adjunct staff.

In summary, community colleges have been leaders in innovation and entrepreneurship in higher education in the past decade, and a number of positive results have emerged from these activities. The concept of creating and rewarding entrepreneurial projects within colleges is a good one, and even if it does not reach large numbers of people, it can still have a significant impact. While this path of emphasizing and rewarding a more entrepreneurial spirit is not going to replace the collegial, political, and bureaucratic ways colleges do things, it may become an even more significant complement to those processes as colleges seek to generate resources externally, reduce costs, and improve quality internally in the decade ahead.

REFERENCES

BALDRIDGE, J.V. 1971. *Power and Conflict in the University.* New York: Wiley.

Chancellor's Office. 1985. Board of Governors, California Community Colleges. *Contours of Change.* Sacramento, Calif.

COHEN, M., and J. MARCH. 1974. *Leadership and Ambiguity.* New York: McGraw Hill.

DEEGAN, W.L., and D. TILLERY. 1985. *Renewing the American Community College: Priorities and Strategies for Effective Leadership.* San Francisco: Jossey-Bass.

DRUCKER, P. 1985. *Innovation and Entrepreneurship.* New York: Harper and Row.

KELLER, G. 1983. *Academic Strategy.* Baltimore: Johns Hopkins University Press.

MERTON, R.K. 1963. *Social Theory and Social Structure.* Glencoe, Ill.: Free Press.

MILLET, J.D. 1962. *The Academic Community.* New York: McGraw-Hill.

PASCALE, R.T., and A.G. ALTHOS. 1981. *The Art of Japanese Management: Applications for American Executives.* New York: Simon and Schuster.

PETERS, T.S., and R.H. WATERMAN. 1982. *In Search of Excellence, Lessons from America's Best-Run Companies.* New York: Harper and Row.

PINCHOT, G. 1985. *Intrepreneuring.* New York: Harper and Row.

11

Governance
IN THE
High-Achieving
Community College

Thomas W. Fryer, Jr.

This chapter on governance in the community college is organized in five main sections. These sections: (1) set forth a working definition of governance; (2) suggest several factors that complicate an understanding of governance mechanisms; (3) propose an overarching purpose for institutional governance functions; (4) present a value-driven theory of ideal governance practices; and (5) briefly describe several institutional characteristics, as well as innovative structures and processes, in six community colleges that may help achieve this ideal.

The chapter's central thesis constitutes a working hypothesis that has grown out of its author's personal observation and experience over a 29-year period in seven educational organizations, principally community colleges, as faculty member, visiting lecturer, staff and line administrator, union member, campus chief executive, and system CEO. The premises that the chapter sets forth, therefore, suffer from all the limitations inherent in personal essays and are subject to one further caveat. The conclusion about which the author is most confident from these three decades is that, in organizations, things are always more complicated than they seem, and treatises on governance could more usefully be published in loose-leaf binders than in hard-bound books.

In overview, the chapter's thesis is that every community college can most effectively achieve its extraordinarily complex, multiple missions when significant numbers of its people exhibit high levels of personal and professional commitment to institutional purposes. Such commitment goes well beyond simple compliance with the minimum requirements of formal job descriptions. It is most profoundly felt and expressed by organizational participants when they perceive themselves as possessing power (as opposed to perceiving they are powerless) in the institution. For its part, the high-achieving organization goes beyond the minimum that is expected of it as employer and attempts to make both work and life at work positive and meaningful for its members.

This author believes that a sense of power or efficacy on the part of organization members—the feeling that they have the ability to achieve results and that what they do makes a significant difference in institutional affairs—is essential to a sense of personal ownership of the organization. This sense of ownership engenders a feeling of responsibility for that which is owned. And the sense of personal responsibility for the organization helps to foster commitment to its purposes.

Governance is defined in this chapter as institutional structures and processes for decision making and communication that is related to decision making. Formal aspects of governance, however, are inextricably linked to the interpersonal behavior of people possessing official authority in the organization. Thus the interpersonal behavior of officials actually becomes a part of institutional governance itself. As much as any other single factor, the operation of governance mechanisms confers or denies the sense of efficacy to organizational participants that is prerequisite to maximum personal commitment.

The exercise of official power in organizations lacks the ability often attributed to it by theorists to control the behavior of organization members. Indeed, such usefulness as formal authority has is limited to achieving compliance rather than eliciting commitment. Certain reasonable, minimum levels of formal control are both necessary and expected to ensure accountability for basic individual and institutional performance. Beyond such reasonable minimums, there is an inverse relationship between the degree of control attempted through formal authority (or the extent of unilateral action by authority figures) and the degree of commitment shown by organizational participants. Furthermore, beyond such reasonable minimums, compliance itself diminishes, and evasiveness and cynicism increase.

Without broad, legitimate participation in institutional decision making (governance)—participation that makes a recognizable difference in the outcomes of decisions—an organization's climate will be perceived as lacking the participant empowerment necessary to elicit and sustain the highest levels of individual commitment to institutional purposes.

Again, however, life in organizations is always more complicated than it seems. Empowerment through participation has its risks and limitations. Utopias do not exist and cannot be created. And every organization consists of a set of separate, unique realities equal to the number of individual participants in the organization.

Thus generalizations are risky. The functioning of organizations is so complex, their relative effectiveness so difficult to understand and to measure, that it is dangerous to claim to know precisely which organizations are working more effectively than others and why that might be so. In addition, responsible people in some organizations may not aspire to maximum achievement for their institutions; for these, being good may be good enough.

But for those community colleges that aspire to achieve their maximum potential as teaching, learning, and service communities— for those that aspire to be the very best they can be—organizational conditions necessary to elicit and sustain high levels of commitment must be present. These organizational conditions, it will be argued, include governance processes that operate effectively in four conceptual domains: structural, human resource, political, and symbolic.

A WORKING DEFINITION OF GOVERNANCE

For purposes of this presentation, governance refers to an institution's structures and processes for decision making and communication that is related to decision making. "Decisions" means *all* decisions: those related to policy development, policy implementation, resource allocation, curriculum development and implementation, institutional planning and priority setting, and so on. In other words, governance, as discussed here, means institutional decision making in its broadest sense, including implementation processes as well as communication structures and processes.

Every organization receives its charter from those who own it or commission its existence. In the case of public institutions, the owners are the people themselves. The charter sets forth the basic purposes for the institution and provides the fundamental grant of authority for the accomplishment of these purposes.

Institutional governance comprises the mechanisms whereby the authority or power of the organization's charter flows through the organization and provides the traction necessary to move the institution toward the achievement of its mission.

An organization's governance structure, therefore, defines the place of both stockholders (owners) and stakeholders (clients and employees) in the organization. In the case of large multiunit systems, it defines the place of institutions; in the case of institutions, it defines the place of individuals and constituencies. In fact, it defines the power and empowerment, or the lack of these, of all organizational participants.

Governance is different from management but closely related to it. Management structures and processes both follow from, and are subordinate to, governance activities. Management implements decisions; governance makes the decisions that management implements.

Leadership is also different from, but related to, governance. However leadership is defined, to the extent that it makes a difference in the course of institutional events, that difference must be expressed through decisions that affect the institution. And *all* such decisions comprise a part of the governance of that institution.

Governance in the American community college possesses special complications. This is because the institution is conceptually and structurally ambiguous, that is, it combines elements of both secondary and higher education, and appropriately so given the institution's history and missions. Historically, many boards of trustees and administrators have tended to rely on secondary, or hierarchical, models of governance, while many faculties have strongly preferred university, or collegial, models.

The strength of hierarchical, "command models" of governance is that they permit the institution to respond quickly to emerging community needs. This responsiveness on the part of the community college is, without doubt, one of the institution's greatest strengths and accounts, as much as anything else, for the remarkable growth of these institutions since World War II.

A major weakness of top-heavy, hierarchical governance structures and processes is that they can lead to feelings of alienation and powerlessness on the part of many organizational participants. These feelings may have adverse consequences, either in direct political action by employees through trustee elections or collective bargaining, or in more general feelings of frustration or cynicism that lead to a lack of commitment to institutional purposes, or both.

The research university or elite liberal arts college model of governance, in contrast, establishes dominant roles for faculties (but not for support staff and not for non–tenure track faculty.) Clearly these roles foster a sense of empowerment and responsibility to institutional purposes, but they also lead to enormous resistance to change and to bottom-heavy decision-making processes that have been described as "organized anarchies."

At least in some community colleges, forms of governance may be evolving that combine the most effective elements of both secondary and university models. Practices in six institutions that may point in this direction will be suggested in the last section of this chapter.

Institutional governance is thus as fascinating as it is important to organization dwellers and external policy makers because it involves one of life's most compelling subjects: power.

FACTORS COMPLICATING AN UNDERSTANDING OF GOVERNANCE

Life in organizations is always more complicated than it seems. This is true because organizations are comprised of unique and mysteriously complicated male and female human beings in interaction with (1) each other, (2) work to be performed, and (3) the terms and conditions under which the work tasks are accomplished. Often both the work and the technology to perform it lack precise definition.

When governing boards, legislatures, executives, and reformers consider the functioning of institutions, a truth they frequently overlook and consistently underestimate is that *the efficacy of official power or formal authority for controlling organizational activities and outcomes is a great deal more limited than it seems.* Karl Weick's paper, "Educational Organizations as Loosely Coupled Systems" illuminates this point. Weick observes,

> For some time people who manage organizations and people who study this managing have asked, "How does an organization go about doing what it does with what consequences for its people, processes, products, and persistence?" And for some time they've heard the same answers. In paraphrase the answers say essentially that an organization does what it does because of plans, intentional selection of means that get the organization to agree upon goals, and all of this is accomplished by such rationalized procedures as cost-benefit analyses, division of labor, specified areas of discretion, authority invested in the office, job descriptions, and a consistent evaluation and reward system. *The only problem with that portrait is that it is rare in nature. People in organizations, including educational organizations, find themselves hard pressed either to find actual instances of those rational practices or to find rationalized practices whose outcomes have been as beneficent as predicted, or to feel that those rational occasions explain much of what goes on within the organization* (emphasis added). Parts of some organizations are heavily rationalized but many parts also prove intractable to analysis through rational assumptions. (1976, 1)

The notion of loose coupling implies that the directives followed by organizational participants doing their daily work are not necessarily the orders of the day that have come down from the top. For example, a faculty member's classroom is "loosely coupled" to the campus chief administrator's office. Certainly the president and the teacher are connected, but, as Weick suggests, "Each retains some identity and separateness and . . . their attachment may be circumscribed, infrequent, weak in its mutual effects, unimportant, and/or slow to respond" (1976, 3).

Since a community college organization achieves its mission to such a large degree by virtue of what takes place in its classrooms and through its student support operations, it follows that, in a given community college, continued excellence in teaching or improvement in educational effectiveness depends on something other than, or at least in addition to, attempting to achieve these qualities through formal direction and control.

Later in this chapter, the idea is suggested that one such added ingredient of governance is the creation of organizational climates. The creation of environments that enhance excellence in performance and attract and nurture people who desire the continual improvement of the work of the enterprise is one of the most important functions of leadership and of its expression through the governance processes of the institution.

Again, however, these matters are greatly more complicated than they seem. It is not currently known whether individuals who pursue excellence and improvement are "born or made" in an organization. Some research points to the likelihood that attempts to make workers happier and more productive in organizations ignore the possibility that "deeply-rooted personality traits can cause an unproductive worker's malaise" (Debley 1986, 7).

Debley notes that researchers have concluded that an individual's satisfaction—or the lack of it—can be predicted from conditions evident in the person in adolescence and that "predictable attitudes toward work appear to remain fairly stable through adulthood" (ibid.). These findings suggest that one should be cautious in believing or claiming that planned or created conditions in organizations can make a controlling difference in the personal job satisfaction and work performance of organizational participants.

Beyond suggesting that "it may be easier to improve organizational morale through employee selection than through organizational development activities," Debley's article does suggest "a realistic option, . . . to lower expectations and develop a reasoned, but sustainable pursuit of the happy and productive worker by using a combination of techniques that recognize strong forces are at work in the individual" (ibid.).

A further interaction of personality factors with organizational conditions is suggested by the observation that "happy" does not always mean "productive" in workers. Job satisfaction and job performance are not perfectly correlated. It is quite possible to have a highly satisfied but unsatisfactory employee—at any level in the organization.

Clearly, personalities do play an enormously complicating role in the operation of institutional governance mechanisms. Indeed, the effects of human similarities are severely limited by the operation of individual differences. Thus people working at the same level, in the same department, in the same room, for the same supervisor, often view the same events in entirely different ways. An examination of governance issues in local institutions demonstrates that perceptions of any subject vary widely from person to person.

They also vary from position to position. Debley's report focuses on the stable aspects of individual personalities that are difficult to change through organizational interventions. And few people, indeed, have not encountered along the way an unhappy soul who was simply going to be unhappy no matter what.

But most organization veterans of any extended tenure have also witnessed great changes occur in the same individual when that person moves from one role to another in the hierarchy. Undoubtedly these changes constitute a complex phenomenon in themselves, but clearly one aspect of the change derives from the different view of the world one gains from different vantage points in the organization.

The realities of governance structures and processes for trustees and presidents are almost never the realities for faculty members and support staff. For example, interviews with faculty and administrators in institutions reveal consistent differences between the two with respect to perceived participation in governance processes.

Almost without exception, administrators report that faculty participate in institutional decision making a great deal more than faculty report they participate. This is true in part because faculty typically participate through representatives, and being represented is often understandably viewed as quite different from being present. It is also true in part because administrators and boards of trustees usually make *final* decisions, and, regardless of how many crucial, controlling decisions (e.g., in personnel selection processes) have been made along the way, a widely held faculty view is that the final decision expunges all the others.

It is also possible that some administrators may actually believe their own rhetoric when they assert that many people actively participate in decisions when in fact (1) decisions were already made before the decision-making process was initiated, or (2) the administrator made his or her preferred decision anyway, disregarding the advice offered through the participatory process.

Clearly, administrators at any level in the organization who are perceived as authoritarian, insensitive, and experts in selective hearing are the bane of some staff members lives. And negative, unhappy, intractable staff or faculty members are similarly regarded by administrators who have to work with them.

However, these matters defy simple explanation and easy understanding. Participation at its best has drawbacks and limitations. As long as human beings are imperfect, organizations will be imperfect. With some individuals, high commitment is always reserved exclusively for their personal interests, not for institutional purposes. Sometimes people who are empowered in an institution abuse this power or use it badly. In some situations, interpersonal relations among parties have deteriorated into the kind of permanent hostilities that no organizational intervention could remedy.

Sometimes trustees and administrators see power as a zero-sum commodity and feel that the empowerment of grass- roots employees diminishes their own power and capacity to exercise control. Processes of participation aimed at producing a sense of empowerment in organizational participants undeniably take a great deal more time for everyone than the simple exercise of authority by officials.

Moreover, it is possible that in some regions, communities, or institutions cultural norms place greater value on action through hierarchies and accord correspondingly less significance to the participation of rank-and-file employees. In such contexts, widespread involvement in governance could be seen as an unnecessary waste of time. Here, probably, some form of benevolent despotism would be the governance system of choice.

These factors merely suggest a few of the complexities inherent in governance processes. One further complication will be mentioned here. As was suggested above, in organizations, *reality itself differs from position to position*. For example, the world that the president looks out upon, including the responsibilities he or she is required to discharge, is simply a different world from the one that the classroom teacher views.

Thus the organization is comprised of multiple realities, all operative, all legitimate, all different. These realities complicate governance immeasurably. They make understanding difficult and generalizations virtually impossible.

In *Modern Approaches to Understanding and Managing Organizations* (1987), Lee Bolman and Terrence Deal develop the notion of organizations as multiple realities by setting forth four conceptual frames of reference through which organizations can be viewed. Bolman and Deal synthesize the research of social scientists into:

- a *structural* frame of reference, based on the work of rational system theorists who emphasize organizational goals, roles, structures, and technology;

- a *human resource* frame, emphasizing the writing of social scientists that has focused on the needs, feelings, skills, and values of the people who work in organizations;
- a *political* frame that sees competition for scarce organizational resources, power, and conflict as central issues; and
- a *symbolic* frame in which the meanings people attach to organizational events dominate the events themselves, and where culture, rituals, sagas, myths, and heroes are more salient than rationality.

Bolman and Deal cogently document that the same organizational events can be, and usually are, seen in entirely different ways depending upon a given participant's frame of reference. Thus, in this framework, institutional governance is most usefully thought of as a complicated mix of structural, personal, political, and symbolic factors, all in interaction with each other.

Bolman and Deal's four frames provide a useful heuristic device for thinking about issues of governance and institutional leadership and administration. Later in the chapter this framework will be used to suggest both the characteristics of an ideal governance system and an approach to examining institutional and individual functioning.

AN OVERARCHING PURPOSE FOR INSTITUTIONAL GOVERNANCE

As was suggested at the outset, governance is sometimes narrowly conceived as comprising merely the channels through which authority flows to control and direct the organization and the people in it. The principal question asked in this formulation is, "Who's in charge here?" This approach almost always tends to confuse governance with accountability, and, while these are related matters, they are, in fact, quite different.

The highly simplistic, factory model of governance constitutes the conceptual basis for much public policy debate concerning governance today. It assumes that organizations function hierarchically, with boards and managers at the top controlling and directing the work of the people below. Everything that happens "down the line" in the organization's structure, according to this theory, results from, and is tightly linked to, the downward flow of policies and directives. To be sure, there is a major hierarchical aspect to the work of all organizations, and properly so. But, as noted earlier, there are inherent limitations in this view of the way organizations operate.

Governance is more usefully thought of as those mechanisms and processes for decision making and communication that enable the institution to achieve its mission most effectively. Governance is not an end; it is a means. This notion introduces the critically important idea that the missions of at least some institutions (among them, this author believes, community colleges) can most usefully be accomplished through governance processes that involve more than structures and processes for control and direction.

Control structures have as their aim achieving compliance from organizational participants. But today there are promising innovations in management theory and practice in the larger world of work. These changes depart from practices that emphasize *compliance*, and move toward those that attempt to elicit *commitment* from workers.

A major premise of this chapter is that community colleges are most effective in achieving their highly complex missions when administrators, faculty, support staff, and trustees all exhibit characteristics that, taken together, can reasonably be described as constituting high levels of commitment to institutional ends.

Margaret Thompson develops this point in her paper, "Mutual Gains Bargaining in the Foothill-De Anza Community College District." Applying the work of Harvard's Richard Walton and others to collective bargaining in community colleges, particularly in California's Foothill-De Anza, Thompson states:

> Control-oriented organizations exhibit adversarial . . . relations. The adversaries—"labor" and "management"—are widely understood to have mutually exclusive interests. . . .
>
> In high commitment work systems, . . . relations stress mutual gains. The parties participate in joint planning and problem solving on agendas expanded far beyond the usual scope of collective negotiations. They emphasize the "integrative issues" which can lead to gains for everyone, and develop methods to jointly manage the "distributive" issues which separate them. Distributive bargaining assumes that the subject of negotiations—such as money—is finite, and that if one side "gets more" the other side "gets less." Mutual gains bargaining produces "principled" bargaining on distributive issues, by stressing shared superordinate goals and nourishing bargaining relationships which keep the organization moving toward these goals throughout bargaining cycles. (1987, 1)

Community colleges cannot, over long periods of time, succeed in their complex, comprehensive missions of serving a rapidly changing society if their governance processes rely predominantly on techniques to achieve compliance on the part of organizational participants.

The reader should make no mistake, however: compliance and accountability in the fundamentals of organization functioning are necessary and appropriate. Both the people and the government they establish are entitled to safeguards and proper accounting for the resources and the trust vouchsafed to institutions.

Beyond reasonable levels of control necessary to achieve basic organizational accountability, however, the attempt to control people and organizations through detailed orders, laws, and regulations is actually destructive of its own ends. When otherwise conscientious people feel themselves abused by intrusive, prescriptive rules, they carefully prepare the elaborate reports such controls always require so as to give rule makers the illusion of compliance. Meantime, they conduct business as usual except that in the process they have grown a great deal more cynical, evasive, and distrustful. And their investment of the energy required for deeper levels of commitment is diminished.

Attempting to employ compliance techniques to achieve the higher order functions of the community college missions is particularly counterproductive. Initiative, entrepreneurship, risk taking, creativity, the investment of extra effort—these are activities that grow out of *commitment* to the enterprise, not compliance with its mandates.

There are no known cases in which boards, legislatures, or managerial officeholders have been successful in compelling faculty members to think, as they shower in the morning, of more effective techniques for presenting a particularly challenging unit of subject matter to an enormously heterogeneous class; or to ponder while driving to work in the morning, how to help a student in difficulty; or to call students at home in the evening to see why they missed class.

Neither are the detailed directives of boards, legislatures, and authority figures effective in compelling administrators to make life more complicated for themselves, for example, by proposing a new program to meet a community need, then absorbing the punishment necessary to guide the proposal through the gauntlet of naysayers and the labyrinth of approvals necessary for implementation. Neither are directives from above useful in motivating a person in a position of responsibility to take that most risky and difficult step of all: disciplining or dismissing an employee who cannot, or will not, perform the duties of his or her position to reasonable standards of quality.

The best teaching and the most effective management almost always depart from the line of least resistance—the compliance line— and the commitment this departure requires has to be freely given by organizational participants. It cannot be obtained on demand.

Creating the climate within which such commitment emerges and is sustained is a key task of institutional leadership. If such a climate is to remain viable over time, the conditions necessary for its preservation must be institutionalized in governance structures and processes.

A VALUE-DRIVEN THEORY OF THE IDEAL GOVERNANCE SYSTEM

The goal of eliciting high levels of commitment from the people who perform the work of the enterprise reflects one of the animating values of this essay. It is linked to another underlying value.

People who work in an organization and receive compensation for their labor are responsible for performing the reasonable duties of their positions. This simple equation—wages in return for compliance with job requirements—is well understood and well accepted in the world of work. This essay, of course, sets forth the premise that institutional governance should take as its goal the creation of organizational conditions that elicit from workers a *desire* to do more— not that they have to do more or are required to, but that they *want* to by their own free choice.

Just as workers are responsible for performing the basic requirements of their jobs, employers are responsible for providing certain basics for the workforce: fair and reasonable compensation, fair and reasonable treatment by superiors, a physically safe workplace, and so forth.

This chapter goes a major step further. It holds that employers have a responsibility to the human beings in their employ to attempt to make work *meaningful* for them in a rich and positive sense. It argues that, insofar as possible, employers should attempt to help workers make lives while they make a living. Thus the sense of commitment to institutional purpose that the organization seeks to evoke *from* the worker is reciprocated by a comparable sense of organizational commitment *to* the worker. Underlying this commitment, of course, is a profound respect for, and a deep sense of the intrinsic value of, every person who is a stakeholder in the organization.

Admittedly this is highly idealistic. The ideal, however, constitutes an overarching goal, something unattainable perhaps but worth striving for, a guide to practice and behavior—a "superordinate" goal. In the case of the Foothill-De Anza Community College District, this goal is stated by the institution's chief executive officer as follows: "to create in Foothill-De Anza two fully functioning community colleges—as teaching, learning, and service communities—for whose members work is joy" (Fryer 1982).

Furthermore, Fryer asserts that people in positions of organizational responsibility hold in trust special authority. By virtue of this trust, they are appropriately held to higher standards of professional conduct in the use of their power than those who hold no such authority. *This view further holds that the exercise of authority in organizations, which includes the interpersonal behavior of authority figures, is one of the most important factors in creating the climate of the organization.*

To be sure, this is not an often-articulated view of governance. Amidst the complicated multiple realities of life in organizations, however, the interpersonal conduct of people who exercise power at all levels in the organization becomes inextricably linked both to the perception and the operation of institutional governance.

This means that, more than anyone else, people in positions of power, including, especially, governing board members, have most to do with what the environment is like. This last point seems to be corroborated by the findings of John Roueche and George Baker: "Many researchers think that managerial personnel contribute more to climate than do others in most organizations" (1987, 105).

These, then, are some of the fundamental premises undergirding this author's concept of institutional governance. A central tenet of this presentation holds that an ideal governance system—governance in the high-achieving institution—is characterized by a balanced combination of qualities in all four of the theoretical domains mentioned earlier: structural, human resource, political, and symbolic. Further, ideal governance mechanisms *must* operate effectively in *all four* domains. A failure in any area significantly damages the whole.

The following two enumerations are designed to indicate how tasks, responsibilities, and behaviors of boards of trustees and administrators can be analyzed into each of the conceptual frames of reference. The governing board is presented first since it bears overall responsibility for the operation of the entire enterprise.

The material is both qualitative and evaluative. It is based on the judgment that a governance system that is maximally effective must work well in four widely divergent conceptual domains. While the particular items listed are suggestive and are not intended as a complete enumeration of all duties and responsibilities, this author does feel that each of them is important. Taken together, they may constitute many of the basic essentials of effective operation in the several theoretical realms.

FOUR CONCEPTUAL FRAME ANALYSES OF IDEAL BOARD BEHAVIOR

STRUCTURAL:

- organizes itself to discharge responsibilities in a timely and effective manner
- handles agendas, meeting conduct, and minutes efficiently

- ensures that policies and procedures are developed, adopted, evaluated, and updated in orderly manner
- behaves with sensitivity to distinction between board's legislative functions and staff's executive functions; demonstrates involvement but not intrusiveness
- operates as a unified board (not necessarily unanimous on every issue) rather than operating independently as individuals (when a board is divided, the board's own policies become an unreliable guide for institutional action)
- exercises oversight of financial and other managerial systems and ensures the balanced allocation of financial resources

HUMAN RESOURCE:

- behaves positively and supportively when dealing with staff while remaining tough-minded and challenging in pursuit of issues and strategies
- shows respect and courtesy toward fellow trustees, staff, students, and community
- demonstrates sensitivity to needs of employees at all levels while balancing these with other institutional and community needs
- listens actively and thoughtfully
- exhibits interested, caring behavior

POLITICAL:

- holds institution in trust for *total* community, not merely one part of it
- remains alert to inherent tensions in the organization among various constituencies and interest groups
- seeks to resolve conflicts constructively for all parties rather than achieve victory
- shows awareness of the power that it possesses but demonstrates wisdom in using it
- shares power rather than hoards it
- resists the temptation to try to control or direct everything
- represents the interests of the total institution rather than the narrow interests of a single issue or constituency

SYMBOLIC:

- acknowledges clearly the legitimacy of *all* constituencies in the organization

- models high commitment to the institution rather than to personal interests or to the gratification of exercising personal power
- comes to board meticulously prepared
- deports itself in board meetings as if its conduct were to be a model for behavior in the entire institution
- sets forth, positively and constructively, high expectations for the institution
- uses first-person-plural rather than first person singular
- projects interest in the institution by attending campus activities

Presentation of the following material assumes, as was indicated earlier, that administrative behavior is also a major factor in creating the climate of the entire organization in the case of the chief executive officer; or one of its operating elements, in the case of any other responsible officer. While the mechanisms that loosely couple the organization serve as buffers for the operating units, the internal environment within which these units and their people operate is created in significant measure by the behavior of people in positions of authority.

FOUR CONCEPTUAL FRAME ANALYSES OF IDEAL ADMINISTRATOR BEHAVIOR

STRUCTURAL:

- provides known organizational structures for multidirectional communication and orderly decision making
- defines organizational roles and relationships so as to minimize conflict and ambiguity
- achieves and maintains a clear sense of the total institution, not just his or her particular part of it
- superintends the development and maintenance of institutional information systems
- directs proper internal control and accountability for financial and physical resources
- guides the development and institutionalization of useful planning mechanisms
- monitors indicators that the institution is achieving its mission effectively

- oversees systems to control financial efficiency in the organization and sees to the balanced allocation of human and financial resources
- establishes sound systems of personnel selection, supervision, and evaluation
- ensures the development and administration of proper compensation and classification systems

HUMAN RESOURCE:

- listens attentively, sensitively, and responsively
- cares personally, genuinely, and deeply about the people in the organization
- provides support and coaching but has high expectations for performance—his or her own performance and that of others
- does not retain marginally competent people in places of responsibility, but achieves needed changes as humanely as possible
- sees organizational participants as human beings and, while expecting top performance from them, wishes to make their work meaningful and their work life a "joy"

POLITICAL:

- recognizes the differing and legitimate interests of the multiple institutional constituencies, both internal and external
- understands the inherent, legitimate tensions among the interests of trustees, administrators, faculty, support staff, and students, and provides mechanisms and processes for reconciling and integrating these tensions
- seldom relies on his/her official authority, and usually does so as a last resort
- empowers every constituency in institutional governance so that no group or individual can reasonably feel impotent or isolated
- empowers individuals within his or her personal span of control
- seeks integration of differing interests and is willing to change to achieve accommodation rather than pushing for victory (wars in educational institutions, even if fought for the right reasons, have no winners)

<u>SYMBOLIC</u>:

- is aware that in his or her person are embodied the values and the mission of the entire institution
- is sensitive to the distances between people that hierarchies create and does everything possible to reduce these distances
- articulates a vision for the present and future of the organization that lifts the aspirations of organization members and draws them to it
- attends to ceremony and ritual that enable both the leaders and the led to celebrate their shared community
- is visible at all levels of the organization and in the community
- supports institutional events and activities and conducts organizational business in ways that emphasize the "joy" of work life

In this author's experience, leaving aside those cases in which people simply lacked the basic ability to do their job, or where there was a controlling personality disorder, most instances in which an individual administrator failed to live up to his or her potential or actually was removed from his or her position could be found to involve *inadequately differentiated frames of reference;* that is, the person lacked a clear sense of one or more of these four major perspectives and thus was unable to operate effectively in that domain or across domains.

The requirements of management and the prerequisites to leadership in today's turbulent, changing world are more challenging than ever. They demand a mastery of new complexities in the traditonal structural and human resource domains as well as sophistication and effective behavior in political and symbolic realms.

Beyond these implications for individuals, it is also possible that, when institutions (or units within them) fail or stagnate, a study of these conceptual frameworks will reveal defects in one or more of the four. For example, failure by the governing board or the institution's chief executive to operate effectively in one or more of these domains may place the entire enterprise in jeopardy, and institutional collapse can almost always be traced to failure at the top.

ROLE OF EMPLOYEE UNIONS

This discussion has so far focused on the crucial importance of boards of trustees and administrators in creating high-commitment environments. But trustees and administrators are not the only actors on the stage. The faculty and support staff also play major roles.

In all cases where faculty or staff are unionized, and in most other cases where they participate significantly in decision-making processes, the responsibilities of these organizations and their leaders are especially important. With collective bargaining in particular, state laws grant union organizations statutory authority, and, by withholding their consent, unions are able to exercise enormous power, in some cases with every bit as much negative effect as the behavior of any board or administrator. Furthermore, as with trustees and administrators, the interpersonal behavior of union officials has an important effect on the climate of the institution.

This author is familiar enough with the history of the American labor movement and has seen enough of college and university administrations, his own and those of others, not only to respect the legitimacy of union organizations but to join a union himself. However, for institutions to achieve their maximum potential, to become "fully functioning" in the words of the previously cited Foothill-De Anza superordinate goal, the unions, the board of trustees, and the administration must mutually engage in the challenging quest to transform the negative energy of confrontation into the positive energy of cooperation.

In thinking about employee unions, it is useful to keep in mind that the workforce is comprised of multiple cultures. In most cases, for example, the culture of the nonprofessional staff, especially "blue collar" workers, is most hospitable to unionization, the faculty culture least so. This author feels more confident of his understanding of operant factors in the faculty and administrative cultures than he does in the cultures of the institution's classified staff.

Among faculties, at least, unions are often organizations of last resort. Sometimes they are created in an effort to protect legitimate faculty interests against very real threats. The creation of unions also suggests a validation of the powerful need for employee empowerment in organizations. Unions also serve in the struggle against real or perceived unilateral, authoritarian action by a board or administration. When this struggle also engages such feelings as "Nobody up there is listening," or "Nobody up there cares," unionization is an almost inevitable result. If economic issues are also salient, unionization *is* inevitable.

Thus unions emerge from an institution's perceived weaknesses, not its strengths. Unions are created, in large measure, as single-purpose organizations to represent, sometimes quite narrowly, the self-interests of their members. Unions, therefore, can become stakeholders in the organization's problems, and it is often difficult for them *not* to focus on real or potential problems as the justification for their existence.

But unions, too, bear a very real responsibility for creating and sustaining the high-commitment, high-achieving institution. Certainly, a union's options are limited if it must deal with a wholly unresponsive or manipulative board and management. But unions have as much responsibility as trustees and managers to engage in the search for positive, mutually beneficial relationships, structures, and solutions to issues. Unless unions are willing to begin and sustain this effort, neither the institution nor the members they represent can ever fully achieve their maximum potential.

So, again, unexpected complexities arise in understanding the operation of institutional governance. Just as the imperfections and deficiencies of trustees and administrative officials have an adverse impact on organizational members and the institution itself, so do the imperfections and deficiencies of union officials and employee organizations have a similar effect.

Here, too, the Bolman and Deal (1987) heuristic is useful in suggesting ideals that may be pursued. In the structural frame, for example, unions in the fully functioning institution

- seek to establish collaborative linkages with the administration for problem anticipation and problem solving
- pursue accurate, complete financial information and present it fairly to all concerned

In the human resource frame, unions

- accord the same decency and respect in public discourse to institutional officials that they do to their members
- listen attentively, sensitively, and responsively to all others in the organization as well as to those whom they represent

In the political domain, unions

- understand and accept the legitimate claim on institutional resources of needs other than their own
- seek mechanisms and processes for reconciling and integrating legitimate tensions and conflicting claims on organizational resources
- are willing to change to achieve accommodation rather than pushing for victory

In the symbolic realm, unions

- demonstrate a sense of responsibility for the *total* institution
- attend to ceremony and ritual that celebrate and affirm their commitment to the community shared by all its members

As Thompson's paper suggests, the creation of high-commitment work systems under conditions of collective bargaining "requires fundamental changes in how people think about organizations [and] labor-management relations. . . . [People] also need to confront their deep-seated assumptions about conflict resolution in the bargaining context" (1987, 2). *Both* sides need to do this.

If unions, therefore, and their leadership, as well as the leadership of *all* groups empowered to play a role in institutional governance, do not buy into, and ultimately behave on the basis of, some concept of a superordinate goal or some overarching sense of the institution that transcends their own self-interest, there can be no achievement of the institution's highest potential or of the ideals this chapter espouses.

PRACTICES AND INNOVATIONS THAT POINT IN THE RIGHT DIRECTION

This presentation will not attempt to establish that any institution embodies all of the ideals that have been articulated here. Probably almost every institution aspires to at least some of them. With over 1,200 community, junior, and technical colleges in the nation, practice varies so widely that attempting to generalize is not helpful. But a research project currently being conducted in California may offer useful illustrations and suggest characteristics and structures that point in the right direction (Fryer and Lovas 1988).

This project is exploring local governance practices in California's 70 community college districts and is attempting to identify and describe models of effective governance practice. Jointly sponsored by the state's Association of Chief Executive Officers, the California Community College Trustees, and the state-wide Academic Senate, the study began by inviting districts to nominate themselves as potential models.

Self-nomination required that the district's CEO, its Academic Senate President, and the President of the Board of Trustees *jointly* sign the following statement:

> We recognize that no human organization is perfect or problem free and certainly no community college district is free of conflicts over decision-making, communication, resource allocation, policy-making, and policy implementation. Yet we believe that in our district our governance process is working effectively, and we wish to be considered as a possible model in the joint study of local internal governance.

Remarkably, 23 districts, approximately one-third of the state total, completed this certification form, indicating a desire to participate. Limited resources made it impossible to examine so large a group of institutions, so a preliminary investigation was undertaken to enable the selection of a smaller number of districts for in-depth study.

This "prestudy" consisted of a mail survey administered to members of key groups involved in institutional governance designated by the districts themselves. Five hundred eighty-six questionnaires were mailed to individuals in 21 districts (two districts elected not to participate at this point) and 414, over 70 percent, were returned.

The questionnaire asked respondents (1) to enumerate the "issues, problems or challenges" they felt their district had experienced over the last several years; (2) to indicate how successfully they felt these issues had been dealt with; and (3) to indicate the role district-level governance had played in dealing with the issues.

Results of this survey, which will be published in the future, were presented to the study steering committee in a format that prevented committee members from identifying individual institutions. Reviewing the survey data, the committee selected six districts for in-depth study.

In making this selection, committee members looked for districts that reported high levels of success in dealing with the issues they faced as well as a strong role for district governance in addressing these issues. In addition, the committee took note of the consistency of responses across the constituent groups. For example, the committee looked for a high degree of consistency between faculty and administration in the levels of success each reported. The committee also considered each district's overall rate of response to the survey and the total number of respondents in each of three critical categories: faculty, administrators, and trustees.

The institutions selected were:

- Allan Hancock College, Santa Maria; established 1920; Fall 1987 total enrollment: 7,733
- Foothill-De Anza Community College District, Los Altos Hills; established 1957; Fall 1987 total enrollment: 39,370
- Mt. San Antonio College, Walnut; established 1946; Fall 1987 total enrollment: 20,657
- Santa Barbara City College, Santa Barbara; established 1908; Fall 1987 total enrollment: 10,500
- Santa Monica College, Santa Monica; established 1929; Fall 1987 total enrollment: 18,594

- Yosemite Community College District, Modesto; established 1921; Fall 1987 total enrollment: 12,175

The Foothill-De Anza District operates the two colleges from which it takes its name. The Yosemite District operates Modesto Junior College and Columbia College. The remaining four institutions are single college districts. These six districts represent a reasonably balanced mix of large and small (by California standards) schools; northern, southern, and central California locations; rural (or small city), suburban, and city institutions. None, however, is located in one of California's major inner-city centers.

As of mid-1987, the average tenure of all California community college chief executive officers was five years. In these six districts, the average CEO tenure was ten years. Roueche and Baker (1987) suggest that institutional climate is affected (either positively or negatively, no doubt) by the longevity of institutional leadership, a view that is consistent with this author's experience. The pace at which deep, lasting change in institutions takes place—the pace, for example, at which environments are created or modified—is a great deal slower than reformers usually imagine.

Two other relevant conditions are reported by the chief executives of these six institutions. The first is that, without exception, the governing board is not significantly involved in the day-to-day management and administration of the institution.

This characteristic is particularly noteworthy since this chapter sets forth the premise that effective governance begins with, and is materially affected by, the quality and behavior of the board of trustees. This author also asserts that effective institutional governance requires a clear separation of powers between legislative (board) and executive (administration) functions, and such a separation seems to be characteristic of these six districts. An intrusive, overly involved board that holds an excessive number of meetings simply makes it impossible for the administration to render maximally effective service.

One trustee who was explaining that her board did not get involved in the day-to-day operations of her institution put it this way, "Our CEO manages this institution. We have enough board members who have made a mistake to know what a mistake is."

A second characteristic emerges in the conversations and writings of these six chief executives. That is a clearly articulated, strongly held sense of the value of people and their vital participation in the governance of the institution. There is, to be sure, wide variability within the institutions themselves as to the perception of the CEOs' commitment to participation. By no means are all these individuals universally perceived as practicing it. When asked, however, "How would you describe your philosophy or values that underlie your institution's governance system?" without exception, the central value of collegial structures and meaningful participation was articulated.

As one chief executive put it, "I am unalterably committed to a participatory style of management which effectively allows anyone who wants or perceives a need to participate in the decision-making process to do so." Another articulated a theme shared by several CEO's when he said, "A lot of personal work goes into a philosophy of participation in decision making with an open, honest system. It doesn't just work on paper."

The following brief summary descriptions of institutional governance mechanisms place primary emphasis on faculty participation in governance, although in most cases structures also include classified staff, students, and others. The material presented here focuses on *structural* elements that are interesting or innovative or that seem to be working particularly well. The chapter's conclusion will suggest implications of these structures for other conceptual domains. At this point, no definitive external evaluation of the effectiveness of any of these structures has been completed. The information presented here is highly selective and is not intended to represent a balanced perspective on the governance mechanisms in each institution.

At the time of this writing, only six faculties in California's 70 community college districts had not unionized. Allan Hancock's was one of these. Santa Barbara's faculty elected an unaffiliated local union to be its representative in the spring of 1987. The Foothill-De Anza and Santa Monica faculties elected unaffiliated locals in the mid-1970s, shortly after passage of the state's collective bargaining enabling statute. The Mt. San Antonio and Yosemite faculties elected the California Teachers' Association to represent them at about the same time. The classified staff in all six districts are represented by the California School Employees Association.

ALLAN HANCOCK COLLEGE. At Allan Hancock, the Academic Senate and an extensive array of Senate subcommittees are the principal vehicles for faculty participation in governance. Notable among these subcommittees is the Academic Planning and Programming (AP&P) Committee, a group of 13–15 predominantly faculty people, appointed by the Senate, who elect their own chair and serve as the principal body for formulating educational policy for the institution. AP&P reports are forwarded to the full senate and from there to the president who "has not found an occasion to override" the committee's recommendations. Faculty and administrators alike report high levels of confidence in this group which is a vital component of the college's governance structure.

The president's cabinet and the Academic Senate Executive Council meet on a monthly basis to discuss issues of concern, anticipate problems, and share information. This structural linkage seems also to be as useful as a problem-seeking and anticipation mechanism as it does a problem resolution vehicle.

The college's Deans and Directors Forum pulls academic and student services people together in routine interaction, a practice that led to the formulation of an institution-wide student matriculation plan thought to be of unusually high quality.

FOOTHILL-DE ANZA COMMUNITY COLLEGE DISTRICT. Foothill-De Anza's Budget and Policy Development Group (BPDG) is a 23-person body representing all institutional constituencies—staff and students—in which the district chancellor formulates his policy and resource allocation recommendations to the board of trustees. The chancellor does not have a cabinet or an exclusively administrative body in which such recommendations are developed. Key management personnel, including the two college presidents, serve on this group, along with faculty and classified union representatives, faculty senate representatives, management association and minority staff association representatives, and students.

A good deal of material has been written and is available on the BPDG. Perhaps of most interest concerning the operation of this group is the fact that the chancellor develops his final recommendations to the board concerning all budget allocations, including compensation, in this forum with the active participation of staff and faculty collective bargaining representatives.

MT. SAN ANTONIO COLLEGE. The hub of Mt. San Antonio's governance structure is the College Council, an 11-person group representing administration, faculty, classified staff, and students. This group reviews all policy recommendations before they are submitted to the board of trustees, and serves as a formal clearinghouse for all college issues. Matters that leave this group are forwarded to the president's Administrative Council. The president reports that he "cannot remember an instance" in which the Administrative Council reversed a decision of the College Council.

The president also has a president's Advisory Council on Budget (PAC-B) that includes faculty, classified staff, and students in addition to administrators. This group reviews the budget process, budget requests, and decisions of the president's Administrative Council convened as a Budget Committee.

Attempts are made in the collegial governance structure to leave matters within the scope of collective negotiations to the bargaining table. Some matters that fall in grey areas are handled in College Council, but only with the consent of the union.

SANTA BARBARA CITY COLLEGE. Faculty in Santa Barbara voted to unionize in the Spring of 1987 and the parties have successfully negotiated their first contract. Of considerable interest in this institution is the apparent desire of both the faculty and the administration to preserve the role of the Academic Senate in college governance.

Centerpiece of the collegial governance structure is the College Planning Committee (CPC), a group representing the faculty senate, classified staff, and students, in addition to the administration. Among its responsibilities, the CPC makes recommendations to the president concerning resource allocation, including priorities for filling instructional positions and allocating both state instructional equipment and lottery funds.

The president of the Santa Barbara Instructor's Association, writing in the association's newsletter, says of the first contract:

> The negotiating team has written an agreement that leaves issues dealing with sabbatical leaves, evaluation, academic calendar, work load and assignment, curriculum, organization, employment, duties and working days, probation and tenure, salary class transfer and academic title policy under the jurisdiction of the Academic Senate. Both the Association and the District are hopeful that current policies covering these areas will continue to work effectively under the guidance of the Academic Senate.

SANTA MONICA COLLEGE. This institution was unique among the participants in California's state-wide study of local district governance in naming the members of the Executive Committee of its community General Advisory Board as being "essential parts of district-level decision making," along with trustees, administrators, faculty, classified staff, and students.

The General Advisory Board is comprised of 100 citizens who meet five times a year. Its Executive Committee meets monthly and is augmented by a subcommittee structure. These groups assist the college both in problem anticipation and problem resolution.

As with the other six institutions being discussed here, Santa Monica has a well-organized and active Faculty Senate. One of the problems of senate leadership typical in many situations derives from the rapid turnover of the organization's presidents. At about the time senate presidents have learned the players, the vocabulary, and the rules of the game, their terms end, and another president takes office.

Santa Monica's effort to develop continuity in senate leadership has taken the form of organizing the past president, current president, and president-elect of the senate into a formal group known as the Three Presidents. This group is employed by the college half-time each summer in some administrative assignment, and during the school year the college president lunches every two weeks with the Three Presidents, the classified staff Forum President, and the district's Vice President for Instruction.

YOSEMITE COMMUNITY COLLEGE DISTRICT. Yosemite consists of three major operating units: two college campuses and a district-wide central services operation. Yosemite's decentralized governance structure attempts, at the district level, to integrate comprehensive planning, budget development, and decision making into a unified process. This process culminates in a written working plan that the institution commits to and that becomes the basis of the institution's decision-making stream.

Thirty-five operating subgroups on the two college campuses and in central services do the initial plan development. As these plans are reviewed and priorities established, in each of the last two years a Budget Review Council, including union representatives, has been convened to examine budget implications of the plans being formulated. Financial information is widely shared through an on-line financial records system.

While this planning process produces the district's annual comprehensive plan, including the proposed allocation of resources, day-to-day operational issues and problems are considered by college and district-level councils comprised of representatives of the support staff, faculty, and administration.

This integrative system, characterized by wide faculty and staff participation, seems to have lessened tensions generally in the district, reduced the "sibling rivalry" between campuses so common in multiunit systems, and helped diminish another typical condition of complex systems, the "we–they" problem between the colleges and central services.

CONCLUSION

Viewed in the context of the conceptual material presented in this chapter, structural components of organizations have implications in human, political, and symbolic domains as well. When chief executives state that they have not had occasion to overrule the recommendations of consultative bodies, they display a respect and willingness to listen responsively that are characteristic of the human resource frame. Through such respect and responsiveness, they empower these groups, a behavior that can be understood within a political frame of reference.

When faculty members reflect that their administration is willing to change its positions and to compromise in order to achieve agreement through consultative processes, implicit in their statements is a sense of empowerment and efficacy essential to maximum individual and institutional effectiveness. When a college president meets regularly with a group comprised, for example, of the Three Presidents, the President of the Classified Forum, and the Vice President for Instruction, this structural link telegraphs messages in the symbolic, political, and human resource domains.

When students and classified staff are included in the membership of consultative bodies, a message is transmitted symbolically that *all* constituencies are legitimate stakeholders and important participants in the enterprise. When structural linkages with internal and external constituencies take as one of their purposes problem *seeking* as well as problem *solving*, they convey messages to human beings in the organization that their concerns are important and deserve to be addressed. When a community group is explicitly included in institutional governance mechanisms, the structure has political and symbolic implications.

When unions engage collaboratively with management in efforts to enhance the effectiveness of the organization, thereby demonstrating a willingness to rise above their own narrow interests in order to pursue institutional purposes, they are displaying a commitment to the enterprise that is operative in all four theoretical realms. On the other hand, when symbolic messages are negative, they also carry enormous power. For example, some years ago in California, during the turbulent time of austerity and cutback following the passage of the state's revolutionary initiative against property taxes known as Proposition 13, a district chief executive's contract provided that he be furnished an automobile at district expense. A red Thunderbird was purchased. Even though it was a used vehicle and was bought at a bargain price, the car became a symbol that operated powerfully in the political arena as a magnet for personal criticisms of all kinds. It energized efforts to remove this administrator from office.

During the same period of time in the same state, a board of trustees, in a single board meeting, took official action both (1) to send termination notices to more than 100 full-time faculty members for reasons of lack of funds, and (2) to grant the use of official district vehicles to a number of administrators as perquisites of office. This action took on explosive symbolic meaning. First, a petition drive and a board recall election were organized. When the recall effort failed, a subsequent board election campaign yielded a new board majority, and following this election a number of district officials found reason to leave their positions.

When, in yet a third institution, the faculty union president, as his first official contact with a new district chief executive, refused the invitation of this new CEO to join other organization presidents and trustees on the speaker's platform at an inaugural fall convocation, a powerful message was telegraphed symbolically that cooperative relations with the union were to be highly unlikely.

In organizations, political and symbolic realities are palpable and compelling. Few institutional events can be as devastating as an error in judgment captured in a symbol that detonates in the political arena. Individuals and institutions that ignore such realities do so at their peril. Even if catastrophes are averted, unless responsible people throughout the organization are sensitive to such factors, the institution can never achieve its full potential.

Thus the requirements of functioning effectively in the political and symbolic domains and of meeting the needs of employees as unique human beings are as potent in shaping institutional character and effectiveness as organization charts, policy manuals, and structural systems.

In all of this, as more than one CEO and staff member in the California study noted, a great deal depends on trust. A great deal also depends on a shared sense of ownership. "Nobody here has *exclusive* possession of anything," one college president said. And everything is always a great deal more complicated than it seems.

Certainly none of the districts mentioned in this chapter is a perfect place; none of the structural elements mentioned in any of them is without those who would disagree with it or feel that it is ineffective in one or more of the conceptual domains that have been discussed. Nevertheless, the spirit of innovation is alive and well in these and many other community colleges, and the quest for more effective governance structures and processes moves forward.

REFERENCES

BOLMAN, LEE G., and TERRENCE E. DEAL. 1987. *Modern Approaches to Understanding and Managing Organizations*. San Francisco: Jossey Bass.

DEBLEY, TOM. 1986. "Less Productive Workers May Be Born, Not Made." *CalReport* (December):7.

FRYER, THOMAS W., JR. 1982. "Part One: Institutional Causes of Individual Responsibility." Occasional paper no. 30, Center for Studies in Higher Education, University of California, Berkeley.

———— and JOHN LOVAS. 1988. "A Study of Governance Practices in California Community Colleges." Los Altos Hills, Ca. In progress.

ROUECHE, JOHN E., and GEORGE A. BAKER III. 1987. *Access and Excellence.* Washington, D.C.: Community College Press.

THOMPSON, MARGARET. 1987. "Mutual Gains Bargaining in the Foothill-De Anza Community College District: Collaborative Employer-Employee Relations in a High Commitment Work System." Los Altos Hills, Ca. 1987 Unpublished.

WEICK, KARL E. 1976. "Educational Organizations as Loosely Coupled Systems." *Administrative Science Quarterly* 21, no. 1 (March):1–19.

12

The Costs

OF

Innovation

Peter R. MacDougall and Jack H. Friedlander

Innovation, for the purposes of this chapter, is defined as "any departure from the traditional practices of an organization" (Levine 1980, 3–4). A facet of innovation that has received limited attention is the cost of innovation; that is, negative consequences that can result when innovations are introduced in community colleges. When costs are considered, the focus is usually limited to direct start-up expenses, expenses for implementation, and, at times, ongoing expenditures. In few cases is attention directed to cost considerations beyond these basics.

The literature on innovation is quite extensive. It addresses such topics as the conditions under which change is likely to occur, characteristics of innovative organizations, plans for, and implementing of, successful innovation or change, and obstacles to successful innovations (Miles 1964; Martorana and Kuhns 1975; Bennis, et al. 1976; Levine 1980; Drucker 1985). Much of what has been written about the process of innovation can be placed into the following four categories which correspond to the sequence in which change takes place: (1) recognizing the need for change, (2) planning a strategy for meeting the need, (3) initiating and implementing the plan, and, (4) deciding to continue or terminate the innovation (Levine 1980, 7).

According to Levine, a great deal is known about the first three stages of the process of innovation. As for the outcomes of innovation,

We wish to extend our appreciation to Ms. Gwen Cain, a librarian at Santa Barbara City College, for her efforts in conducting the interviews for the project and to our colleagues at the colleges who participated in the interviews.

the current literature speaks generally of only two possibilities—success and failure. An innovation is deemed successful if it persists in the organization. An innovation is regarded as a failure if it does not persist. The question of what costs or negative consequences can occur in colleges during the stages of innovation has not been systematically addressed.

The focus of this chapter is on the range of possible negative consequences (costs) that can occur when an innovation is introduced. The purpose is to heighten awareness of how the dynamics of an organization can affect and be affected by change. Applicability of what is stated rests on the premise that, when proceeding with an innovation, a knowledge of the possible consequences on the organization will increase the probability of deriving maximum benefits while minimizing negative consequences to the college from the innovation.

A range of cost categories to be considered in planning for innovation is identified and analyzed. This economic-based classification is adopted to make apparent the negative consequences that may result from innovation. To serve colleges in planning for, and evaluating how to proceed with, an innovation, a checklist is then presented.

Conclusions were developed by establishing the cost classification categories, reviewing the literature, conducting structured interviews with individuals representing ten institutions in which significant innovation has occurred, and direct experience with other professionals. An additional interview took place with a representative of a firm that conducts workshops for organizations interested in creating an environment that supports innovation. Through the interviews with individuals from ten community colleges at which innovation occurred, analyses of the cost categories were derived. The literature review sought understandings as to how categories of the costs have been addressed and to determine what other significant elements should be included in the development of the checklist. Direct contact with other professionals at administrative workshops allowed for further refinement of the cost categories.

Costs were classified as follows: funding (direct expenditures), innovation without attachment, neglect of core institutional functions, institutional harmony, staff burnout, institutional reputation, and leadership.

The structured interviews were held with staff members from colleges known for having an innovative program in the following areas: staff development programs (Dallas County Community College District [Texas] and Humber College of Applied Arts and Technology [Ontario]); alternative methods of instructional delivery (Coast Community College District [California]); an off-campus hotel and restaurant operated by the college's hotel, restaurant, culinary program (Santa Barbara Community College District [California]); computers in education (Miami-Dade Community College [Florida] and South-western College [California]); outreach to business-industry and gov-ernmental relations (Foothill-De Anza Community College District [California]); telecommunications improvement project (Maricopa County Community College District [Arizona]); small business de-velopment center (Lane Community College [Oregon]); and inter-national education (Broward Community College [Florida]).

The innovations ranged from high tech (telecommunications and computers in education) to open-ended programs (staff development/ alternative methods of instructional delivery) to targeted innovations (off-campus hotel/restaurant facilities and a small business devel-opment center). This range of innovations and the geographical dis-tribution of the colleges, combined with the literature review and discussions with numerous practitioners, provided a broad base for refining the cost categories and for developing a checklist that could be used by educational leaders in determining whether or not to pur-sue an innovation.

IDENTIFICATION OF COST CATEGORIES

The cost categories were developed by the authors and refined through a review of the literature pertaining to innovations, field re-search with colleges that are known as innovative institutions, and discussions with colleagues. A definition and discussion of each of these categories follows.

FUNDING

What are the direct expenses associated with the innovation? There was universal agreement in the literature and in each of the structured interviews that there were direct costs in terms of dollars, staff, fa-cilities, and supplies involved in the launching of an innovation. If it can be assumed that maximum resources go into current operations and maintenance, then the development and implementation of new programs would appear to require either the addition of money and staff beyond that required for the present operation of the college (Miles 1964) or the redistribution of existing resources to support the new enterprise. One of the conditions for successful innovations iden-tified by B. Lamar Johnson (1969) was the availability of adequate funds. Johnson illustrated the consequence of not providing adequate resources to support innovation when he observed expensive innovative instructional equipment lying idle and the faculty returning to using traditional methods of teaching because they were not given sufficient time to devote to the innovative activity.

The ten institutions included in this study proceeded with their innovations by anticipating additional direct expenses resulting from the innovation. Frequently, however, new and unanticipated needs for staff arose when moving from the conceptual to the implementation stage of the innovation. Some innovations had greater unanticipated costs than others in terms of direct financing and human resources. For example, technological innovations generally resulted in greater direct expenditures than anticipated in such areas as the commitment of staff time, expenditures for upgrading equipment, modification of systems, facilities modifications, and staff training for use of the new technology. Costs in the implementation stage, for example, ongoing staff training and retraining, product enhancements, and upgrading facilities, should be anticipated and specified in the plan for change.

In the current climate of limited resources, the fiscal means used to support innovations in the ten colleges were most often drawn from existing resources of those institutions such as cost savings, borrowing from support departments, and direct costs for services.

The need for systematically determining the direct expenses for all stages of the innovation and for revenue sources to support these expenses is obvious (for examples of the stages for innovation, see Levine, 1980, 7). However, what is not so obvious are the negative consequences of failing to assess expenses and income—a condition that quite often appears without being anticipated. These negative consequences may include premature halting of the innovation, taking funds from other budget areas, commitment of staff time to raise funds, underutilization of the innovation, an inability to expand the innovation to meet demands that it has stimulated, and less receptivity for future innovations.

INNOVATION WITHOUT ATTACHMENT

What cost considerations result if the innovation is seen as an end in itself and not related to the mission or functions of the college? Innovation without attachment can occur when managers introduce new programs at their institutions, not because they are part of a systematic process of planned change, but because they are responding to opportunities that are available in the immediate environment. Factors that can result in the addition of new programs not directly related to the college's core functions include: availability of external grant funds intended to support a particular activity; offers of funds by donors to initiate their pet projects; and pressure from influential members of the community, governing board, and/or staff to implement a new program that will solve a particular problem. Martorana and Kuhns (1975) state that such a band-aid approach is liable to set in motion inappropriate changes completely unrelated to the goals of the institution and which in the long run may prove to be more liability than asset. Martorana and Kuhns observed that change for the sake of change, that is, without regard to whether or not the proposed change will accomplish institutional goals more effectively than current practice, is the norm in community colleges.

In his chapter on principles of innovation, Drucker warns managers that innovations straying from the core of an institution's activities are likely to become diffuse. Drucker notes that, to succeed, innovators must build on their strengths. Successful innovators look at opportunities over a wide range, but they also ask, "Which of these opportunities fits me, fits the company, puts to work what we are good at, and have shown capacity for in performance?" (Drucker 1985, 138). Costs of innovating without attachment identified by Martorana and Kuhns (1975) and Drucker (1985) include the diversion of staff time and energy from building on a college's strengths by spending time to manage programs that are on the periphery of the institution's core functions and the loss of staff enthusiasm resulting from needing to support an innovation which is perceived as unimportant to the viability of the institution.

Respondents to the ideas in this chapter highlighted the necessity of assuring that the innovation is related to the institution's function. Although perceiving their innovation as related to the mission and functions of the comprehensive community college, respondents acknowledged that at times an innovation does not fit neatly into the existing institution's organizational structure. An example was the small business development center introduced at Lane Community College. Unanticipated staff time was required not only to modify the college structure to accommodate the innovation but also to explain to staff the relationship of the program to the college's mission.

One of the respondents recommended that institutions should conduct "random harvesting" to assure that colleges are "using the most effective means to achieve the diverse ends of the comprehensive community college." Such harvesting has cost considerations if the activities are perceived as "unattached", that is, not related to institutional practices or purposes.

Respondents cautioned that colleges should not chase dollars that are available or seek "quick fixes" without adequately verifying the institution's need. It was noted that the best way to get into trouble was to innovate for innovation's sake and not to have developed adequately the institution's connection to the ends sought through the innovation.

In the literature, *compatibility* is identified as one of the critical characteristics for success in effecting the innovation. Compatibility is defined as "the degree to which an innovation is perceived as consistent with the existing values, past experiences, and needs of the receiver" (Shepard 1969, 168). If the innovation is not attached to the institution's purposes, failure may result. Consequences from such failure may include a lack of enthusiasm to seek out and support subsequent change and deep resentment from the use of limited funds and staff resources to support activities seen as tangential.

NEGLECTING CORE INSTITUTIONAL FUNCTIONS

What costs does the innovation have in regard to time, energy, and fiscal resources diverted from fundamental tasks of the college? According to Drucker (1985), perhaps the most difficult task for top managers is to balance the needs of existing programs against the needs of potential programs. Drucker urged managers to think carefully about how innovation fits into their strategy and then structure their technology, resources, and organizational commitments accordingly.

At a recent state-wide leadership conference attended by one of the authors, there was a consensus among the participants (program directors, deans, vice presidents) that over the past few years they had been asked to supervise a number of new programs that were initiated at their institutions. Participants noted that the time and effort required to administer these new activities was being diverted from the core functions that they were initially hired to manage. To illustrate, community colleges in a number of states have only recently emerged from a five- to ten-year period of retrenchment in which the resources provided to operate the institutions did not keep abreast with increased costs caused by inflation (CPEC 1986; Schoening and Terry 1985). Nevertheless, during this time of declining or steady-state funding, many colleges continued to respond to the changing needs of their constituents by adding new programs within their existing funding and staffing allocations (Schoening and Terry 1985). Quite a few managers have noted that, while there may have been an excellent rationale for why each new initiative was introduced at their respective colleges, the sum total of these innovations was having the unintended consequence of undermining the quality of existing programs because staff time and institutional resources were being spread too thinly.

Because the individuals interviewed from the ten colleges saw their innovations as being consistent with their institutional missions, expenditures were often viewed as investments rather than costs alone. This view is not always embraced that simply by all constituent groups in a college community. In a time of budget constraints, there is competition for funds among numerous valid institutional programs. Frequently the issue is: how can funds be spent for new programs when that requires diverting them from underfunded, ongoing functions?

Most of the individuals interviewed for this project agreed that introducing an innovation into a college does divert staff from their core responsibilities and functions. The consensus of those interviewed was that this cost could be minimized by providing adequate staff to meet the demands of the innovation. However, even with added support, other responsibilities of staff members may have to be set aside during the implementation phase of the project. To illustrate, Miami-Dade's Audiovisual Department installed and now maintains the hardware needed for the college's computer lab. To accomplish this task, existing staff allocated all their time to support this new program which forced them to set aside their existing responsibilities. After six months, the Audiovisual Department needed to create a new line position to support the new program. At this college, implementing a new program diverted existing staff time away from their assignments to the point where additional staffing was needed to handle the increased workload generated by the innovation. In an era of limited funds, many community colleges are not in the position to add additional positions to relieve their staff of the added workload resulting from the innovation. To the extent that this occurs, significant portions of a staff member's time will be diverted from his or her core job responsibilities to the operation of the innovation.

In situations where the innovation was perceived as peripheral to ongoing programs, as having significant start-up and ongoing costs, and as having results that were uncertain, consequences (costs) related to neglecting core institutional functions emerged. The contract education program at De Anza College was initially located within the college's existing organizational structure with the mission to market the college's programs to organizations in the community. In the beginning, the only new additional staff member was a part-time program developer hired from outside the campus. As the contract education program grew, however, it became a problem to participating academic divisions. The program became a burden to the ongoing operation and caused program managers to divert staff and resources from the core functions of their divisions. This problem was solved by adding additional staff to the contract education program to perform much of the administrative work required to operate the program.

A situation in which the innovation may be taking unanticipated and unwanted direction may result in a need to "curb" the innovation. In an analysis cited by Levine, "curbing the innovation begins to take so much time that the host organization is unable to satisfy its more basic needs, which makes the innovation unprofitable and termination is the result" (1980, 159).

This condition occurred in the case of the Santa Barbara Community College District's venture into the operation of an off-campus, 114-room hotel and major restaurant for its well-known Hotel, Restaurant, and Culinary (HRC) program. The project was intended to provide the staff and students with a unique, real-world educational laboratory by their operating all phases of a prominent hotel and restaurant in the community. Though the plan was well received in the extensive planning stage, unanticipated and unwanted directions resulted. These included millions of dollars in claims being filed against the district by a culinary union, inquiries by the state legislature, a decline in student enrollment for the HRC Department, reduction of some on-campus food services, and considerable press— not all of it complimentary.

The time commitment for district staff, particularly the president, vice president for academic affairs, the business manager, the HRC department chairman, and the board of trustees became burdensome; it affected the college's capacity to deal effectively with its more basic needs. These conditions, coupled with income-expense estimates not in keeping with original projections, resulted in termination of a project all parties supported because of its educational benefits.

The scope and magnitude of the innovation has bearing on the neglect of core institutional functions. Whether an innovation is met with some resistance or support, or a combination of both, neglect to other functions of an organization may occur or be perceived as occurring. Ongoing staff commitment to the core functions of the college may be undermined to the extent to which each of the following reactions to the innovation occurs:

1. the view that funds and staff resources required to support the innovation could be used better to support the existing programs;
2. the perception that basic functions are receiving less attention from the administration and, thus, are being devalued; and
3. the emergence of a gap between those who support the innovation and those who do not.

Each of these can cause conflict and divisiveness which in turn can divert staff involvement from basic college programs.

INSTITUTIONAL HARMONY

Are there factors regarding the innovation's implementation that may lead to institutional conflict? Miles (1964) and Drucker (1985) have each observed that reforming or introducing a change in the operation of an existing college often requires a change in the behavior of college staff and students. According to Miles (1964), some members of the college may be eager to try the idea; but inevitably others will be opposed, and overcoming these negative forces requires a major effort which represents a significant cost in staff time and energy.

Several of the respondents to the structured interviews noted that there were members of the staff who did not support the innovation when it was first introduced. The lack of support for the innovation ranged from initial skepticism among some staff at one college to widespread resentment and personal vilification of the president at another college.

For example, when the study-abroad program was first introduced at Broward Community College, a number of people within and outside the institution questioned why the college was involved in international education. Many of the faculty and staff who were not involved in the program viewed it as a "boondoggle," feeling it was just a way to take a nice trip.

Another illustration is the contract education program at De Anza College. The program initially caused resentment among some staff who questioned whether a program that diverted resources from the ongoing activities of the academic division fit the mission of the college. Divisiveness over the program was at its peak two to three years after it was initiated because, as it grew, it became more and more of a burden on the existing resources of the academic divisions. At one of the colleges, an internal advisory committee was formed to alleviate concerns individuals had in how the new program would affect their own programs. While this effort proved to be successful, it did require a significant investment of administrative and faculty time to overcome the concerns expressed by members of the college community.

At two of the institutions, the divisiveness caused by the innovation contributed to the decision of the colleges' governing boards not to renew the contracts of the presidents. The former president at Southwestern College (California) was committed to making her college a leader in the use of computer technology in instruction and management. Upon her arrival at the college in 1981, the president's assessment of the curriculum was that it was woefully out of date in many areas and that it could be updated and upgraded through the use of computer technology. A $6 million reserve was used to provide for salary increases as well as to pay for the implementation, maintenance, and enhancement of the innovation. Criticism over the computer project began almost immediately. The faculty had been in place at the college for many years, and many had a fear of automation. To some, the innovation was interpreted as a negative statement about their work and how they taught all those years. It was met with tremendous, consistent resistance with a great deal of personal vilification.

The automated computer system required increased resources each year to accommodate the growing demand for the technology. As the funding for the program increased, college staff and board members became critical and questioned whether too much money was being spent on computers. Ironically, however, even the critics did not want to give up their terminals.

This project attracted substantial contributions of computer technology from the private sector and enhanced the reputation of the college as a leader in the use of computers in instruction and management (Southwestern was the only community college selected to participate in the prestigious Inter-University Consortium for Educational Computing). Nevertheless, it caused a tremendous amount of institutional stress which resulted in substantial costs in time and emotional well-being. The time spent participating in board of trustees and campus politics diverted the president, her management staff, and the faculty from focusing on the main aspects of their jobs. Emotional costs were incurred from responding to attacks on the sponsor and supporters of the innovative program.

A somewhat similar scenario occurred at the Coast Community College District (California). The district's use of alternative methods of delivering instruction established the institution as one of the leaders in the nation in the use of instructional technology and helped to attract substantial sums of money from the private sector to support the project. However, it also caused a great deal of debate and divisiveness within the colleges. The dissension was over the allocation of resources needed to support the project and the use of media rather than in-class "live" instructors to deliver instruction. The extensive internal debate surrounding this successful innovation dominated the agenda of the district for a prolonged period of time and served to divert staff energies from their jobs to their participation in campus politics.

In each of the case studies, the innovation appeared to be sound. However, the divisiveness that was initially present intensified when there was a decline in state funding, which was followed by losses in student enrollment and subsequent additional declines in revenues. In order to cope with the decline in revenues, both districts considered reductions in staff and programs. At this point, staff members singled out the expenditures from the innovations as the major contributor to staff layoffs and program reductions. The innovations and their principal advocates became the target of the disharmony within the institution.

Because anxiety is often associated with change, some conflict may be a concomitant condition of innovation. However, anticipating and addressing anticipated sources of discontent may help to reduce such negative effects (costs). For example, it was the general view of those interviewed that tension results when finite resources must be shared further "for something new." Also, whether the innovation is perceived as imposed from above or emanating from a staff solution is an important variable.

The research of Rogers and Shoemaker (1971) is instructive in preventing institutional disharmony from occurring as a result of the innovation. Basing their conclusion on more than 1,500 empirical and nonempirical studies, they identified five critical characteristics that determine an innovation's success or failure:

1. *relative advantage* (the degree to which the innovation is perceived as better than the idea it supersedes);
2. *complexity* (perceived difficulty to understand and use);
3. *observability* (the degree to which the results are visible to others);
4. *compatibility* (the degree to which the innovation is perceived as consistent with the existing values, past experience, and needs of the receiver); and
5. *trialability* (the degree to which an innovation may be experimented with on a limited basis).

To the extent these characteristics can be advanced during the innovation will the potential for disharmony be reduced.

The Telecommunications Improvement Project, which was initiated at the Maricopa County Community College District (Arizona) in 1985, serves as an innovation that has met each of these five critical characteristics and that has resulted in maximum benefits with minimum costs to the district. This project was designed to replace the district's antiquated telephone systems with an intercollege, integrated telecommunications network that allowed for voice, data, and video communications among the nine locations in the district.

This massive, complex, and expensive project did not result in divisiveness among staff members in this multicollege district for the following reasons. The relative advantage of the proposed communications systems over the one it was designed to replace was established through an intensive six-month needs assessment study that involved consulting with numerous members of the district's staff.

In addition to documenting the need for an alternative communications system, this study aggressively sought staff members' reactions to the proposed project. In order to circumvent problems that could have arisen from staff perceptions that the new system was too difficult to learn how to use, the vendor was required to develop a customized training program. To ensure that staff members would use the new system, the district mounted an internal marketing campaign to promote the availability of the training program. This campaign resulted in over 90 percent of the staff in the district participating in the training program called, "Don't Be Puzzled by Your Telephone."

With respect to observability (the degree to which the results of the innovation are visible to others), the district publicized the advantages of the system to its staff and to the community through newsletters and articles in the press. An important feature of this public awareness campaign was the fact that the money borrowed to pay for the new up-to-date communications system was being paid back through the savings the district realized from operating its older, more costly telephone systems.

It is likely that the new communications system would have been regarded as a costly boondoggle and been the cause of much divisiveness if the project staff had not taken time to demonstrate the relative advantage of the proposed system over the one it replaced, the ease of using the new system, and the actual benefits of the system to the college community.

STAFF BURNOUT

This cost results where there is a depletion of contributions from individuals resulting from intense involvement over time. Job satisfaction appears to be a basic need. Until that need is satisfied, there is little likelihood, states Levine "that solution to more advanced needs will be sought, "thus reducing the potential for innovations because they will appear unprofitable (1980, 172). It became equally clear in this investigation that staff burnout is a cost element that must be dealt with as a precondition and possible consequence when innovation is being considered.

In identifying one of the three conditions of successful innovation, Drucker stated that "innovation requires hard, focused, purposeful work making very great demands on diligence, on persistence, and on commitment. If these are lacking, no amount of talent, ingenuity, or knowledge will avail," (1985, 138). The substantial commitment of time and energy needed to develop, to implement, and, in many instances, to maintain an innovation was confirmed in the literature

(Johnson 1969; Miles 1964) and in each of the structured interviews conducted in conjunction with this project.

The premise that innovation cannot be accomplished without overextension was also concluded from discussions with respondents. For innovation to succeed, "a terrific commitment is required." The ultimate concern for the manager, it was noted, must be moving from burnout due to lethargy, cynicism, and resentment to burnout resulting from enthusiasm.

There are a number of conditions through which the introduction of innovations can result in the unintended consequence of staff overextension, burnout, and resentment. Such conditions can occur when:

1. The same administrators and faculty members are asked to assume responsibility for an innovation year after year.
2. Staff members are not provided with adequate release time and/or resources to develop and implement the innovation.
3. No additional funds are available to relieve staff members of the excessive workload they endured during the early stages of the project or to accommodate the increased work activity resulting from the success of their program.
4. The workloads of support staff are not taken into account in decisions to add new programs at the institution.
5. Unrealistic goals are set for the innovation.

These conditions can cause frustration, fatigue, internal blaming, and perhaps failure (Miles 1964).

These views were echoed by those interviewed who noted that the tendency at their institutions was to reward good work with additional responsibility. Respondents highlighted the need for sensitivity regarding the extent of staff time being invested, balancing time off with time-on tasks, and providing support programs when individuals "run out."

Recognition for contributions made was identified as a means to alleviate burnout along with the basic, but central, consideration of the intrinsic rewards that come from quality of effort and achievement. That individuals are rejuvenated through innovation was clear. Equally clear is the need for a sensitive, supportive environment to assure that the costs for overtaxing staff are limited.

Attention to this cost area was felt to be particularly important to individuals supervising staff working in college centers for innovative projects. For example, individuals responsible for innovation centers that focus on staff development or alternative methods of instructional delivery work consistently with applications from different teachers. This requires ongoing enthusiasm, commitment, and dedication at an intense level. For the applicant, the innovation is new, exciting, and often releases great supplies of energy. The center staff is supposed to mirror this response. Initially, it is possible; month after month of such energy levels may result in burnout. The results may become costly for the individual and program. As was noted in the interview with staff from the Dallas County Community College District, "There is no panacea for the problems of burnout involved with staff development programming. It is a rare individual who can avoid burnout over the long term because of the total commitment required to run the program."

For other program innovations, once the initial demand is over, there is often a leveling out in the maintenance stage. The open-ended innovation center must be attended to in order to assure that a depletion of staff contributions does not occur. The rotation of staff, staff support and recognition, adequate staff for the project, and setting realistic goals are among the actions helpful in reducing costs associated with staff burnout.

Costs in this area may include resentment at being used, unwillingness to participate in future projects, increased staff cynicism regarding innovation, and, thus, a decline in overall institutional effectiveness.

INSTITUTIONAL REPUTATION

What will be the effect of the innovation on the college's reputation, or, will the innovation enhance or detract from the institution's reputation? This potential cost of innovation was addressed in a recent article in the *Harvard Business Review* where the author noted: "A company that wishes to move a concept from innovation to the marketplace must absorb all potential failure costs itself. The risks may be socially or managerially intolerable, jeopardizing the many other products, projects . . . the company supports" (Quinn 1985, 73).

Almost without exception, the conclusion reached from the structured interviews with leaders from the innovative community colleges was that successful innovations have had positive institutional effects, including enhancement of the college's reputation and increased staff morale. The consensus from the respondents was that, once an institutional value for innovation is in place, a base is established for other innovative endeavors to be undertaken. In one case when the innovation failed, the conclusion was that it was, at worst, neutral. Moreover, failing may have enhanced the institution's reputation because of the perceived educational soundness of the idea, the perception that failure was greatly influenced by external factors the college could not control, and the willingness to risk.

However, as noted in the article by Quinn, the cost, or negative consequences, of the effect of the innovation on the institution's reputation is an element colleges should consider before proceeding with the innovation. The effects are often lasting because of the high visibility associated with innovation. For example, during the time of high oil prices, the leaders at Lassen College (California) decided to build a cogeneration plant on their campus with funds raised from the sale of certificates of participation. This alternative energy project was initiated with the expectation that it would generate much-needed funds for the financially strapped district by: (1) selling the surplus energy produced by the plant to a gas and electric company; (2) saving money in its own gas and electric bills; and (3) attracting students to enroll in the college's new alternative energy program.

For a variety of reasons, including the faulty design of the cogeneration plant and rapidly declining oil prices, the cogeneration plant proved to be unsuccessful and put the college on the verge of financial bankruptcy. An unintended consequence of this innovation was that it focused a great deal of local and state-wide attention on the financial instability of the institution. This episode has had a long-term negative effect on the reputation of the college.

Both the probability of success and the educational value of the innovation are important elements to evaluate because of their relationship to the institution's reputation and the subsequent climate produced for initiating future innovations. Levine states, "The fact of the matter is that innovation is more likely to occur in some types of organizations than others" (1980, 168). Innovation-resisting versus innovation-producing organizations are referred to by Shepard (1969, 108). The *cost* of failure may be upon the institution's reputation and thus upon the institution's self-perception and place on the continuum of "resister" to "producer" organization. In short, if the institution's reputation is negatively affected by innovation that fails or by an innovation seen as inappropriate for the college, the potential for institutional effectiveness may be reduced. Such a cost occurs when an institution spends insufficient time contemplating both the risks and the alignment of the innovation with the institution's *raison d'être*.

EFFECT ON LEADERSHIP

What are the costs (consequences) that may affect the institution's leaders as a result of innovation? Considerations in this cost area became evident during the interviews. Three leadership considerations appeared: the importance of the leader maintaining credibility, of the leader staying out in front (but not too far), and of the leader encouraging others in the organization to take on responsibilities as "leaders and developers."

If the leader is too far in front of his or her constituents, a lack of support can result in negative effects (costs) for the college's leadership. In the interview with the President of Humber College, he noted, "You want to be pushed by the followers, and not be so far out in front that you can't pull them with you. It does not matter what kind of a visionary mission the leader has; if the leader is not closely in touch with the followers, the leader will have a problem." In one case, the leader's continued commitment to the innovation and the inability to develop broad-based faculty support appeared to be directly attributable to the loss of a job. This cost was in spite of clear evidence of the innovation's success and tangible benefits accrued from it.

To a less dramatic degree than the leader's loss of a job, a failure to deliver can affect the leader's credibility. Again, the Humber College President's comments are instructive. "You also have to deliver on what you say and promise. Otherwise, you lose your credibility. Once you lose your credibility, staff are reluctant to put out energy to follow in other categories." Thus, credibility is important as a precondition in establishing the momentum to initiate the innovation. It is also a consideration in all stages of the innovation because its loss is costly if a healthful climate for future innovations is to be maintained.

The importance of presidential leadership is well established. However, in today's complex institutions, the president cannot do it alone. The need for leadership to emerge at all levels becomes linked to the college's vitality and ultimate success. As observed by the Humber College President, if key players are alienated, the president becomes a demigod. He or she has to work in the structure to give incentives to faculty and encourage managers. "They are all leaders and developers."

The risks of leadership are apparent when innovations are considered. Institutional change creates unease, and reactions can be unpredictable. The costs emanating from innovation that may affect the leader include loss of credibility or a loss of position. The likelihood of these conditions occurring can be lessened if the leader is able to deliver on what is promised (credibility), if there is support for the change being pursued, and if leadership throughout the organization is encouraged.

CHECKLIST FOR DETERMINING POTENTIAL COSTS ASSOCIATED WITH INSTITUTIONAL INNOVATION

The literature review and interviews with respondents from colleges involved with innovation led to the conclusion that a review of the seven cost categories can be of value in reducing negative consequences and increasing the benefits to be derived from an institutional innovation.

An assumption that has guided the authors is that innovation in the community college is essential to community colleges meeting their broad, diverse, and challenging mission. Moreover, a less- than-thorough approach to planning for and implementing an innovation can have negative consequences, including significant internal disharmony, damage to the college's reputation, and loss of jobs by capable leaders. Such results hinder receptivity to needed innovation. By understanding and anticipating the potential costs related to innovation, the institutional leader will not be paralyzed by a fear of failure but will be supported in efforts to improve the college. The checklist that follows is intended to support and enhance leadership for innovation.

The purpose of the checklist is to provide a means for practitioners to consider potential consequences of their actions while determining whether or not to pursue an innovative program. Based on his extensive experience with organizations, Drucker observed that "successful innovators have one thing in common: they are not 'risk-takers.' They try to define the risks they have to take and to minimize them as much as possible" (1985, 143). Drucker urged organizations to develop a guide to the practice of innovation. Such a guide should provide specific suggestions on what colleges have to do to innovate, what they have to watch for, and what they should avoid doing. Although a number of authors have proposed guidelines that managers should follow in developing strategies for change in educational organizations, most of the suggestions either focus on the process of change or are very general. None of the guidelines or checklists focus systematically on the potential consequences of innovation once it has been implemented.

For example, Martorana and Kuhns (1975) advanced a series of guidelines for educational change leaders that focused on strategies that managers should take into account when initiating, directing, and implementing change. The list did not include any strategies for addressing the consequences of change identified in this chapter that can take place after an innovation has been implemented.

In his discussion of the principles of innovation, Drucker identified several "Do's and Don'ts" of innovation as well as three conditions of innovation. He states that successful innovation requires hard, purposeful, and focused work; it must build on the strengths of the organization and should be close to the market, focused on the market, and be market-driven (1985, 138–39). While the suggestions forwarded by Drucker make good common sense, they tend to be general and do not focus on the consequences of innovations other than ongoing expenses.

The checklist is meant to provide the community college leader with a guide for a review of the potential costs of proceeding with an innovation. The results of such a review should help the leader to determine whether or not to pursue the new venture. If a decision is made to proceed, the checklist should assist the leader in planning successful strategies for instituting the innovation.

QUESTIONS TO BE ANSWERED WHEN PLANNING AN INSTITUTIONAL INNOVATION

A. FUNDING

1. What direct and indirect expenditures are anticipated for the innovation from its inception through implementation to maintenance or expansion?
2. Are the costs appropriate for the benefits to be derived?
3. What are the sources of funds and the probability of their continued availability?
4. Are there sufficient contingency funds available to cover unanticipated costs?
5. When is the program to become self-supporting, and are the bases for these assumptions clear to program managers?
6. What administrative, faculty, and support staff are needed to initiate, implement, and maintain the program?
7. What training costs are required to upgrade staff skills to fully utilize the innovation?
8. Have equipment purchases, upgrades, and facility requirements been accurately determined?

B. INNOVATION WITHOUT ATTACHMENT

1. Does the innovation relate to the institution's mission? If so, who (faculty, students, administrators, community) will benefit, and how?
2. Have the connections of the innovation to the college's fundamental purposes been well established and communicated to staff?
3. Is there a perceived need for the change?
4. Who is providing the impetus for it?
5. Has there been sufficient involvement of staff at all levels in the decision to pursue the innovation?

6. Has information regarding the benefits of the innovation to the institution been widely disseminated?

C. NEGLECTING CORE FUNCTIONS

1. Will the innovation require significant time from existing staff? How much, and for how long?
2. What ongoing responsibilities will receive less staff time, and what will the effect be on those responsibilities?
3. What steps are required to assure adequate attention to core functions during the time of heavy staff commitment to establish the innovation?
4. Is the investment in time and resources warranted by the benefits to be received by the innovation?
5. Have contingencies been identified to modify or curtail the innovation if necessary?
6. What ongoing functions will not receive funds for program maintenance or enhancement because of the expenditures for the innovation?

D. INSTITUTIONAL HARMONY

1. What will the innovation allow the college to do better?
2. Are the results readily observable, and how can they be made so?
3. Do individuals understand the innovation, and are they able to use it?
4. What, if any, resentment is likely to surface, and can it be addressed effectively?
5. Has broad-based support been developed for the innovation?

    __ Board of Trustees   __ Faculty
    __ Management Staff   __ Support Staff
6. Have individuals who are likely to express concerns been included in the planning?

E. STAFF BURNOUT

1. Are there sufficient human resources available to support the innovation during all stages?
2. What support programs are available to assist staff if the innovation runs into problems and significant commitments on time are required?

3. Is it possible to alternate staff without losing impetus for the innovation?

4. Is there a core of staff members enthusiastic about, and committed to, the project?

5. What intrinsic and extrinsic rewards will be available to project staff?

6. Who is responsible for monitoring the effect of the innovation on the workloads and attitudes of the project staff?

F. INSTITUTIONAL REPUTATION

1. What are the potential effects, both positive and negative, of the innovation on the institution's reputation?

2. Is the institution prepared for criticisms from internal and external constituencies—whether the innovation succeeds or fails?

3. What is being done to promote understanding of the benefits of the innovation within and outside the institution?

G. LEADERSHIP

1. Have the potential liabilities and assets of the innovation been accurately identified?

2. What possible consequences will the innovation have upon the:

_____Board of Trustees

_____CEO

_____Other administrators

_____Faculty leadership

3. Are the lines of management and organizational responsibilities clearly delineated for all phases of the innovation, including its place in the organizational structure?

4. Is there an institutional willingness and capacity to maintain the innovation after its implementation?

5. Is there a sufficiently skilled technical staff and system support for the innovation?

6. Is there an evaluation plan that will produce information for the consequences of the innovation?

CONCLUSION

In addition to direct financial expenditures, there are other institutional costs to be considered when innovation is contemplated.

In an evaluation of direct costs, unanticipated and often hidden costs should be contemplated. The structured interviews conducted with individuals from a variety of colleges verified that projections of direct expenditures frequently underestimate the actual costs. Thus, innovations may require an infusion of unanticipated funds or curtailment of the project.

The amount of staff time required and the direct expenses related thereto were most significant, particularly for staff not directly involved with the innovation. The time required on the part of senior administrators and others associated with the innovation was highlighted as costs associated with neglecting "core" functions.

The necessity of close affiliation with the institution's mission, that is, a capacity to be "institutionally attached," was seen as a necessary element with cost implications if that does not occur.

That institutional harmony can be jeopardized through innovation was clear. Change under the most favorable of circumstances induces uncertainty within the organization and, thus, steps must be taken to anticipate and respond to this effect.

Staff burnout and institutional reputation and leadership were identified as cost areas that, if not attended to, could offset the value achieved through the innovation.

In summary, the intent of the authors has been to demonstrate that, when considering innovation, colleges must take numerous costs (consequences) into account in addition to direct expenditures. These cost areas include: (1) unanticipated funding, (2) innovation without attachment, (3) neglect of core institutional functions, (4) institutional harmony, (5) staff burnout, (6) institutional reputation, and (7) effects on leadership. An awareness of these areas and institutional efforts to give them full consideration in all phases of the innovation should reduce costs and increase the benefits resulting from institutional change.

REFERENCES

BENNIS, WARREN G., KENNETH D. BENNE, ROBERT CHIN, and KENNETH CORY. 1976. *The Planning of Change*, 3rd ed. New York: Holt, Rinehart, and Winston.

California Postsecondary Education Commission. (CPEC). 1986. *Impact of 1982–83 Budget Constraints on the California Community Colleges*. Sacramento.

DRUCKER, PETER R. 1985. *Innovation and Entrepreneurship: Practice and Principles*. New York: Harper and Row.

JOHNSON, LAMAR. 1969. *Islands of Innovation Expanding:Changes in the Community College*. Beverly Hills: Glencoe Press.

LEVINE, ARTHUR. 1980. *Why Innovation Fails*. Albany: State University of New York Press.

MARTORANA, S.V., and EILEEN KUHNS. 1975. *Managing Academic Change.* San Francisco: Jossey-Bass.

MILES, MATTHEW, B. 1964. *Innovation in Education.* New York: Bureau of Publication, Teachers College, Columbia University.

QUINN, JAMES BRIAN. 1985. "Managing Innovation: Controlled Chaos." *Harvard Business Review* 63, no. 3:73–84.

ROGERS, E., and F. SHOEMAKER. 1971. *Communication of Innovations.* New York: Free Press.

SCHOENING, DON, and JOHN TERRY. 1985. "The Consequences of Financial Retrenchment: An Impact Study in Washington State." Paper presented at the 67th Annual Convention of the American Association of Community and Junior Colleges, April 14–17. ED 264–933.

SHEPARD, H. 1969. "Innovation-Resisting and Innovation-Producing Organizations." In *The Planning of Change,* edited by W.G. Bennis, K.D. Benne, and R. Chin. New York: Holt, Rinehart, and Winston

13

The Future

OF THE

Community College

PREMISES, PRIOR QUESTIONS, AND IMPLICATIONS FOR INNOVATION

Nancy Armes

The Commission on the Future of Community Colleges is a commission of 20 leaders in higher education. It was appointed in the fall of 1986 by the Board of Directors of the American Association of Community and Junior Colleges (AACJC) and chaired by Ernest Boyer. In the spring of 1988, at the national AACJC convention in Las Vegas, the commission presented its formal report and announced that it will continue its work, perhaps for several additional years. In its next stage, it hopes to identify and showcase exemplary practice (i.e., innovation) among community colleges, especially those practices that illustrate recommendations stressed in the report.

As Executive Director participating in these deliberations, this author has had the opportunity to engage in a fairly intense analysis (some 100 hours of work as a group), considering both what the future will bring community colleges and how the movement will meet this future. This analysis has, again and again, focused on past, current, and promised innovations as a litmus test for what indeed will be possible, not in the "blue-sky" future, but in the more foreseeable future of the next decade or so.

These deliberations have real merit in an analysis of the future of community college innovation because they provide both context and content for the analysis. If innovations are the application of creativity to real world problems, then their success will closely parallel what can be accomplished in the community college future. The chapters that have preceded this one are rife with examples of the types of innovations that have been discussed by the commission. On a number of issues, for example, our discussion included a habit of reviewing educational innovations that have worked in the past, that are just beginning to work, that have not worked, perhaps that have taken us off on tangents—all to better understand what might work in the future.

But this was only one strategy in our deliberations that seems to complement similar deliberation about the future of community college innovation. What follows is a fairly informal accounting of various elements that contributed in positive ways to the problem-solving tasks we had set for ourselves. They are offered as both an anecdotal record of the work of the Futures Commission and as a primer for those who wish to look in concrete ways at the future of their college and its long-range plans for innovation.

PREMISES

In its process of analyzing issues and then extrapolating future impact, the Commission first reached general consensus on how it would plan for the future. It established premises on which its deliberations would be based. These premises were not formally set forth in the report, but they became fairly universal givens during the discussion, were the result of much soul searching, and were especially useful in the final stages of work as recommendations were formed. They may serve a similar function for any community college contemplating its future. They include the following:

- The community college will continue to meet needs presented by multiple, overlapping constituencies. Its student body will continue to be complex, attending in intermittent patterns. Its external partners will grow more numerous and will sometimes bring competing agendas to the fore.
- The community college will not change its basic modus operandi—it will continue to embrace the complexity brought by its constituents through a range of programs. It will not retrench, in the classic sense. It will not back away from its comprehensive mission, although there will continue to be

those who preach caution and advocate some greater focus by protesting the movement's "add-on" tendencies. Such cautions should be taken into account. But in the final analysis, the community college has been a "fill-in-the-gap" institution. It will continue to be so and will continue to find innovative ways to support this work.

- Nevertheless, some institutions will have more money, others less. Taking its cue from fiscal realities and the passions of local and state policy shapers, each community college will, in the next decade, make clearer determinations of its *own priorities* within this comprehensive mission.

- In good part because it will serve growing diversity, the community college will continue to be the scout of innovation in higher education. It will, out of both need and commitment, continue to try new things which make problems and opportunities more approachable. Especially in matters that push teaching and learning effectiveness, the community college will seek to expand its frontiers.

- In spite of this, or some would say because of it, the community college will not have high status within the higher education community. It will not have the status it frankly would like to have. It will continue to be thought of by many as "on the margins."

- Even though it lacks this element of status, since it will be scouting, trying new things, borrowing others, the community college will be often imitated—some would say the sincerest form of flattery.

- The community college will continue its practitioner bent, trying the new thing "on the job," evaluating it there rather than in some more controlled laboratory setting. This bent has definite pluses and minuses for innovation. It speeds the development and implementation, but it often impedes the refinement of innovation because practitioner evaluation is frequently cursory or lacks follow-through.

- This is, in fact, the final premise. The community college does not evaluate itself as well as it should. It does not collect data and analyze results in sophisticated ways that include practitioners in the feedback loop. Since those in higher education who have borrowed innovations from the community college have improved them precisely because of more sophisticated evaluation and refinement of the practice, the community college must improve in this area if it is to take full advantage of its scouting and innovating tendencies.

PRIOR QUESTIONS

In its final report, the commission makes rather specific recommendations, addressing thorny issues whenever possible and, in the process, advocating innovation. Understandably, although these recommendations have grown out of much debate and some clear resolution of a group of prior questions, the report does not attempt to capture the flavor of these interesting debates. For our purposes, in our discussions a prior question became one that needed to be answered *first*—before more deliberation on a particular issue was useful or even made sense.

Because prior questions were then very much on the table as specific recommendations were being formed, and because they now provide a backdrop against which a college might plan for the future, it seems worthwhile not only to identify them here, but to indicate the flavor of the discussion surrounding them. Each of these questions overlaps with others and contains the paradoxes implicit in the mission of the community college, but together they indicate fundamental questions that must be resolved if innovation is to thrive. For the purposes of this article, each discussion is followed by a section that more directly links the issue to the future of innovation.

The following prior questions were identified, discussed, debated, and in some sense resolved by the commission.

Are community colleges truly "communities of learning"? Or "Is there a there, there?"

This question seemed particularly urgent to the commission because the overarching theme of the report became *Building Communities.* As the report stipulates, community was to be defined in broad terms, not only as a "region to be served, but as a climate to be created." In a time of fragmentation, of splintered purpose, with special interest groups pushing discreet goals, the matter of building or, perhaps, renewing community was deemed fundamental.

The commission chose to hold its feet to the fire on this prior question with a fairly searching application of the quandary it represents to the internal, institutional community. The discussion went something like this: Can we help to build or rebuild the larger neighborhood into a community if the college is not a community? Perhaps, the group acknowledged, it is naive to try to be a community—given commuter patterns, part-time students, and faculty; given a comprehensive mission that requires so many different major undertakings to be underway at once. Perhaps it is more realistic to place value on smaller enclaves of learning and professional effort within the college—to the classroom, for example. Perhaps these smaller units have become the way to define community.

At a pivotal night session, midway through the meeting schedule, our Chair, Ernest Boyer, recalled a visit to Sinclair Community College in his hometown of Dayton, Ohio. He described Dayton as a city that seemed in many respects to have lost its center, and he expressed a fear that our cities may provide vivid examples of the reality that we are losing our sense of community. Too many times, he said, "There is no there, there." In this particular case, at Sinclair Community College, however, he had sensed the college itself drawing the downtown area together. The college seemed to him a place where the whole was indeed greater than the parts, where the college had become a community, bonded in a way that empowered it to do its work.

It was a view quickly internalized by the larger group. After that agreement, the commission sought to attend to the process of building community within the college, asking hard questions all through the discussion: Is there an environment of mutual trust and open and honest communication at community colleges? How has collective bargaining affected a sense of community? If we are honest, is there not a pecking order in many community colleges that discourages connectedness? Do not some groups have more status than others—instruction more than student services; transfer more than technical or vice versa; credit more than noncredit; full-time more than part-time; faculty more than administration or the reverse? What does the future hold if we become still more compartmentalized by discipline? How can we foster collaboration across programs at the college?

As we probed, the question became even more fundamental: are our students part of the learning community? Do part-time students, in particular, feel meaningfully connected to the college? Surely that is possible if community begins in the classroom and if college-wide activity supports what takes place in the classroom. And what of racism, sexism, age discrimination—separators all. Are we "tracking" the students, as critics claim, keeping them unnecessarily compartmentalized, or are we rather meeting students at their point of need and encouraging them to collaborate?

Through such questioning and discussion, the commission came to reiterate a strong belief in the value of *summoning* the college to become a community and to rebuild this sense, if necessary. Our professionals hunger for community as do our students. As research and experience indicate, it has the potential to renew our staff and to increase learning for our students.

IMPLICATION FOR INNOVATION

Further, if the question is specifically the future of innovation, that future will be strongly affected by how well the innovation is connected to institutional life. Students of the change process have long warned against isolating the innovation, failing to institutionalize it. Too often in community college programs that have pioneered innovation—developmental studies and continuing education programs, for example—the impact has been diminished because the work has seemed to be set apart, not *really* part of the college community.

In the most basic terms, a sense of community supports innovation. It encourages trust, the open sharing of ideas, and risk-taking. Creative problem solving is much more likely to flourish in such a setting. The original gleam of an idea is more likely to be shared, as is the freedom to pursue an idea in the first place.

Thus, those who have interest in encouraging innovation have a two-sided responsibility: first, to help create, renew, and become a contributing part of the larger college community; and, second, to integrate the particular innovation they sponsor into the full life of the college.

Are we as good at teaching and learning as we think we are? Or can the community college lay legitimate claim to the mantle "teaching institution"?

Community colleges have regularly rehearsed the elements that make them uniquely suited to be celebrated as teaching institutions. As Commissioner Frank Newman began to remind us a number of years ago, our colleges take on the most difficult teaching assignments in higher education. Our faculty are generally not involved in specialized research that pulls their minds and hearts away from teaching. They are student-centered, ready to meet students at their point of need and, using teaching as the transforming tool, ready to help them learn.

The commission staked its claim to this rationale and to the designation *teaching institution* at another notable evening meeting midpoint in the schedule of meetings. That night, Pat Cross developed a maypole image. She rehearsed for us the fact that four-year colleges and universities do not seem to be able to push the recognition and reward of teaching to the forefront. Reward continues to be based much more on publication than teaching; graduate school preparation is almost exclusively discipline-specific, with little or no reference to pedagogy, even though many of these same students will become the college faculty of the future. She went on to indicate an even more fundamental concern: we know a good bit about what works in teaching for learning, but we are not developing new ways to apply what we know to the undergraduate experience.

What if, she postulated, we truly lay claim to the teaching-institution designation, see it as central, like a maypole, a source of celebration to which all other aspects of college life are willingly aligned. The commission played with the image and looked at what it meant to connect issues of leadership and access more directly to teaching. What does it really mean to make teaching the celebrated center, the maypole?

And even as the image emerged and invited us to focus on what a teaching institution should be about, the prior question emerged: how good are we at teaching, really? The commission repeated some of what it had heard in testimony from community college faculty. They had heard that faculty were often overextended—with classes too large, time too short, too many essays to grade, too many problem students with which to cope. What of the reality, true in some community colleges, that faculty have little or no contact, either in pre-service or in-service experience, with educational practice that will improve their teaching? Are our faculty poorly equipped to teach underprepared students, of whom there are many? Do faculty tend only to teach the way they were taught? Do they lecture most of the time, an approach research would indicate is less likely to succeed with underprepared students? The commission looked at the reality that faculty are often more loyal to their disciplines than to a particular teaching assignment. It looked at the role of part-time faculty and rehearsed the familiar concerns that these faculty are disconnected from much of institutional life, especially from students.

Finally, it looked at a still larger, related quandary: the methods that research has found successful in teaching for learning are not always easy to apply in a community college setting. What may work in ideal circumstances—with residential, full-time, young, well-prepared, free-of-responsibility students—may not work with adult, commuting, part-time, community college students who have family and work responsibilities.

From there, it was a straight line to how we evaluate good teaching. How effectively do we establish a relationship between teaching and learning? Evaluation has often been at the program or institutional level, but has failed to amplify the relationship between teaching and learning and, therefore, to evaluate on that basis.

This emphasis on evaluation, in fact, became the key to how we resolved this prior question. Yes, we believe ourselves to be good at teaching. Our anecdotal evidence strongly supports this view. But to continue making this claim, community colleges must evaluate more thoroughly that process in creative and helpful ways, beginning in the classroom.

IMPLICATION FOR INNOVATION

This prior question underscored an area ripe for innovation. We must learn how to evaluate teaching, more effectively, how to involve faculty in that process, and how to better apply what research clearly indicates will work in the classroom.

Because it focuses on one such area, the commission made a specific recommendation regarding Pat Cross's "classroom researcher" concept, a concept that asks faculty to evaluate their own teaching in terms of the learning that occurs. Specifically, a classroom researcher is trained to be a careful observer of the teaching process, to collect feedback on what and how well students learn, and to evaluate the effectiveness of instruction. This approach asks faculty to make a clear connection between how they teach and what students learn. It establishes the classroom as both a teaching *and* research environment, a place where pedagogical questions can be thoughtfully pursued, not in theory but in the laboratory of the classroom.

Recommendations related to teaching included other areas ripe for innovation. The commission stressed the need for professional development of experienced faculty and, more particularly, for the careful selection and professional development of new faculty.

Fundamentally, if teaching in community colleges is to thrive in the future, it must be more carefully evaluated, adapted, and improved, and this will require thoughtful innovation.

Are we overextended in dangerous ways? Or have we moved into a dangerous form of mission blur?

Especially among community college representatives on the commission, there seemed no unwillingness to admit that the comprehensive mission our institutions have carved out has from time to time threatened to overwhelm our good intentions. But there was a corollary and generally more powerful feeling that, warts and all, the way community colleges have come to see their mission is profoundly aligned with their identity and success. Because these colleges have been more open and flexible, they have grown in ways that are powerful and that have positioned them well for the future.

Commission representatives from the broader educational arena helped us identify positives in our expansive tendencies. Because we are not tied to some of the most inhibiting traditions of academe, we are ahead in important respects—in the "catbird" seat was one assessment. The relationships many community colleges have been cultivating with business and industry over the past decade was an example we looked at. These partnerships with the private sector have put community colleges where many universities now wish to be—in long-term, mutually beneficial collaborations with the private sector. Similarly, our continuing education and noncredit programs are more flexible than their university counterparts, which were more typically developed as shadow systems using parallel staffs that are expensive and have less impact on the college as a whole. And we surmised, as a result, lifelong learning had become a much more integral element of our institutional philosophy.

In yet another arena, in our partnerships with public schools, community colleges have put emphasis on shared programs in such a way that they now have the potential to be legitimate brokers among community-based groups dealing with the pressing social issues related to dropouts.

In all of this, however, commissioners continued to express concerns about mission blur. As Paul Elsner put it, "Even though we take on the most difficult assignments, there may be no reward in heaven!" He not only linked quality concerns to mission blur, but fiscal concerns as well. Members found themselves remembering testimony of faculty who indicated that new initiatives tended to steal attention and resources away from the classroom.

So the discussion went, with genuine agonizing over variations on these themes. How do we frame our work so that there is a reward in heaven? How do we impress our newfound friends in business and industry with their responsibility to help us present our funding case at local and state levels? How do we truly integrate new programs into college life so that they renew our institutions and give them energy? Collaborations need not be tangential. They can revitalize our programs, helping us solve resource and equipment needs.

In one lively debate, the commission wrestled with whether the image concerns associated with noncredit leisure courses was a dangerous instance of mission blur. Is this a case in which the mission goes too far and the media and public use it to trivialize our comprehensive mission? The group could not decide. In fact, this was one of those fairly infrequent times when compromise recommendations were carefully worded because clear consensus could not be reached.

IMPLICATION FOR INNOVATION

Whether or not mission blur is a frequent enough phenomenon to become debilitating is a matter of judgment, the exercise of which must be made in good part by community college leaders. Decisions to be made regarding mission and the expression of this mission in focused ways is one of the most important roles of leadership.

Thus, because this particular prior question often became a discussion of when, how, and even whether to innovate, it raised an equally urgent question of when and how does the leader intervene. The same dynamics seemed to apply—whether taking on new assignments and, therefore, running the risk of mission blur or deciding when to innovate, as the following litany suggests.

- Significant innovation is generally a remedy sought to a pressing need or problem in the community college, often one of large proportions.

- Risks, options, and creative opportunities are inevitably seized by change-agents, early adopters and, of course, by leaders.

- Sometimes the innovation will succeed, will be institutionalized. At least as often, the new idea will not succeed. Ask among community college veterans and they can provide at least as long a list of failed as successful innovations.

- In other words, a winnowing process occurs and that process is not only inevitable, it is healthy. To wit, one can encourage but not guarantee the success of an innovation.

- Leadership is a key in making judgments and increasing the likelihood that innovation will succeed.

It may not be much of an overstatement to say that this winnowing of innovation at times contributes to mission blur, but by the same token, because it is a sorting process, it becomes a great part of the genius of the community college.

Are we learning communities of integrity? Or will we look at "closet issues"?

From midpoint on through the commission's discussions, there were occasional uneasy pauses that followed someone's raising a particularly difficult question. Generally, one member would raise the question almost inadvertently, as though thinking aloud. But, once raised, the query often touched on an issue that was immediately recognized by all to be volatile, fraught with controversy, not to mention difficult to solve.

It was Paul Elsner who coined the term "closet issue," as he asked the question, "Would we be willing to look at some of the really difficult issues?" Would we be willing to look at quandaries for which we either might not find a solution or for which the solution would alienate an important constituent group?

Perhaps any duly constituted group charged with such a task as ours wrestles with these difficult questions. But the Futures Commission, in seeking to address these closet issues, uncovered a ticklish prior question: Can we claim we are institutions of integrity if we do not consider these issues—not because some outside agent has forced us, but because to so deliberate is necessary to the health of our educational enterprise?

Without exception, when one of these difficult issues came to the fore, the commission chose to look at it and for solutions. Sometimes the group turned a surprising corner, finding a good, if not perfect, response, and answering a particularly difficult question with a concrete recommendation. Sometimes, even though there was not enough understanding or consensus to make a specific recommendation, there remained the desire to bring the issue to light.

Each member's list of these closet issues would be different, but here are some we remember: the growing predisposition to hire more part-time faculty; overload policies for teaching faculty; differences in services provided day and evening students; the growing confusion and overlap between internal and external college governance; the lack of strong professional evaluation processes; burnout; the incoherence of the general education curriculum; the impact of collective bargaining on the college community; the abysmally small numbers of minority faculty.

There are recommendations that address most of these issues. If they do not offer neat solutions, they propose steps for progress. However, the greatest value of this particular self-imposed prior question, dealing as it did with our sense of integrity, was in the discussion itself. It is impossible to wrestle with difficult educational issues and not come nearer the truth, hold oneself more accountable, and, it is interesting to note, look toward innovation for help.

The discussion dealing with part-time faculty was notable. By increasing the number of part-time faculty, by relying less on full-time professionals, are we acquiescing to a law of diminishing returns? Should we make a case for holding the line, warning that community colleges that increase their reliance on part-time faculty are in jeopardy of losing their integrity as institutions? Or do we simply need to ensure accountability within our teaching institutions? Research, we reminded ourselves, indicates that part-time faculty do provide quality instruction. They do bring special skills and expertise from the business community. They do enable flexibility in building programs. But, in light of declared interest in our building strong internal communities, the question became: Are part-time faculty full members of our learning communities—truly? Are they as available to students? Do they interact with their full-time counterparts? Are they provided the support they need to do their job well? And, finally, are they carefully evaluated?

Eventually, the commission adopted a both/and response to this particular closet issue. On the one hand, the commission recommended that as a general rule a majority of credits awarded by a community college should be earned in classes taught by full-time faculty. But this was only a guideline. The more fundamental principle was that the use of part-time faculty in a learning community was *only* as effective as the administrative and support systems that undergirded their work. It is wrong, we concluded, to rely on part-time faculty and not provide them adequate help nor hold them to high expectations.

IMPLICATION FOR INNOVATION

It is not too idealistic to suggest that there is a clear relationship between an institution's integrity and its capacity to innovate. If the college does not confront the difficult questions, the closet issues, then in all likelihood:

- it has less positive motivation;
- thus, it becomes more reactive than active;
- it develops a pattern of looking, almost exclusively, at short-term solutions;
- it does not evaluate itself in comprehensive and substantive ways; and
- it demonstrates a lack of strength in its top leadership.

The opposite of these characteristics—taking aggressive action, thinking long term, evaluating carefully, leading by example—invariably creates a more positive environment for innovation.

Are we bound by unrealistic forms, traditions, and patterns? Or should we move from a "flow-through" to an "in- out" model?

This particular prior question insinuated its way into the discussion from the beginning but was not clearly articulated until a final lengthy discussion, as the commission began to focus almost exclusively on specific recommendations. In the early deliberation stages, clues came with frequent reminders that community colleges are no longer "two-year" institutions or that to describe our students as "young people" or, worse, as "kids" is clearly misleading. Certainly some of our students are quite young, but more are not. Members corrected one another good-naturedly, and occasionally someone would acknowledge how difficult it is to change the language we grew up with—educationally speaking.

Somewhat less frequent and more substantive discussions centered on part-time as opposed to full-time student realities and on commuter as opposed to residential experiences. The commission constantly remembered that our colleges deal with large numbers of working adults who often carry spouse and family responsibilities. Again and again, the commission reminded itself that policy shapers and the general public carry inaccurate pictures in their heads of the community college experience, that, if we cannot change this, we are likely to languish from lack of support.

But it was not until early in that final meeting that Jan LeCroy shared what consultants had found when they analyzed a great deal of data at his own institution. Based on their analysis, they estimated only 20 percent of students at the large metropolitan Dallas Community College District followed the "flow-through" model typically laid out in catalog descriptions. Rather, some 80 percent followed an "in-out" pattern. Tracing a community college cohort over several semesters, the research found large numbers who not only attended part time, but who did not complete a program without at least a semester's interruption, and who returned to the college at different periods of their lives, sometimes for different reasons. Nevertheless, the consultants reminded, the programs and policies of the institution, having been designed on a flow-through model, remained. Their question to Dallas Community College leaders had been: given the patterns the data now describe, do you want to make changes?

It was as if a tinderbox had been lit for the commission with the sharing of this illustration. Other CEOs corroborated. Several talked about the difficulty in changing a flow-through model since professionals and systems have been so choreographed through a number of years. Perhaps, one theory ran, those following an uninterrupted pattern are indeed the core student group and to treat them as such is reasonable. Perhaps, another suggested, if our support systems were stronger (i.e., advising and financial aid), more would attend without "stopping out."

On the other hand, since so many are in-out, commissioners wondered aloud how we could build true learning communities if our systems and traditions did not appropriately acknowledge this more current reality? Why do we continue to structure most of our literature on two-year time frames? How can we change funding patterns that are based on a flow-through model and in some fundamental ways penalize the in-out patterns to which our institutions find themselves responding? Can we adequately build a funding base on full-time equivalent formulas?

The commission concluded the obvious. The framework within which our colleges function is not sacrosanct. Certainly there is great value if the student can attend full time and complete a course of study in a sequential and timely manner. But community colleges are not in the business of coercing adults to become full-time students. They can encourage persistence, especially through strong student support systems, but they must not only make room for, but authenticate, other part-time, in-out patterns, carefully evaluating the quality of services they provide these students.

It was at this point that a familiar warning came. If community colleges evaluate their more complex reality using an old yardstick designed to measure a flow-through reality, the result will be, at best, misleading and, at worst, dead wrong. In other words, when the commission addressed this prior question, a fundamental inconsistency in how community colleges do business emerged, one for which more enlightened responses must be found.

IMPLICATION FOR INNOVATION

Here again, the issue is one basic to the process of innovation in the community college. This prior question speaks eloquently to the need for an innovation to match the environment. Community colleges are basically in the business of applied or targeted innovation. They target solutions for existing or anticipated problems. They must establish a fit between a new idea, current reality, and earlier patterns and traditions. When there is no fit, the chances of success diminish, and there is the equally dangerous possibility that the innovation will needlessly use up resources that could better be applied elsewhere.

This particular quandary sets in high relief the reality that innovation must thrive in the midst of ambiguity.

What constitutes an educated person? Or must we choose between a liberal education and preparation for work?

This prior question was almost not raised, at least not legitimately so, because the "correct" answer came so glibly, quickly. "Of course, we must do both!" But we were to find there were important, subliminal elements to this question.

The commission tackled the meaning of a liberal education early on. They rallied around the need for a core of learning. The core was not to be satisfied by a distribution of courses, but by something more coherent, by a program of common learning which offered greater substance and continuity. But, even in these early discussions, there were underlying, unresolved tensions. What did these requirements mean for tightly sequenced technical programs? There was a concern, perhaps truthfully a fear expressed by some that, when too much emphasis is placed on general education, more specific vocational/technical preparation for work becomes a step-child.

Later, midway through the 18-month deliberations, Frank Newman and others began to come at the issue from a slightly different tack, emphasizing that a liberal education that provides core learning may indeed be the best preparation for work. Narrow specializations will simply not serve well enough, long enough. Again, there was little apparent quarrel with the basic supposition: our students need the necessary general education tools for lifelong learning if they are to work productively.

But the unasked dimensions of this prior question contained the seeds of dissonance. Surely our students must develop generalizable skills for living and learning, but what of specific skills and knowledge? What of the value of fast-track education that leads to immediate employment, growing as does from the most basic need on Maslow's hierarchy of needs. Many of our students need to learn to earn a living wage, and quickly. Does such effort become "mere" technical training as one member framed the question? Have we shortchanged our students if that is the primary goal?

There were a number of closet issues in this prior question, even though it soon became clear that the answer was going to be a "both/ and" not an "either/or" response. At the last meeting, there was the most open discussion on the unresolved tensions between these two mandates that many of us had ever heard or been part of. Is a liberal education or preparation for work more important? If the student wants to go from specific training for work to more general learning goals later in life, is that bad? From a different vantage, if community colleges *really* value a liberal education, why are there no more exemplary general education programs, programs in which a core of learning is required? Fundamentally, is one educational mandate more ennobling than the other?

It goes without saying that these two polarities—liberal education (transfer curriculum) and preparation for work (the vocational/technical curriculum) are the two components of our mission that have been with the community college movement since its earliest days. Indeed, some of the commission's dialogue harkened back to ideological questions framed earlier still in our nation's history by Thomas Jefferson and others. By the time the dust had settled, several principles were endorsed:

- that in the matter of these two seminal components of our mission, when we get to the point of saying one or the other is more important, we are in a zero-sum game;

- that there is prejudice on both sides of the house which prevents authentic collaboration from taking place for the good of students;
- that if we image community college students as returning to us a number of times through the years, the opportunity for both breadth and depth of preparation gains legitimacy;
- that improved literacy skills are the glue that holds the educational experience together and, if those learning experiences are shortchanged, all educators—on both sides of the house— have failed; and
- that if we cannot break down a certain provincialism among the disciplines and between these mandates, there will indeed be little chance for a liberally educated technician or for a technically literate generalist.

IMPLICATION FOR INNOVATION

It was during this prior question discussion, perhaps more than any other, that the commission probed the phenomenon of resistance to change. Such resistance is certainly the specter that constantly threatens innovation. The recalcitrant can slow progress, sometimes to a crawl. In this case, we had uncovered a fairly pervasive resistance of this variety—perhaps because the liberal and vocational functions are so long-lived within our movement; perhaps because the populist and elitist stereotypes associated with these functions have real power; perhaps because of self-interest, that is, is my program, my job, to continue unabated if we collaborate.

There are important innovations to be accomplished in this arena, and there are a few highly creative efforts underway. But they are not only few, they remain infrequently replicated. Interdisciplinary projects are often developed using grant monies and then are not sufficiently institutionalized after these funds are gone.

In effect, this prior question becomes a case study highlighting the reality that success in innovation is a matter of timing. There are windows of opportunity that can be lost with real damage done. There is the tendency for resistance to become so burdensome, so entrenched, that it precludes an innovative response, in spite of warning signals.

In this particular case, there are those who maintain that liberal education in the community college falters and that this weakening is to the detriment of our historic transfer function. At the same time, there are those who maintain that vocational-technical programs are dead-end, with students tracked at the college and graduates destined for unfulfilling and short-lived work. Neither need be the case.

The seeds of renewal and innovation seem to bear most fruit

through collaboration. That the motivation to collaborate, to elimi-
nate traditional dichotomies seems sorely lacking in areas most in
need of innovation is comment both on the power of tradition, even
among community colleges, and on the need for still more effort in
breaking down artificial barriers and impediments to progress.

Index

A

Access, 4–7, 27, 71, 88–90
Access and Excellence: The Open-Door College (Roueche, Baker, and Roueche), 49
Accountability, 202
Action plans, 85
Adler, Mortimer, 36, 37
Administrative Information Systems: The 1985 Profile and Five-Year Trends (Thomas and van Hoesen), 116
Administrator behavior, analyses of ideal, 229–231
Adult literacy, 166–167
Adult students, 100, 101
Advisement and graduation information system (AGIS), 126
Agency for International Development (AID), 150, 154
Alabama Technical Training, 164–165
Alberta Career Development and Employment (Canada), 65–66
Allaire, Sandra, 52
Allan Hancock College (California), 235, 237–238
Alternative delivery systems, 5–6
Aluminum Company of America Tennessee, 165
American Association of Community and Junior Colleges (AACJC), 11, 12, 88, 138, 140–141, 161, 179, 181, 266
American Association of Junior Colleges, 137–138
American Association of Women in Community and Junior Colleges, 88
American College Personnel Association, 88
American College Testing Program, 78–79, 88
American Council on Education (ACE), 23, 24
Anandam, Kamala, 98–112
Anthony, Joe, 56–57
Apprenticeship training, 164–165
Arizona State University, 20, 123
Armes, Nancy, 74, 266–282
Ashland Community College (Kentucky), 56
Assessment, 80–82, 88–90
ASSET system of testing, 78–79, 83
Athos, A. G., 213
Attendance, 50–51
Austin Community College (Texas), 60, 167
Automotive Service Education Programs (ASEP), 164
Automotive Student Service Educational Training (ASSET), 43, 164
Automotive technology program, 42–43
Axelrod, Joseph, 25

B

Bahruth, Robert, 60
Bainbridge Junior College (Georgia), 165
Baker, George A., III, 49, 227, 236
Baker, J., 185
Bakersfield College (California), 19, 38
Baldridge, J. V., 201
Barnes, Cynthia A., 66
Barth, Roland S., 65
Basic skills training, 6, 37–38, 62–63, 166–167
Baskin, Samuel, 3

Bay de Noc Community College (Michigan), 107

Beaufort Technical College (South Carolina), 78–80

Beene, Jo, 90

Bennis, Warren G., 244

Bertch, Julie, 66–67

Bessemer State Technical College (Alabama), 164, 165

Betts, L. J., 198

Bleed, Ronald D., 113–135

Bloor, Earl G., 65–66

Board behavior, analyses of ideal, 227–229

Bolman, Lee G., 222–223, 233

Boris, Edna, 52–53

Boyer, Ernest, 266, 270

Brevard Community College (Florida), 141, 147, 148, 165, 168

Brigham Young University, 124

Brookdale Community College (New Jersey), 105

Brooklyn College (New York), 31–32

Broward Community College (Florida), 148, 246, 252

Brubacher, John S., 2

Budd, Gary, 62–63

Bunker Hill Community College (Massachusetts), 142

Bunker Hill Community College (New Jersey), 145

Burlington County College (New Jersey), 67

Business and industry, alliances with, 17–19, 42–43, 159–175, 274
  dual-purpose partnerships, 167–169
  international education and, 144–146
  partnerships for economic development, 169–172
  partnerships for human resource development, 163–167
  trend assessment, 173–174

Business development, 171–172

Bystrom, Valerie, 15

C

Calendar management system, 123

Calibration, 63–64

California Teachers' Association, 237

Carter, Jimmy, 138

Case I. H. (International Harvester), 166

Case Western Reserve University, 18

Castleton State College (Vermont), 67–68

Catonsville Community College (Maryland), 164

CAUSE, 116

Centra, J., 192, 193

Central Oregon Community College, 50, 75

Central Piedmont Community College (North Carolina), 34, 43, 80–81, 101, 145

Change magazine, 3

Changing American School, The (Goodlad), 3

Charner, I., 163, 169, 170

Chemeketa Community College (Oregon), 170

Chicago City College (Illinois), 6, 50

Clackamas Community College (Oregon), 93–95

Clayton State College (Georgia), 30–31, 37

Cleveland Advanced Manufacturing Program, 18

Cleveland State University, 18

Coast Community College District (California), 6, 245, 253

Cochise College (Arizona), 166

Cohen, Arthur M., 27, 177

Cohen, M., 201

Colby Community College (Kansas), 39, 53, 61–62

Collaborative learning, 14, 15–16

Collective bargaining, 232

College Board, 80, 126

College Consortium for International Studies (CCIS), 138, 141–142

College of DuPage (Illinois), 7

College of the Sequoias (California), 62–63

College Responses to Low-Achieving Students: A National Study (Roueche, Baker, and Roueche), 49

Collegiality, educational, 65

Columbia College (California), 236
Commerce, Department of, 171
Commission on the Future of
    Community Colleges, 14, 29,
    266–281
Commitment, 224, 225
Communications technology, 12,
    20, 113–135
  communication system, 121–124
  future trends, 129–132
  historical perspective, 113–116
  human resource system, 127–
    129
  keys to success, 132–134
  library automation, 117, 119–
    121
  registration system, 124–125
  student services system, 125–
    127
Communications Workers of
    America, 168
Community College of Allegheny
    County (Pennsylvania), 168
Community College of Aurora
    (Colorado), 66
Community College of Rhode Is-
    land, 165
Community College Transition
    Program (CCTP), 87
Community colleges
  future of, 266–282
  predecessors of, 1–2
  See also Innovation
Community Colleges for Interna-
    tional Development (CCID),
    138, 141–144
Community Colleges of Spokane
    (Washington), 165, 166
"Community Colleges on The Pla-
    teau" (Cross), 8
Community development, 169–170
Compact-Disc Interactive (CD-I),
    107–108
Compatibility, 249
Competency-based curriculum, 24,
    25, 27–28
Competition, 13, 203
Compliance, 224, 225
Computer-assisted education, 24
Computer-assisted instruction, 20,
    34
Computer-based education, 24, 100
Computer literacy courses, 114–
    115

Computer-managed instruction, 20
Computer Placement Testing (CPT),
    80–81
Computer testing, 80–82
Computers, 10, 20, 74, 93. *See also*
    Communications technology;
    Technological innovations
Concurrent Resolution, 301, 139
Control structures, 224–225
Cooley, William W., 103
Cordova, J. A., 75
Core curriculum, 29–31
Core functions, neglecting, 249–
    251, 262
Cornell University (New York),
    58
Corse, Larry, 30
Costs of innovation, 244–265
  checklist for determining, 259–
    261
  effect on leadership, 258–259,
    263
  funding, 246–247, 261
  innovation without attachment,
    247–249, 261–262
  institutional harmony, 252–255,
    262
  institutional reputation, 257–
    258, 263
  neglecting core functions, 249–
    251, 262
  staff burnout, 255–257, 262–263
Counseling, 5
Course sequencing pathways (CSP),
    126
Critical thinking, 14, 16, 26, 36–37
Cross, K. Patricia, 8, 9, 103, 271–
    273
Crowe, Richard, 59–60
Curricular innovations, 23–45
  collaborative learning, 14, 15–16
  competency-based versus objec-
    tive-based, 24, 25, 27–28
  critical thinking, 14, 16, 26, 36–
    37
  developmental studies, 10, 40–
    41
  general education, 10, 14–15, 24,
    25, 28–32
  honors programs, 10, 14–15, 26,
    41–42
  interdisciplinary studies, 24, 26,
    39–40, 60–62
  internationalizing, 146–149

Curricular innovations (*continued*)
technological change and, 33–
35, 42–43
writing-across-the-curriculum,
14, 16, 24, 26, 37–38
Cuyahoga Community College
(Ohio), 18, 34, 105, 149
Cynicism, 9

D

Dallas County Community College
District (Texas), 6, 14, 29, 39,
128–129, 169, 245, 257, 278
Danville Area Community College
(Illinois), 18–19
Daytona Beach Community Col-
lege (Florida), 171
Deal, Terrence E., 222–223, 233
Debley, Tom, 220, 221
DeCabooter, A. W., 75
Deegan, William L., 200–214
Delta College (Michigan), 164
Demographics, changing, 11, 203
Des Moines Area Community Col-
lege (Iowa), 169
Developmental psychology, 71
Developmental studies, 10, 40–41
Digital Video Interactive (DVI),
107–108
Dislocated Worker Educational
Training Program, 168
Displaced worker programs, 168
Doig, James, 30
Dollar, D., 183
Drucker, Peter, 134, 135, 201, 206,
209, 213, 244, 249, 252, 255,
260
Dundalk Community College
(Maryland), 166
Durham Technical Institute
(North Carolina), 167

E

Eastern Iowa Community College
District, 183–184
Eastern Kentucky University, 68
Eastman Kodak Company, 34, 43
Easton, John, 50
Eaton, Judith, 32

Economic development, partner-
ships for, 169–172
Education, Department of, 145,
178
"Educational Organizations as
Loosely Coupled Systems"
(Weick), 219–220
Educational Testing Service, 80,
81, 139
El Paso Community College (Tex-
as), 153–155
Electronic file cabinet, 123
Electronic mail, 106, 123, 130
Elgin Community College (Illi-
nois), 117
Elizabethtown Community College
(Kentucky), 187–188
Ellison, Nolen, 87
Elsner, Paul, 70, 93, 122, 274, 275
Employee Selection Services, 167
Encounter group process, 5, 7
Engineers and Scientists Guild,
168
Entrepreneurial management,
200–214
Equipment sharing, 165–166
Esso Foundation, 3

F

Faculty
decline of innovation and, 8–9
development: *see* Staff develop-
ment
shortages, 204
Faculty unions, 8, 9, 231–234
Feedback, 63–64
Fersh, Seymour, 147–148
Fisch, Linc., 58–59
Fisher, Glenn, 100
Florida Collegiate Consortium for
International/Intercultural
Education, 142
Florida Committee for Staff and
Program Development, 183
Florida Community College at
Jacksonville, 169, 189–191
Florida State University, 209
Floyd, D. L., 88, 89
Fluid Power Systems, 165
Foothill-De Anza Community Col-
lege District (California), 15,

224, 226, 232, 235–237, 238,
246, 250, 252
Ford Foundation, 3, 87, 137, 138
Ford Motor Company, 164
Forsyth Technical Institute (North
Carolina), 166
Fox Valley Technical Institute
(Wisconsin), 167, 170
Fox Valley Technical Research In-
cubator Park (Wisconsin), 170
Frederick Community College
(Maryland), 15, 41–42
Friedlander, Jack H., 244–265
Fryer, Thomas W., Jr , 215–243
Fund for the Improvement of Post-
secondary Education, 32, 179
Funding, 3, 8, 12, 246–247, 261

G

Gaff, J. G., 179
Gannon, Philip, 152, 156
Gantz, John, 131
Gateway Community College (Ari-
zona), 164
General education programs, 10,
14–15, 24, 25, 28–32
General Motors Corporation, 164
German university model, 1
Gifted students, 19
Gleazer, Edmund J., Jr., 136–158
Goals, marketing and retention,
84, 85
Gold, G. G., 163, 169, 170
Golden West College (California),
65
Gonzaga University (Washington),
166
Goodlad, John I., 3
Governance in community colleges, 215–243
  employee unions' role, 231–234
  factors complicating understanding of, 219–223
  practices and innovations, 234–
  240
  purpose for, 223–225
  value-driven theory of ideal,
  226–231
  working definition of, 217–219
Government, partnerships with,
166

Green, Connie, 90
Greene, William, 148
Greening, John, 62–63
Greenville Technical Community
College (South Carolina), 18,
105, 170, 171
Griffith, J. S., 74
Group for Human Development in
Higher Education, 178–179
Group Ten for the Seventies, 4, 8
*Guidelines for Library and Media
Automated Systems* (League for
Innovation in the Community
College), 121
Guilford Technical Community
College (North Carolina), 105,
164

H

Hammons, J., 180
Handicapped students, 100, 101
Harper, William Rainey, 2
Harrisburg Area Community Col
lege (Pennsylvania), 141
Harvard University, 1
Hausen, D. W., 193
Hazard Community College (Ken-
tucky), 59–60
Henderson, Algo D., 2
High schools and colleges, alli-
ances with, 17, 19–20
*Higher Education: Some Newer De-
velopments* (Baskin), 3
Higher Education Act of 1965, 139
Higher Education Act of 1980, 145
Hodes, Elizabeth, 60–61
Hodgkinson, Harold, 27
Honors programs, 10, 14–15, 26,
41–42
Hopper, Grace, 131
Horne, Christina, 30
Human development education, 5,
7
Human resource development, 160
  business and industry and, 163–
  167
Human resource system, comput-
  erized, 127–129
Humber College of Applied Arts
and Technology (Canada), 21,
245, 259

I

Illinois Community College Educational Development Association, 172
Indian Valley Colleges of the Marin Community College District (California), 7
Information access literacy, 133
Innovation
  business and industry and: see Business and industry, alliances with
  costs: see Costs of innovation
  curricular: see Curricular innovations
  decline of, 7–10
  entrepreneurial management, 200–214
  in governance: see Governance in community colleges
  international education: see International education
  of 1960s, 4–7
  of 1980s, 13–21
  renaissance of, 10–13
  in staff development: see Staff development
  Student Success Systems Model, 70–97
  in teaching: see Teaching, innovations in
  technological: see Communications technology; Technological innovations
Innovation Abstracts, 50, 65, 102, 182
Innovation and Entrepreneurship (Drucker), 134
Inquiry, 56–57
Institutional development, 170–171
Institutional harmony, 252–255, 262
Institutional reputation, 257–258, 263
Instituto Politecnico de Panama, 154
Inter-University Consortium for Educational Computing, 253
Interactive video, 20
Interactive videodisc, 107
Interactive videotape, 107

Interdisciplinary studies, 24, 26, 39–40, 60–62
International Association of Machinists and Aerospace Workers, 168
International corporations, training for American workers of, 167
International education, 10, 21, 136–158
  business and, 144–146
  change in, 155–158
  curriculum and, 146–149
  development of, 137–141
  orientation/acculturation courses, 149–153
  partnerships in, 141–144
  technical training in Spanish, 153–155
  work-study program with Japan, 152–153, 156
International/Intercultural Consortium, 138, 142
Intervention, 89, 90
Invitational National Seminar on the Experimental Junior College (1967), 3–4
Islands of Innovation Expanding: Changes in the Community College (Johnson), 4
Islands of Innovation (Johnson), 4
Itawamba Community College (Mississippi), 101

J

Japan
  management concepts, 211, 212
  work-study program with, 152–153, 156
Jefferson Community College (Kentucky), 36, 54, 186–187
Jenrette, David, 63–64
Johnson, B. Lamar, 4, 246, 256
Johnson County Community College (Kansas), 18, 36–37, 105
Johnson Foundation, 138
Joint degree programs, 11
Joint service compacts, 11
Joint technical training, 163–164
Joliet Junior College (Illinois), 1–2

Journal of Staff, Program, and Organization Development, The, 182–183
Jung, Donald, 67–68

K

Kaiser Aluminum Corporation, 165
Kalamazoo Community College (Michigan), 106
Kanter, Sanford, 54–55
Kassebaum, Nancy, 29
Kastner, H. H., 178
Keller, George, 204, 206, 213
Kellogg, W. K., Foundation, 137, 179
Kelly, J. T., 100, 103
Kennedy, John F., 95
Kerr, Lornie, 83
Kettering, Charles F., Foundation, 3
Keyser, John, 70–97
King, Max, 142
Kirkwood Community College (Iowa), 141–142
Kirtland Community College (Michigan), 172
Korn, Ellen, 36
Kreider, Paul, 147
Kuhns, Eileen, 244, 248, 260

L

LaGuardia Community College (New York), 52–53
Land grant colleges, 1
Lane Community College (Oregon), 246, 248
Laney College (California), 41
Lansing Community College (Michigan), 152, 156
Lassen College (California), 258
Lauderbaugh, Stanley, 147
Leach, E. R., 83
Leach, Ernie, 71–72
Leadership, costs of innovation and, 258–259, 263
League for Innovation in the Community College, 4, 8, 21, 74, 92, 111, 121, 126, 133

Learning, Assessment, Retention Consortium (LARC), 90, 92
Learning laboratories, 6
LeCroy, Jan, 278
Lectures, 51–55
Leonard, George, 111
Lester, Barbara, 56
Levine, A., 244, 247, 251, 255, 258
Lewis, C. T., 83
Lewis and Clark College (Illinois), 101
Lexington Community College (Kentucky), 56–57, 58–59
Liberal arts curriculum, 31
Library automation systems, 117, 119–121, 130, 132–133
Lilly Foundation, 179
Lindblad, Jerri, 42
Lindemann, William, 75–76
Lingle, Ronald, 19
Linkages, 182
Literacy, adult, 166–167
Little, Judith Warren, 65
Lockheed California Company, 168
Lombardi, John, 3
Long, James P., 159–175
Loop College (Illinois), 145–146, 157
Los Angeles Community College District (California), 168
Los Medanos Community College (California), 14
Lovas, John, 234
Luckenbill, M., 182
Lutz, L. L., 83

M

MacDougall, Peter R., 244–265
Management by objectives, 7
March, J., 201
Maricopa County Community College District (Arizona), 15, 20, 66–67, 121, 124, 131–132, 134–135, 246, 254–255
Marketing, 13
Marketing-retention system, 83–86
Martorana, S. V., 244, 248, 260
McCabe, Robert H., 110
McCadden, Joseph F., 67
McDonnell Douglas Astronautics Company, 165

McKeachie, Wilbert J., 102
Megatrends (Naisbitt), 98
Mentoring system, 66, 67
Mercer Community College (New Jersey), 141
Metropolitan Technical Community College (Nebraska), 168
Miami-Dade Community College (Florida), 6, 11, 14, 29, 39, 76–78, 95, 103, 110, 124, 125–127, 191, 245, 250
Michelin Tire Corporation, 170
Midlands Technical College (South Carolina), 40–41
Miles, Matthew B., 245, 246, 252, 256
Miller, Bob, 68
Miller, D. J., 194–195
Mills, B. J., 185
Milwaukee Area Technical College, 170, 171
Ministry of Education (Panama), 154
Minutes, classroom, 52–53
Mitchell, Kenneth, 61–62
Mitchell, Vicki, 53
Mitsubishi Company, 167
Modern Approaches to Understanding and Managing Organizations (Bolman and Deal), 222–223
Modesto Junior College (California), 62, 236
Monroe Community College (New York), 20, 43
Moore, W., 193–194
Moraine Valley Community College (Illinois), 18
Motorola, Inc., 163
Mt. Hood Community College (Oregon), 81–82, 95, 147, 170–171
Mt. San Antonio College (California), 235, 237–239
"Mutual Gains Bargaining in the Foothill-De Anza Community College District" (Thompson), 224

N

Naisbitt, John, 98, 111
National Association for Developmental Education, 88

National Association of Student Personnel Administrators, 88
National Center for Education Statistics, 203
National Community College Hispanic Council, 88
National Council for Staff, Program, and Organization Development (NCSPOD), 181–813
National Council of Instructional Administrators, 88
National Council on Black American Affairs, 88
National Council on Student Development, 88, 89
National Governors' Association, 139
National Institute for Staff and Organizational Development (NISOD), 50, 182
National Tooling and Machining Association, 165
NATURAL, 128
Network, 182
Networking, 117, 119, 129–130
New innovations, 13, 17–21
New Staff for New Students (American Association of Community and Junior Colleges), 179
Newman, Frank, 271, 280
Niagara County Community College (New York), 171–172
Nissan Company, 164
Nock, M., 191
Nontraditional students, 4–6
North Central Association of Colleges and Secondary Schools, 3
North Central Technical Institute (Wisconsin), 172
North Florida Community College, 142
North Seattle Community College (Washington), 39–40
Northern Virginia Community College, 55–56, 140
Northwest Conference on Student Success Strategies, 90
Northwest International Education Association, 142, 147
Northwestern Bell Telephone Company, 168
Northwestern Michigan Community College, 83

O

O'Banion, Terry, 1–22, 133, 177, 180
Oberholtzer, Dwight, 53–54
Objective-based curriculum, 24, 27–28
Obler, Susan, 92
Office automation, 122
On-line processing, 114
On-site training, 165
Open-entry/open-exit programs, 6
Orangeburg-Calhoun Technical College (South Carolina), 166
Orientation, 82–83
   required courses for international students, 149–151
Outreach centers, 5, 7

P

Pacific Lutheran University (Washington), 53–54
Palitz, Merriem, 38
Parnell, Dale, 86
Partnership testing, 56
Pascale, R. T., 213
Pauk, Walter, 58
People's colleges, 1
Peters, T. S., 213
Petersen, Donald, 43
Pima Community College (Arizona), 147, 150
Pinchot, G., 202, 213
Place strategies, 84, 85
Plato system, 107
Portland Community College (Oregon), 27, 172
President's Commission on Foreign Languages, 138, 139
President's Commission on Higher Education (1947), 29
President's National Advisory Council on Education Professions Development, 17
Price strategies, 84, 85
Prince George's Community College (Maryland), 83–86
Private sector. *See* Business and industry, alliances with
Product strategies, 84, 85
Productivity, 202

Profiling Excellence in America's Schools (Roueche, Baker, and Roueche), 49
Project ABLE, 101
Project ACCESS, 12
Project Bridge, 41
PROJECT CHANCE, 31–32
Project Homebound, 101
Promotion strategies, 84, 85
Proposition, 13, 96, 241
Pueblo Community College (Colorado), 172

Q

Quality, 10–11, 202
Questioning, 56–57
Quick, Gail, 79
Quinn, James Brian, 257, 258
Quinn, Sandra, 54–55

R

Ramer, M. H., 92
Rancho Santiago College (California), 185–186
Ratcliff, J. L., 194–195
Refurbished innovations, 13, 14–17
Registration system, touch-tone, 124–125
Remedial/developmental courses, 46–48
Resource Handbook for International Business (Loop College), 145–146, 157
Richardson, R., 193–194
Richland College (Texas), 19
Rickey, Herman G., 3
Rio Salado Community College (Arizona), 106, 163
Risk capital, 207
Risk taking, 9–10
R. J. Reynolds Tobacco Company, 166
Rockland Community College (New York), 141
Rogers, E., 254
Roth, Carolyn, 55–56
Roueche, John E., 46–69, 182, 227, 236
Roueche, Suanne D., 46–69

Rowray, Richard D., 79
Rudy, Willis, 2

S

San Antonio College (Texas), 56
San Jacinto College (Texas), 54–55
Santa Barbara City College (California), 60–61, 235, 237, 239
Santa Barbara Community College District (California), 245, 251
Santa Fe Community College (Florida), 7
Santa Monica College (California), 235, 237, 239–240
Savio, Mario, 5
Schinoff, Richard B., 127
Schoening, Don, 249
Science Research Associates, 3
Scott Community College (Iowa), 184–185
Seattle Central Community College (Washington), 15–16
Self-assessment, 5
Self-pacing, 48
Shaw, Ruth G., 14, 23–45
Shawl, Bill, 65
Shepard, H., 249, 258
Shigematsu, Megumi, 152
Shively, Harold, 142
Shoemaker, F., 254
Simon, Herbert A., 102
Sinclair Community College (Ohio), 270
Situation analysis, 84, 85
Smith, Al, 177–199
Smith, Janet, 87
Socrates, 49, 68
Southeastern Community College (North Carolina), 38
Southern Association of Colleges and Schools, 44
Southwestern College (California), 245, 252–253
SPOCAD Educational Center (Washington), 166
Spokane Falls Community College (Washington), 147
St. Louis Community College (Missouri), 168
Staff burnout, 255–257, 262–263

Staff development, 14, 16–17, 21, 65–68, 111, 112, 177–199
early beginnings of, 177–178
early guidelines for success, 180–181
early writings on, 178–180
future, suggestions for, 197–198
innovative models, 183–191
new leadership, 181–183
research on, 192–195
special problems, 195–197
Stansberry, Kay, 120
Stansbury, Don, 38
State control, 204
State Technical Institute (Tennessee), 165, 169
Stewart, Bill F., 142
Student codes of conduct, 5
Student Development Model, 71–72, 93, 94
Student leadership, 5
Student processing system, 16, 20
Student Services Model, 71–72, 93, 94
Student services system, computerized, 125–127
Student Success: The Common Goal (Lindemann, DeCabooter, and Cordova), 75
Student Success Systems Model, 70–97
Student tutoring, 5
Students' rights, 5
Study Commission on Global Education, 139
Systems thinking, 72–74, 87, 93

T

Tacoma Community College (Washington), 39
Tagle, Tessa, 56
Tai Sung Kim, 152
Taiwan, 142–144
Tandem testing, 55–56
Tarrant County Junior College (Texas), 119–121
Task Group for the Commission on Instruction, 29
Teachers for Tomorrow: Staff Development in the Community-Junior College (O'Banion), 17

Teaching, innovations in, 46–69
  attendance, 50–51
  feedback and calibration, 63–64
  interdisciplinary programs, 60–62
  lectures, 51–55
  practical applications, 59–60
  questioning, 56–57
  strategies, 57–59
  testing, 55–56
  writing assignments, 62–63
Team teaching, 54–55, 68
Technical Education System (TEC), 169
Technological innovations, 10, 12, 33–35, 98–112, 203
  communications: *see* Communications technology
  from one-way to interactive communication, 99, 106–108
  from teaching to learning focus, 99, 109–110
  from technology-instigated to education-instigated technology, 99, 100–103
  from uniform to customized information, 99, 103–106
Telecourses, 6–7, 104, 106
Telephone service, 115
Terrell, Roland, 183
Terry, John, 249
Testing, 55–56
Texas Association for Higher Education, 121
Texas Instruments Company, 167
Thomas, Charles R., 116
Thompson, Margaret, 224, 234
Tillery, D., 204
Toward Mastery Leadership in Access, Assessment, and Developmental Education (Keyser and Floyd), 88, 89
Transfer agreements, 11
Traverse City conferences, 89, 94
Tri-County Technical College (South Carolina), 188–189
Triton College (Illinois), 164
Trout, Lee, 74
Two-plus-two programs, 19
Tyler, Ralph, 29

U

Umpqua Community College (Oregon), 172
Undergraduate International Studies and Foreign Language Program, 148
Union County College (New Jersey), 124–125
Union for Research and Experimentation in Higher Education, 3
Unions, faculty, 8, 9, 231–234
United Auto Workers, 166
University of Akron's Community and Technical College (Ohio), 164
University of California at Los Angeles Junior College Leadership Program, 3
University of Chicago, 2
University of Florida, 196
University of Illinois, 107, 157
University of Minnesota Technical College, 52
University of Texas at Austin, 102, 182
University of Washington, 87
Urban Community College Transfer Opportunity Program (UCCTOP), 87
U.S. Army Information Systems Command, Fort Huachucs, 166
U.S. Office of Education (USOE), 142

V

van Hoesen, Dana S., 116
Venditti, Phillip, 60
Venture capital, 207
Verbatim, 34
Vocationalism, 27

W

Wallace-Smith, T. H., 180
Walstrum, John, 164
Walton, Richard, 224
Washington Center, 15–16

Washington State Student Services Commission, 92
Waterman, R. H., 213
Watts, G., 180
Weber, John, 50
Weick, Karl, 219–220
Weinstein, Claire, 57–58
Wilhelmson, Nancy, 52
Wilson, Woodrow, 23
Wranosky, Vernon, 61–62
Writing-across-the-curriculum, 14, 16, 24, 26, 37–38
Wygal, Benjamin, 142

Y

Yarrington, R., 179
Yavapai College (Arizona), 51–52
Yosemite Community College District (California), 236, 237, 240

Z

Zeiss, P. Anthony, 172
Zumwalt, Joan, 51–52